P9-EEQ-967

The Wobblies

PREAMBLE

The working class and the employing class have nothing in common. There can be no peace so long as hunger and want are found among millions of working people and the few, who make up the employing class, have all the good things of life.

Between these two classes a struggle must go on until the workers of the world organize as a class, take possession of the earth and the machinery of production, and abolish the wage system.

We find that the centring of the management of industries into fewer and fewer hands makes the trade unions unable to cope with the ever growing power of the employing class. The trade unions foster a state of affairs which allows one set of workers to be pitted against another set of workers in the same industry, thereby helping defeat one another in wage wars. Moreover, the trade unions aid the employing class to mislead the workers into the belief that the working class have interests in common with their employers.

These conditions can be changed and the interest of the working class upheld only by an organization formed in such a way that all its members in any one industry, or in all industries if necessary, cease work whenever a strike or lockout is on in any department thereof, thus making an injury to one an injury to all.

Instead of the conservative motto, "A fair day's wage for a fair day's work," we must inscribe on our banner the revolutionary watchword, "Abolition of the wage system."

It is the historic mission of the working class to do away with capitalism. The army of production must be organized, not only for the every-day struggle with capitalists, but also to carry on production when capitalism shall have been overthrown. By organizing industrially we are forming the structure of the new society within the shell of the old.

THE IWW PREAMBLE

THE WOBBLIES

The Story of Syndicalism in the United States

PATRICK RENSHAW

1967
Doubleday & Company, Inc., Garden City, New York

LIBRARY OF CONGRESS CATALOG CARD NUMBER 67–14123

PRINTED IN THE UNITED STATES OF AMERICA
FIRST EDITION

To my mother and father,
who know what it means to be rebels.

No more tradition's chains shall bind us
Arise, ye slaves! no more in thrall!
The earth shall rise on new foundations,
We have been naught, we shall be all.

The Internationale by Eugene Pottier
(sung at the I W W's first convention).

Contents

Illustrations

Acknowledgments

In writing this book I have incurred more debts than I can adequately acknowledge, much less repay. It started life as a piece of graduate work when I was Ochs-Oakes Senior Scholar at The Queen's College, Oxford, and Northwestern University, Illinois, in 1959–61. The first of my many obligations is to the late George W. Oakes and his brother John B. Oakes, who founded this scholarship, to Queen's and Northwestern, who financed my studies, and to the Essex Education Committee, the Rockefeller Foundation, and the British Association for American Studies, who provided further funds.

My supervisor at Queen's, Dr. Henry Pelling, subjected my early efforts to unsparing, but beneficial criticism; while Professor Ray A. Billington and members of his seminar at Northwestern helped modify and, I hope, improve my ideas by forcing me to defend them.

Professor Hugh Clegg first suggested I should turn my efforts into a book, while my former tutor, Philip Williams, made endless, irritatingly accurate observations about the first draft and was a constant source of advice and encouragement. The Warden and Fellows of Nuffield College, Oxford, provided a generous award to help pay for further research in the United States for which I am specially grateful.

Many people gave freely of their time and knowledge to clarify certain points. In particular, I should like to thank the late George Hardy, Charles Ashleigh, Tom Barker, Dr. Frank Bohn, Bill Friedland, Benjamin Kaminsky, Jack Ryan, Fred Thompson, and Bill Waters. Mrs. Joyce L. Kornbluh put her great knowledge of the IWW at my disposal and guided me to many valuable documents; she also read the final draft and made some illuminating comments. I must also thank Carl Keller, the general secretary of the I W W, for permission to use verses from *The Little Red Songbook* at the head of some of the chapters, and the staff of the I W W headquarters at 2422 North Halsted Street, Chicago, Illinois, for their assistance.

The staff of many American libraries helped my work, especially those of the State Historical Society and the University Library at Madison, Wisconsin, the Newberry Library in Chicago, the Library of Congress, Washington, D.C., the Industrial and Labor Relations School at Cornell University, the Labadie Collection at the University of Michigan Library, Ann Arbor, and the Library of the Institute of Industrial and Labor Relations at the University of Michigan—Wayne State University, Detroit. Wayne State also provided all the illustrations in this book, except for the frontispiece. The staff of three libraries in Oxford—Rhodes House, Nuffield College, and the Bodleian—and one in London—the London School of Economics—were also most cooperative.

Lack of space prevents me naming all the many Americans who showed such boundless hospitality during my travels, but I must mention members of Telluride House who made me so welcome at Cornell. Other people found time to undertake the chore of reading the manuscript at various stages. Professor Henry A. Landsberger read a partial first draft; Professor Clegg and Michael McNay read first and final drafts; and my sister-in-law, Mrs. Janet Renshaw, read the proofs. They excised many errors and infelicities, but are in no way responsible for any which remain, nor for the opinions expressed in these pages.

I would like to thank my colleagues and friends at Newspaper House, Oxford, for much patience and kindness. My final debt is to my wife Mary, who not only helped prepare the index, but also endured many months when I seemed to have forsaken her company for that of a chattering typewriter in what spare time I could snatch from a full-time job on a newspaper.

Oxford,
January, 1967.

Abbreviations

AF of L	American Federation of Labor
ALU	American Labor Union
ARU	American Railway Union
AWO 400	Agricultural Workers' Organization 400 of the IWW
BAIU	British Advocates of Industrial Unionism
BBRR	Bronco Busters and Range Riders Union
CGT	Confédération Générale du Travail
CIO	Congress of Industrial Organizations
CLP	Communist Labor Party
EPs	Emergency Program faction of the IWW
FOTLU	Federation of Organized Trades and Labor Unions
GEB	General Executive Board of the IWW
GRU	General Recruiting Union of the IWW
IU	Industrial Union of the IWW
IWGB	Industrial Workers of Great Britain
IWW	Industrial Workers of the World
LWIU	Lumber Workers' Industrial Union
MTW	Marine Transport Workers' section of the IWW
NEC	National Executive Committee of the Socialist Party of America
NLU	National Labor Union
OBU	One Big Union
RILU	Red International of Labor Unions
SDF	Social Democratic Federation
SLP	Socialist Labor Party
SPA	Socialist Party of America
ST & LA	Socialist Trade and Labor Alliance
TUC	Trades Union Congress
UAW	United Auto Workers
UMW	United Mineworkers of America

UTW	United Textile Workers
WFM	Western Federation of Miners
WIIU	Workers' International Industrial Union
WLU	Western Labor Union

The Wobblies

Introduction

Who were the Wobblies? This nickname for the Industrial Workers of the World, a revolutionary syndicalist trade union founded in Chicago in 1905, has passed into the vocabulary of labor and socialist movements everywhere. But few who have heard of the Wobblies know much about their history, aims, or achievements. The IWW planned to combine the American working class, and eventually wage earners all over the world, into one big trade union with an industrial basis, a syndicalist philosophy and a revolutionary aim. Its industrial departments were to act as syndicalist shadows of American capitalism, so that after the revolution they could quickly step in and help govern the workers' commonwealth. The revolution was to be achieved by a series of strikes, leading to a general strike which would force the capitalists to capitulate. Thus the IWW was to be both the embryo of the new society and the revolutionary instrument for achieving it.[1]

The term "Wobbly" was apparently first used in print by Harrison Gray Otis, the stanchly antilabor editor of the Los Angeles *Times,* whose offices were dynamited by the McNamara brothers during the open shop dispute in 1911. But its exact origin is still a matter for contention. Legend ascribes it to a Chinese restaurant keeper on the West Coast who agreed to feed some IWW strikers. When he tried to ask "Are you IWW?" the nearest he could manage was "All loo eye wobble wobble?" Mortimer Downing, an IWW member who told this

[1] Paul F. Brissenden, *The IWW: A Study of American Syndicalism* (New York, 1920), 351–52 prints the preamble to the IWW constitution, including the controversial political amendments of 1906 and 1908.

story, added "Thereafter the laughing term among us was 'I Wobbly Wobbly.'"[2] H. L. Mencken, in his book *The American Language,* doubts this explanation. Another possible derivation is from the "wobble saw," a circular saw mounted askew to cut a groove wider than its own thickness, though when Max Hayes, the American socialist, first used the word "wobbly" he meant simply "unstable."[3] The initials IWW were variously interpreted by opponents as "I Won't Work," "I Want Whiskey," "International Wonder Workers," "Irresponsible Wholesale Wreckers," and (during the First World War) "Imperial Wilhelm's Warriors," while the most common error among historians is to refer to the IWW as the *International* Workers of the World.

The IWW still has a paper existence, with a small office in Chicago. But its effective life span was from 1905–24. In those years it seemed to fall far short of its objectives. It led some strikes among poor, illiterate immigrant workers on the East Coast, in the grain fields of the Plains states, at lawless logging camps and mining towns in the Rocky Mountains, the Far West, and the South. Its "free speech fights," not unlike the "sit-ins" of the modern civil rights movement in conception, won much free publicity and created sympathy for down-trodden sections of the American working class. Yet the IWW's membership rarely exceeded 100,000 at any one time. On the other hand, the turnover in members was so high, averaging 133 percent a year from 1905–15, that perhaps as many as one million workers held IWW cards, and were exposed to IWW propaganda, at one time in their lives.[4]

[2] *The Nation,* September 5, 1923.

[3] A point I owe to Joyce L. Kornbluh, whose IWW anthology *Rebel Voices* (Ann Arbor, 1964), captures magnificently the true Wobbly spirit.

[4] Brissenden, *op. cit.,* 350; John S. Gambs, *The Decline of the IWW* (New York, 1932), 164–69.

Never attracting more than 5 percent of all trade unionists, the IWW looks like a grandiose failure—though in its heyday it was feared as a sinister plot, hatched by foreigners, anarchists, and Bolsheviks, against the American way of life. With some exceptions in textiles and agriculture it apparently did little to improve the lot of American wage earners, or further the cause of world revolution. Internal faction fights between anarchists and syndicalists dragged on for years. Then, during a period of wartime hysteria in 1917–18, over a hundred leading Wobblies were convicted of sabotage and subversion and given sentences of up to twenty years in jail and $30,000 fines. After this blow the IWW was never the same again. When Moscow tried to persuade the IWW to join the Red International of Labor Unions the movement split in 1924 into Communist and anti-Communist factions and lost all chance of recovering its old strength.

Yet despite its small success, the IWW has secured for itself a unique place both in left wing revolutionary mythology and in American folklore and literature. Why should this be? American society has long been taken as a model of freedom and order. Its constitution, the first of the modern world, is the oldest written document of its type in existence. It has survived the impact of agrarian and industrial revolutions, the trauma of a civil war, the upheaval of emancipation and immigration, the shock of two world wars and a great economic depression, and the prolonged strain of the cold war.

In the last decade hate and violence have often erupted to the surface, and cries of protest are frequently heard. But these have more often come from the right wing of the political spectrum than the left. The permanent, authentic voice of social and political protest has seemed to belong to the "radical right," from the Know-Nothings and the Ku Klux Klan to the John Birch Society and the zealots for Goldwater. The Wobblies, who spoke with the voice of the "radical left," held the stage for a briefer spell. But they inspired fear among their enemies and warm affection among sympathizers which has lasted until today.

Respectable, conservative Americans still speak with something approaching hatred of the "I Won't Work" IWW as a threat to the ordinary decencies of civilization. Liberals often confess to a sneaking affection for the Wobblies' virile, uncomplicated philosophy of action. Some of their popular revolutionary songs, like *Casey Jones* or *The Preacher and the Slave*, both written by the IWW's most famous folk poet and martyr, Joe Hill, whose tough, skeptical, humorous verses and parodies captured the imagination of a whole generation of workers,[5] have become part of the American tradition. These and other songs, by men like Hill, Covington Hall, T-Bone Slim, and Ralph Chaplin, show that the IWW was a radical movement with both a sense of humor and a singing voice. And beyond this, the romanticism that has enveloped all manifestations of the old West, that area of primitive vitality where the United States experienced its heroic age, has undoubtedly contributed to the IWW mythology.

Still, we need further explanation for the endurance of the Wobbly legend in a country where the labor movement has always been ideologically conservative. It gained fresh life from the emergence in the 1930s of the Congress of Industrial Organizations. The CIO injected a new militancy into the American labor movement, and by founding a whole crop of unions on industrial rather than craft lines vindicated the idea of industrial organization which the IWW helped pioneer.

[5] *IWW Songs* (Chicago, various dates) contains the best known Wobbly songs. For the story of Joe Hill, see below, chapter 7.

In addition the Wobblies were more than simply an American phenomenon. Both in name and in fact, the IWW was an international organization. It flourished at a time of great labor unrest, when anarchist and syndicalist ideas were making their most determined challenge to the conventional wisdom of the day. As the editor of the *San Francisco Labor Clarion* put it in March 1912, when the IWW was at the crest of its power: "In this country this movement is represented by the Industrial Workers of the World; in England by the Transport Workers; in France by the Confederation of Labor, and in other continental countries by small groups of fanatics struggling for supremacy. New Zealand, Australia—the entire civilized world—is today pestered by this insane theory." The Wobblies made an impact not only in English-speaking countries, like Canada, Great Britain, Australia, New Zealand, and South Africa, but in Mexico and other South American states as well as Norway and Sweden. At home, apart from pioneering the task, eventually undertaken by the CIO, of organizing the unskilled and foreign-born in the mass-production industries, they stimulated investigations into the problem of migratory agricultural labor, aroused public concern about conditions in prisons or convict labor camps, gave the most depressed sections of the working class a sense of the dignity of their labor and dramatized the whole question of the persecution of dissidents.

In the last analysis, perhaps, the Wobblies are famous because they run counter to the mainstream not only of the American labor movement and American life, but of Western society as a whole. Though still surviving, with principles intact, the IWW must be regarded as a failure. "Give flowers to the rebels failed" runs the first line of an Italian anarchist poem which the poor fish peddler, Bartolomeo Vanzetti, translated in prison before his execution in 1927. Many have been prepared to give flowers to the IWW, the failed rebels of American revolutionary history.

Despite this, the IWW had roots deep in American history. Not only were some of its leaders Americans of old stock, like William D. (Big Bill) Haywood and Vincent St. John, but their stand came from a long American tradition of outspoken opposition to inequality and social injustice. In 1905 the Wobblies spoke for those who had no voice of their own. If the Populist and Progressive movements at the turn of the century can be interpreted as the response of those who were displaced or dispossessed by the march of American capitalism, the IWW was the desperate response of the "submerged fifth": the immigrant and migratory workers, the unskilled, unorganized and unwanted, the poorest and weakest sections of labor. Recently, as the traditional left seems to be emerging from the long sleep which followed the McCarthy era, Americans have become uncomfortably aware that, in the midst of affluence, the problem of the submerged fifth is still with them.[6] For this reason, perhaps, and also because the submerged nations of the world are today in revolt, a study of the IWW may be of more than academic interest.

[6] Michael Harrington, *The Other America* (Penguin Books, 1963), *passim,* esp. 4, 171–86, estimates between a fifth and a quarter of the American people live in poverty. For the continuing hardships of migratory workers see John Steinbeck, *The Grapes of Wrath* (Penguin Books, 1951), and Ed Murrow's controversial CBS television documentary, *Harvest of Shame,* shown on television in 1961 in both Britain and the United States. The problem is discussed fully in Louis A. Ferman, Joyce L. Kornbluh and Alan Haber, eds., *Poverty in America* (Ann Arbor, 1965).

1
LABOR AND THE LEFT

DUMP THE BOSSES OFF YOUR BACK

(Tune: "Take It to the Lord in Prayer")

Are you poor, forlorn and hungry?
Are there lots of things you lack?
Is your life made up of misery?
Then dump the bosses off your back.
Are your clothes all patched and tattered?
Are you living in a shack?
Would you have your troubles scattered?
Then dump the bosses off your back.

JOHN BRILL, *I W W Songbook*

When a small group of men and women met to launch the Industrial Workers of the World in Chicago in 1905, there was little precedent for such a movement in American history. The industrial revolution, and with it organized trade unions, began much later in the United States than in Britain. Slavery, or convict and indentured labor, did not favor the growth of ideas about free associations of workers designed to improve wages and conditions. Neither did the agrarian values America's Founding Fathers had believed were the only basis for the good society. From Colonial days until the Civil War, America remained predominantly agricultural. Even as late as 1900, census returns showed that 60 percent of the population lived in rural surroundings. Not until 1920 was a majority living in towns.

In this environment, the American dream of equality seemed easily realized. New immigrants pushed earlier arrivals onward and upward, while to the West the expanding frontier provided an apparently endless opportunity for free enterprise. Though Karl Marx accepted this as the reason American capitalism failed to develop along class lines, few historians now think the frontier acted as a "safety valve" in the way Frederick Jackson Turner argued in his seminal essay *The Significance of the Frontier in American History*.[1] But it remains true that contemporary wage earners thought that it did, and their dreams of escaping from wage slavery to a new

[1] Fred A. Shannon, "A Post Mortem on the Labour-Safety-Valve Theory," *Agricultural History*, XIX (January 1945), 31–37. For every worker who went from factory to farm between 1860–1900 twenty deserted farm for factory.

world in the West made them unlikely to be moved by the appeals of labor unions or the millennial promises of socialists and utopians.

Moreover, appeals to proletarian solidarity found little sympathy among farmers forced to leave their own holdings and work for wages in towns. Craftsmen's wages remained higher than in Europe, and there was an apparent absence of any class structure, as foreign observers, from Tocqueville to Laski, have noted. Thus American labor remained far less class conscious than trade unions in Europe. The major fact of industrial life in the United States was not class but race. From 1820 until 1920 some 35,000,000 immigrants made the often arduous journey to American shores.[2] Deep cultural and religious differences cut across any attempts to forge working class unity, while language barriers hampered understanding, communication, and trade union propaganda.

Immigration patterns created a complex ethnic hierarchy on the labor market. In 1885 in Illinois 33 percent of the workers were German, 19 percent Irish, 12 percent Scandinavian, 10 percent British, 5 percent Polish, Czech, and Italian, and only 21 percent American-born.[3] Workers of Anglo-Saxon descent, skilled and in regular employment, were the aristocrats; next came Irish, Germans, and Scandinavians, refugees from mid-century hunger and persecution; then south and east Europeans, Catholic peasants, who dominated the last great wave from 1880 until 1920 and found life difficult in a predominantly Protestant, industrial country, and many Jews who were active in the socialist and labor movements. The Wobblies made

[2] Oscar Handlin, ed., *Immigration as a Factor in American History* (New York, 1959), 5–7.

[3] Joseph G. Rayback, *A History of American Labor* (New York, 1959), 156–57.

great efforts to organize this most recent group, printing propaganda leaflets and newspapers in Polish, Russian, Serbo-Croatian, Italian, and Spanish in an attempt to reach them. Recent immigrants, nearest the bread line, were always readiest to attack Negroes who, freed from slavery after the Civil War, constituted the mud-sill below which it was impossible for a white worker to sink. The IWW did, however, organize among Negro workers and even formed some integrated locals.

Significantly, when the American Federation of Labor was founded in 1886 one of its first actions was to devise union labels to show which goods were made by white American workers. But before the AF of L was launched few of its predecessors had shown any militancy or imagination. There was no real counterpart to Chartism or Robert Owen's Grand National Consolidated Trades Union of England and Ireland. True, at the time of Owen's experiment in 1834, there was some discussion among members of the tiny American National Trades Union about the attitude they should adopt toward the social, civil and political questions of the day that faced the working class. In the end they drew up a resolution which omitted the word "political,"[4] foreshadowing the attitude of most subsequent American unions, including the AF of L.

American trade union history in the nineteenth century emphasizes this deep-rooted aversion to any form of political action. In 1864 came an abortive attempt to organize a national federation of trade unions; and in Baltimore, two years later, another conservative body, the National Labor Union, was launched. The NLU lived barely three years before succumbing to what one contemporary observer called "the disease

[4] John R. Commons, ed., *Documentary History of American Industrial Socialism* (Cleveland, 1910–11), vol. iv, 211–16. Reprinted from *The Man*, September 6, 1834.

known as politics."[5] Its leader, William Sylvis, overtaxed its feeble financial resources on ambitious political projects, taking up cudgels for many diverse political causes: Negroes (he admitted nine as delegates to the union's 1869 congress), women's emancipation, European workers, the monetary theories of Edward Kellogg, and the Greenback movement.[6]

After Sylvis died the NLU tried to back a presidential candidate in 1872 and collapsed ignominiously. Its successors in the American labor movement took the failure of the NLU very much to heart and were determined to avoid a similar fate by keeping out of politics. Until the end of the century and beyond, politics was left mainly to socialists and other "undesirable foreign elements."

Just as the American labor movement was unwilling to enter the political arena, so American socialists were unwilling, or unable, to make effective contact with trade unions. In the 1870s the anarchists were the strongest faction in an American socialist movement of only some 5000 members. In 1872 Marx sent the First International, mortally sick from the wasting disease of Bakunin anarchism, to New York to die in peaceful obscurity. But the local anarchists managed to keep it alive for a few years and later to bring the threat of bloody revolution to the attention of a horrified American public.

A wave of strikes during the Panic of 1873 and the Year of Violence in 1877 rippled the complacency of the Gilded Age. At the same time ten Irishmen were executed on charges of murder and conspiracy for belonging to a secret society of Pennsylvania coalminers called the Molly Maguires. Yet it was the Haymarket riot in Chicago on the evening of May 4, 1886, that really created widespread concern.[7]

[5] Richard T. Ely, *Labor Movement in America* (New York, 1890), 69.
[6] Henry Pelling, *American Labor* (Chicago, 1960), 56–59.
[7] Henry David, *The History of the Haymarket Affair* (New York, 1936), contains a full account.

The riot began as a perfectly peaceful demonstration for an eight hour day. The newly formed AF of L was cautious in its attitude to the eight hour movement, which had been largely taken over by the Social Revolutionaries, an anarchist party. In the middle of an orderly demonstration in Chicago's Haymarket a bomb exploded. It killed seven policemen, and sixty-six were wounded in the rioting that followed.[8] Afterward, eight anarchists were found guilty and four were executed for their alleged part in the outrage,[9] including Albert R. Parsons, the only English-speaking member of the group, whose widow Lucy helped found the IWW. The bomb was believed to have been thrown by one Rudolph Schnaubelt, who disappeared from the scene.

The Haymarket affair was a major setback for the American socialist and labor movements. The size and strength of unions in the 1880s is difficult to estimate exactly. From the Civil War to the turn of the century membership figures fluctuate wildly. In 1883, total union membership was about 200,000, but early in 1886 it had leapt to nearly a million. After the Haymarket episode union membership declined sharply, and a decade afterward total membership was only 447,000 of whom 264,000 belonged to the AF of L. However, unionism expanded rapidly during the next ten years, and when the IWW was born in 1905 union membership had leveled out around the two-million mark. Only half of these belonged to the AF of L, and the figure was still less than 10 percent of the total wage-earning labor force.[10]

Organized labor was divided, with several groups struggling for leadership. The AF of L was founded in 1886 to oppose the first of these, the Knights of Labor. This curious move-

[8] *Ibid.*, 206–18.
[9] *Ibid.*, 528.
[10] Rayback, *op. cit.*, 142–68.

ment, which combined radical ends with conservative means, was founded by Philadelphia clothing cutters as a secret society in 1869. Under the leadership of its General Master Workman, a mystical Roman Catholic named Terence V. Powderly, it grew rapidly. After the 1885 Gould strike, which ended in complete victory for the strikers, they were the unchallenged leaders of the labor movement with over 700,000 members out of a total of just under a million union members.[11] But the zenith of the Knights proved short-lived. Severe recessions and a series of desperate strikes broke their loose structure and emptied their coffers. Membership dwindled; and Powderly, a poor administrator, proved unable to cope.

In their days of influence the Knights of Labor placed little, if any, emphasis on collective bargaining, union rules, or other traditional features of labor organizations. Their chief interests were education, cooperation, temperance and discussion of the land question. Powderly described the union as a "connecting link between all branches of honorable toil."[12] Thus, as the first union to cut across lines of demarcation and attempt serious recruitment among both skilled and unskilled workers, white and Negro, the Knights of Labor in one important respect anticipated the aims of the Wobblies.

In his efforts to forge his "connecting link" Powderly had paid scant respect to the jurisdictional claims of the older Federation of Organized Trades and Labor Unions, which represented the craft unions and skilled workers. Determined to prevent further incursions by the Knights into the ranks of their own trades, the FOTLU reconstituted itself into a new body called the American Federation of Labor at Philadelphia

[11] John R. Commons and Associates, *A History of Labor in the United States,* 1896–1932 (New York, 1935), vol. iv, 13–19.
[12] Philip Taft, *The A F of L in the Time of Gompers* (New York, 1957), 22.

in 1886, electing Adolph Strasser and Samuel Gompers, of the Cigarmakers' Union, to leading positions.

By the early 1890s Gompers, destined to become one of the most influential leaders of American labor, found himself in command of much of the organized labor movement. Born in London in 1850 of Dutch-Jewish parents, Gompers did not come to the United States until he was thirteen years old.[13] But his cautious philosophy of conservatism was in the long tradition of American labor history.

Under his leadership, the AF of L emphasized immediate demands rather than the collectivist or utopian ends of the Knights. It held that the workers could improve their lot and enlarge their freedoms through organized trade union action and collective bargaining. It opposed political activity on principle. Far from seeking the aid of the state in its battle with the employers for better conditions, it feared the state as a possible source of fresh oppression.

So Gompers and the other AF of L leaders agreed completely with the employers that state intervention in economic matters should be resisted and minimized at all times. Their critics quickly pointed to the development of the vast and powerful trusts, like United States Steel and Standard Oil. These corporations, they argued, greatly benefited from the doctrine of non intervention in economic affairs. The puny workers' organizations, however, reaped no reward from this support for laissez-faire policies. At best, most employers simply refused to recognize their existence, much less enter into collective bargaining. At worst, the unions found themselves at the mercy of bosses who broke up union shops by force. By the end of the

[13] Samuel Gompers, *Seventy Years of Life and Labor* (New York, 1948), vol. i, 22–23, 417; Howard H. Quint, *The Forging of American Socialism* (Columbia, S.C., 1953), 142.

century the AF of L reluctantly began to rethink its attitude toward politics and to press its case before state and Federal legislatures. By 1905, the effective counterlobbying of the National Association of Manufacturers forced the AF of L to seek direct influence during elections, a policy the hero of the eight hour movement, Ira Steward, called "reward your friends and punish your enemies."[14]

Others attacked Gompers because he emphasized craft unions, as opposed to industrial ones. Though the AF of L was founded by craft unionists and developed primarily on a craft basis, the leadership was not initially opposed to industrial organization. Gompers believed in high dues and per capita payments, but opposed increases in the early days because this would have prevented unskilled workers from joining.[15]

But limited financial resources precluded extensive organizing drives in the great industries, like coal, steel, and the railways. Here, to be successful, unions would have had to break down craft lines of demarcation, joining skilled and unskilled workers in the same union. Nevertheless by the turn of the century the AF of L had won the right to speak for organized labor, and its attitude still reflected the aspirations of the majority of the organized labor movement. But for some this traditional craft union conservatism seemed too old-fashioned for the 1890s. It smacked of the horse and buggy in the age of the railway trust. And it embraced only 5 percent of the wage labor force. Almost as many workers belonged to unions that were not affiliated with the AF of L.[16] So the AF of L was vulnerable to the challenge that came from the advocates of

[14] Commons and Associates, *op. cit.*, vol. iv, 531.

[15] The figure of one cent *per capita* every four months was still very low when compared with the Knights rate of six cents every quarter. Pelling, *op. cit.*, 82.

[16] Rayback, *op. cit.*, 212–13.

industrial unionism in brewing, coal, and metal mining, and on the railways.

The National Union of Brewery Workmen of the United States was organized in 1884. It had an industrial structure, admitting all workers employed in and around breweries—drivers, maltsters, engineers, firemen, even stenographers. When the union left the Knights of Labor in 1896 and affiliated with the AF of L it insisted on keeping its industrial structure. Some of its own skilled members wanted to join AF of L unions that represented their own craft, and inconclusive wrangling between the industrial and craft factions continued for several years. Because the brewing industry was largely a German-American monopoly many of the leading brewery workers were also German-Americans, and often socialists too. One of them, William E. Trautmann, editor of the Brewery Workers' rank-and-file paper *Brauer Zeitung*, later became a founder of the IWW and an influential figure during its early history.

Another challenge to craft unionism came from the mineworkers. The United Mineworkers of America was the largest industrial union in the United States at this time. Founded in 1890, its industrial structure sprang naturally from the camaraderie of life in mining communities, with the result that the UMW faced none of the internal opposition that rent the Brewery Workmen. Opponents of industrial unions within the AF of L were consequently obliged to concede the mineworkers' right to organize as they saw fit and accept them on their own terms. The UMW was not always happy within the AF of L; but its leadership was too conservative to think of forming its own federation and so joining the ranks of the "dual unions," as unions which threatened the jurisdiction of the AF of L soon came to be known.

The most significant of these dual unions was the American Railway Union. Founded by militant elements in the old craft-oriented railway brotherhoods after the failure of the Buffalo signalmen's strike in 1893, the ARU was not slow to break away from the AF of L. The ARU's first president, a balding, lanky, thirty-nine-year-old footplate man named Eugene Victor Debs, was an able, enthusiastic exponent of industrial unionism. With the possible exception of Norman Thomas, Debs is the most widely admired figure in the history of American socialism. Five times the socialist candidate for President from 1900 to 1920, Debs polled 6 percent of the popular vote in 1912—the best showing by any socialist in American political history. Born at Terre Haute, Indiana, in 1855, Debs fired his first locomotive at the age of fifteen, and soon joined the newly formed Brotherhood of Locomotive Firemen. In 1878 he became editor of the *Loco-Firemen's Magazine* and later was elected secretary-treasurer of the Brotherhood. He resigned in 1893, despite a unanimous effort by the union's annual convention to make him stay, because of differences over the industrial form of organization.

He lost no time in forming his own union—the American Railway Union—and making it the center of dual unionism in the United States. At first relations between the ARU and the AF of L were cordial enough, if only because the other railway unions were at loggerheads with each other and with Gompers. But the AF of L was, of course, strongly opposed to dual unions in principle and soon began to regard with alarm the infant ARU which in less than a year enrolled 465 branches with 150,000 members. Since the other railway unions, perhaps the most conservative in the labor movement, found themselves in serious disarray at this point, the ARU threatened to control the organization of most railway workers before long.

But it was not to be. Against their better judgment Debs and his comrades allowed the ARU to be drawn into the Pullman strike and boycott of 1894.

The details of this dispute—which, with the Homestead steel strike of 1892, is one of the most celebrated in American labor history—are too complex to be dealt with here.[17] But the strike broke the ARU and put Debs in jail (not for the last time) where, incidentally, he completed his conversion to socialism. The hostility of the Pullman Company, the use of Federal court injunctions against the strikers, and the intervention of Federal troops by President Grover Cleveland aroused the whole Illinois and Midwestern labor movement as nothing had since the Haymarket affair. Yet despite pressure from those unions that sympathized strongly with the strikers, Gompers resisted the demand for a general strike on behalf of the ARU. Even if Gompers had wanted a general strike his lack of influence on the other, more conservative railway unions would have made the bid futile. The ARU was not ruined by perfidious Gompers but by the very lack of solidarity among railway unions that had created it.

The most important consequence of the Pullman strike was the new militancy it injected into some sections of the labor movement by its demonstration of the power of industrial unionism. Gompers had saved the AF of L from possible extinction by keeping out of the dispute; but to many workers his type of "pure and simple" unionism now seemed less attractive than ever.

[17] The best account of the Pullman strike is Almont Lindsey, *The Pullman Strike* (Chicago, 1942). Shorter summaries can be found in Thomas G. Manning, "The Chicago Strike of 1894," *Select Problems in American Historical Interpretation* (Henry Holt, New York, 1960), and Colston E. Warne, ed., "The Pullman Boycott of 1894," *Problems in American Civilization* (D. C. Heath, Boston, 1955).

Just as American labor was in a state of flux at the turn of the century, so American socialism was in a transitional phase. Marxist socialism came to the United States with the German immigrants in 1850.[18] The most outstanding of these early German socialists was Joseph Weydemeyer,[19] a newspaper editor and union organizer for whom Marx had high regard.[20] Weydemeyer led the German-American labor movement at a time when German-speaking elements dominated American socialism. This trend was continued by the new waves of German immigrants who arrived in the 1860s, or fled Bismarck's anti-socialist laws in the 1870s and 1880s. The refusal of many German socialists to learn English and their often arrogant superiority in theoretical matters gravely hampered their effectiveness. As late as the 1880s, meetings of the Socialist Labor Party, at both local and national level, were conducted in German—a fact greatly deplored by Marx.[21]

The conflicts of European socialism left their mark in America. Karl Marx's *Communist Manifesto* had a profound influence on socialist ideas in both continents. But when Marx helped found the International Workingmen's Association—the First International—in London in 1864, he quickly ran into opposition from anarchists like Pierre Joseph Proudhon and Mikhail Bakunin, whose ideas stemmed from earlier European thinkers like William Godwin and Jean Jacques Rousseau.

Marx supported revolutionary activity on all fronts—in trade unions, by strikes, at the ballot box. The anarchists despised

18 Carl Wittke, *Refugees of Revolution* (Philadelphia, 1852), *passim*, esp. 166–75 contains a contemporary account of the first great wave of German immigration.

19 Others were Wilhelm Weitling, editor of *Die Republik der Arbeiter*, and Victor Sorge, a close friend of Marx.

20 Carl A. Landauer, *European Socialism* (Los Angeles, 1959), vol. i, 116.

21 Marx and Engels, *Selected Correspondence 1846–95* (New York, 1942), 464–67, 502.

political activity. Marx's main anarchist adversary in the First International, Mikhail Bakunin, thought any political activity by the working class merely strengthened the position of their bourgeois oppressors. Moreover, while both agreed that after the revolution the state must wither away, for Bakunin this was an immediate goal, while for Marx it was distant. The real point at issue was neatly summarized by Friedrich Engels, Marx's friend and ally in the long and bitter dispute. "They say 'abolish the state and capital will go to the devil,'" he wrote.[22] "We propose the reverse."

This conflict about the place of politics in revolutionary movements, which was refought forty years later between American socialists and Wobblies, hastened the collapse of the First International in 1871. After this the main division in American socialist ranks was between Marxists and the disciples of the German socialist Ferdinand Lassalle, who wished to concentrate exclusively on political activity.[23] The latter accepted Lassalle's "iron law of wages" and regarded economic action by the working class to improve their position as futile. Since the European goal of universal manhood suffrage had been achieved much earlier in the United States, Lassallean socialists in America concentrated on founding workers' political parties which would vote money to found producers' cooperatives.

The Socialist Labor Party, formed in 1877 from a merger between the Social Democratic Workingmen's Association, the rump of the First International and the Illinois Labor Party, was torn by this Marxist-Lassallean controversy, which became even more animated during the Haymarket affair and continued throughout the years after 1886. According to Justus Ebert, a member of the SLP who became an active IWW publicist,

[22] Marx and Engels, *op. cit.*, September 4, 1867.

[23] Quint, *op. cit.*, 37–72, 142–75, 319–50 gives a full account of this dispute.

the Haymarket incident "involved the SLP in a fierce discussion of the right course to pursue in the emancipation of labor."[24]

The Marxists, for their part, were not opposed to political activity as such—indeed, they supported it strongly—but only to the Lassallean idea of its place in the strategy of revolution. They held that political action must begin not with parliamentary parties, which would be too small to influence anything at the start, but with trade unions on the economic front. Eventually, the Marxists argued, this industrial activity would provide a basis broad enough for effective parliamentary political action—a view that later seemed vindicated by the growth of the British Labour Party.

While the Lassalleans continued their own political agitation, Marxist socialists made repeated attempts to gain a foothold within the American labor movement. At first they used the technique of "boring from within": rather than establish their own socialist unions on a slender basis they tried to infiltrate existing unions. However, this penetration was blocked at almost every turn. Since some leaders of the AF of L were themselves former socialists they were well versed in socialist ambitions to take over their unions and thus able to frustrate them. Only in New York City, among the German trade unionists, was any real socialist progress apparent. Within the Knights of Labor the socialists, though often disruptive, were in the long run hardly more successful.

The plain fact was that the American working class, in general, was just not interested in socialist theory with its millennial promises. The organized workers preferred less exciting but more immediately practical policies like those Gompers gave them. Under Gompers' leadership the craft-dominated AF of L

[24] Justus Ebert, *American Industrial Evolution* (n.p., n.d.), 63.

had developed in the conservative, non political tradition of the American labor movement. But by the turn of the century the AF of L was facing a mounting challenge from industrial unionists, syndicalists, anarchists, and other revolutionaries who were among the most disruptive elements of a nation in flux.

2

THE BIRTH OF A MILITANT UNION

ARE YOU A WOBBLY?

(Tune: "Are You from Dixie?")

Are you a Wobbly? then listen, Buddy,
For the One Big Union beckons to you—
The Workers' Union, the Industrial Union;
Tell every slave you see along the line:
It makes no difference what your color,
Creed or sex or kind,
If you are a worker, then it's kick right
in and join.
Become a Wobbly and then we'll probably
Free ourselves from slavery.

JOE FOLEY, *IWW Songbook*

The ferment in the American labor and socialist movements at the turn of the century was just another symptom of the ferment agitating American society as a whole. In less than forty years, since the end of the Civil War, the United States had changed out of all recognition. Its population in 1860 was 31,000,000. In 1880 it had more than doubled to 63,000,000, and by 1910 leaped to 92,000,000. During that period immigration, mainly from Europe, had changed from a trickle to a torrent. From 1871–1880 about 2,500,000 immigrants came to American shores. From 1891–1910 about 12,500,000 arrived.

More interesting than the rise in physical numbers was the change in the sources of immigration. Until 1880, the large majority of immigrants came from northern and western Europe. American racial stock at this time was still chiefly English, Irish, Scotch, German, and Scandinavian. The change came with the rise of the new cities and the new industries. Between 1881 and 1890 southern and eastern Europe sent a million immigrants; between 1891 and 1900 there were 2,000,000; between 1901 and 1910 it rose to 6,000,000—or 70 percent of the total immigration for that decade.[1]

Thus during the twenty years from 1891–1910, more than 8,000,000 of the 12,500,000 foreigners who settled in America came from Italy, Poland, Hungary, Bohemia, Slovakia, Croatia, and Greece. These people, from peasant farming or trading stock, were alien by race, religion, language, and customs

[1] Herbert Agar, *The Price of Union* (Boston, 1950), 561.

to the American way. The sharp transition bewildered, often angered them, much more than it had the Irish or Germans of an earlier era. So it was among this new, many-tongued nation, called into being to nourish the appetites of industry, that the Wobblies concentrated much of their revolutionary effort.

These appetites of industry were prodigious. Before the Civil War the United States counted for little as an industrial power. After 1870 the pace of industrial development was breathtaking. "The old nations of the earth creep on at a snail's pace," the industrialist Andrew Carnegie wrote in 1886. "The Republic thunders past with the speed of an express."

The figures supported Carnegie's colorful image. Bituminous coal production expanded from 43,000,000 tons in 1880 to 212,000,000 in 1900, anthracite from 30,000,000 to 57,000,000, pig iron from less than 4,000,000 to 14,000,000, steel production from 1,250,000 to 10,000,000. From the viewpoint of Europe, the United States was not a rival economic power, but a rival continent. Her coal production equaled that of Great Britain and Germany combined, her iron and steel production surpassed all Europe.[2] A vast communications system sprang up to link these centers of growth. Employment on the railways rose by over a third in the 1890s alone, to reach more than a million by 1900.

New industries, some based on new inventions like the telephone, the typewriter, the adding machine, grew up almost overnight. The spread of these great industries brought with it the concentration of ownership and control predicted by Marx and analyzed by Lenin. The first and best known of the "trusts," as the vast corporations soon came to be called, was

[2] Pelling, *op. cit.*, 79–81; A. J. P. Taylor, *The Struggle for Mastery in Europe* (Oxford, 1954), xxix–xxxi.

William D. ("Big Bill") Haywood, the one-eyed giant of the Western metal miners.

Elizabeth Gurley Flynn, the original "Rebel Girl."

Tom Tracy, who was acquitted of murder after the Everett "massacre."

Charles Ashleigh, a British-born Wobbly, delivers the funeral oration for the Everett victi

John D. Rockefeller's Standard Oil Company, which by 1904 controlled about 85 percent of the domestic petroleum trade and 90 percent of the export trade.[3]

The climax of the trust movement came at the turn of the century when J. P. Morgan finally consolidated his celebrated "Billion Dollar Trust," the United States Steel corporation. The actual value of U. S. Steel's tangible property was estimated by the Federal Commission on Corporations at $682,000,000 and it was capitalized at nearly $1,500,000,000,[4] paying dividends on common stock for all but three years until 1932.

The personal fortunes and power represented by the trusts, and the resulting inequality and injustice, caused widespread alarm. But efforts to break the power of the corporations, through the Sherman Anti-Trust Act and other measures, proved ineffective. As early as 1890, the year of the Sherman Act, the Ohio Supreme Court ordered the dissolution of the Standard Oil trust. But the trust retained its character and in 1899 reincorporated under the laws of New Jersey as a holding company. In 1907 it was fined $29,240,000 and in 1911 the United States Supreme Court ordered its dissolution again. Nevertheless, in 1913 Standard Oil declared a 60 percent dividend and in 1922 a 400 percent stock dividend.[5]

However much President Theodore Roosevelt might thunder against the "malefactors of great wealth" (much as his namesake, Franklin, attacked the "economic royalists" during the New Deal) these "robber barons" and industrialists knew the attacks were largely moral and ceremonial in character—and that anyway they could often control corrupt state and even

[3] Harold U. Faulkner, "Consolidation of Business," *Roosevelt, Wilson and the Trusts,* Edwin C. Rozwenc, ed. (Boston, 1950), 11.
[4] *Ibid.,* 8.
[5] E. M. Hugh-Jones, *Woodrow Wilson and American Liberalism* (London, 1947), 50.

national legislatures, as well as the judiciary. "Law!" cried Cornelius Vanderbilt. "What do I care about law? H'aint I got the power?"[6]

Vanderbilt was right: he had got the power. Based on this cynical realism the trusts continued to grow prodigiously until, in 1931, the Federal Trade Commission estimated that the House of Morgan controlled, through interlocking directorates, one-quarter of America's total corporate assets. The founders of the IWW sought to meet the challenge of the trusts with one union of all the workers, a concentration of labor power to meet a concentration of ownership.

These rapid, complex changes in American society inevitably led to social dislocation and political protest. Much of it was directed against a system that encouraged the growth of overwhelming wealth and power side by side with squalor and poverty—and in some places, like New York City, it was literally side by side. At a time when $700 a year was considered the minimum on which a family could be raised without serious hardship between one-fourth and one-third of men employed in factories and mines earned less than $10 a week, while over half the women in industry or trade were paid less than $6 a week.[7] Apart from pay and working conditions the accident rate in industry was appalling. In the Pittsburgh steel mills alone in the 1890s about 300 workers were killed each year and another 2000 injured.[8]

By the turn of the century Populism, the great agrarian protest movement, had been largely overtaken by Progressivism, a broader-based, middle class protest movement of the towns and cities. The Progressive era, in which Populism continued to

[6] *Ibid.*, 53.
[7] Pelling, *op. cit.*, 119–20.
[8] Leon Wolff, *Lockout* (London, 1965), 34–38.

play an important part, is the name given to the widespread impulse toward criticism and change so conspicuous after 1900. The urban middle classes, though still more securely placed in American society in 1900 than either farmers or industrial wage workers, were no longer the powerful social arbiters they had been at the time of the Civil War.

They above all were alarmed by the wave of change sweeping across the land. Thomas Jefferson, who had held that freedom depended on free land, believed there would be room for westward expansion in the United States for a thousand years after the Louisiana Purchase had virtually doubled the nation's size. But in less than a century the frontier was closing. The future seemed doubtful. From 1860–1900 the urban population zoomed from 12,000,000 to 48,000,000. "What shall we do with our great cities? What will our great cities do with us?" were the questions that tormented middle class minds. The questions were made more urgent by the work of a group of writers like Ida M. Tarbell, Upton Sinclair and Lincoln Steffens, who soon became popularly known as "the muckrakers."

The political expression of the Progressive movement was the Progressive (or Bull Moose) party, formed by Republican insurgents who supported Theodore Roosevelt for the presidency in 1912. Its general theme was the effort to restore the nation to the economic individualism and political democracy that was widely believed to have existed earlier in America, before it was destroyed by the trusts, the corrupt urban politicians and the labor unions clamoring for more. Thus the Progressives blamed management and labor equally for this loss of civic innocence. So by 1900 the United States, the land that seemed to have been mystically blessed with immunity from grave economic maladjustments, appeared to be threatened by social upheaval and revolt. For in the midst of the Populist and Progressive movements America also faced a mounting socialist challenge.

Out of the Marxist-Lassallean conflict about the relative importance of industrial and political action in achieving revolution which had rent American socialism in the 1880s came eventual unity—a unity imposed on the Socialist Labor Party by its newest recruit, a thirty-eight-year-old Venezuela-born, European-educated son of Dutch-Jewish stock named Daniel DeLeon. Dismissed from a teaching post at Columbia University for radicalism, he began campaigning in 1889 for Henry George's idea of the single tax as an economic and political panacea. At this stage he had read scarcely a word of Marxist theory, though he was familiar with Edward Bellamy's vastly influential utopian romance *Looking Backward*, and regarded Bellamy's Nationalist movement as "one of the most important . . . of the forces of progress in the United States."[9] As late as October 1890 he was still being introduced to SLP audiences as a Nationalist rather than a socialist.[10]

By the end of the year he had reunited the American Marxist party and refashioned it in his own image. Daniel DeLeon dominated American socialism for the next fifteen years, played an important part in founding both the IWW and (by reaction against him) the Socialist Party of America, and died in 1914 with a reputation even Lenin reportedly held in the highest regard. "Premier Lenin is a great admirer of Daniel DeLeon," wrote John Reed, an American socialist and author of a classic eye witness account of the Russian Revolution, *Ten Days That Shook the World*. "He considers him the greatest of modern

[9] *Workmen's Advocate*, March 15, 1890.
[10] *Ibid.*, October 18, 1890.

socialists—the only one who has added anything to socialist thought since Marx."[11]

Next to Debs, DeLeon is probably the most famous American socialist of the period, certainly the most controversial. A dedicated doctrinaire who used his pen not merely for propaganda but to heap vituperative abuse on political opponents and allies alike, he excommunicated his own son, Solon, for daring to question his interpretation of Marx's theory of value. Not surprisingly, he was known as "the Pope" because of his claim to infallibility in matters of socialist faith and morals. On one occasion he told a hostile audience, "I am here . . . to establish a principle, and when that principle is sinned against, I am here to illustrate the principle by the sin."[12] On another, he wrote, "The SLP has all the 'tyranny' of truth."[13]

The mood and the method are that of Lenin. DeLeon, like his Russian counterpart, was an impossible friend and comrade. He split every organization he belonged to, as much for personal as political reasons. Of course, there were serious political disagreements behind all the socialist schisms. DeLeon himself probably bore no malice; but his abusive verbal and editorial attacks made his political opponents believe he did. They contributed to the bitterness of the disputes, and made DeLeon the outstanding "that man" of American socialism, as Lenin was of Russian socialism.

For good or ill Daniel DeLeon left an indelible mark on the American socialist and labor movements. But it was quite un-

[11] Arnold Peterson, *Daniel DeLeon: Socialist Architect* (New York, 1941), 61. For other tributes see Robert Minor's interview with Lenin in *The World*, February 4, 1919, and Arthur Ransome, *Russia in 1919* (New York, 1919), 120–21.
[12] *Proceedings of the Second Convention of the IWW* (Chicago, 1906), 438.
[13] *The People*, January 7, 1900, 5.

characteristic of him to begin his socialist career by uniting a divided movement, as he did with the SLP, rather than dividing a united one. More adept at synthesizing than inventing ideas, he quickly assimilated the rival Marxist and Lassallean arguments about the place of political action in the working-class struggle.

He soon convinced both sides that their controversy within the SLP was futile. The overthrow of capitalism, he argued, could be achieved only by continuous attack on both political and economic fronts. "Iif you have an economic organization alone," he wrote, "you have a duck flying on one wing; you must have a political organization or you are nowhere. . . . Make no mistake: the organization of the working class must be economic and political. The capitalist is organized on both lines. You must attack on both."[14] This argument is significant in the light of the dispute about politics that broke out in the early years of the IWW, and the part DeLeon played in it.

More immediately, DeLeon's policy represented a victory for Marxist ideas within the SLP. By 1891 his new policy was universally accepted within the SLP. But his intellectual gifts were not allied to basic political prerequisites. He never saw the distinction between differences of opinion and political treason, and rarely knew when to make a compromise. The failings of this "perfect American prototype of Russian Bolshevism," as the American socialist Morris Hillquit called him,[15] prevented him from founding a Bolshevik party in the United States.

Although DeLeon advocated activity on both political and economic fronts from his earliest days with the SLP, there was no doubt in his mind at this stage that "thanks to universal

[14] Daniel DeLeon, *Revolution or Reform* (New York, 1945), 31–32.
[15] Morris Hillquit, *Loose Leaves from a Busy Life* (New York, 1934), 46.

suffrage, the ultimate, bloodless socialist revolution will be achieved at the ballot box."[16] He showed little interest in industrial unionism, syndicalism, or direct action until he was forced into a political alliance when helping to found the IWW. He began his political career with the SLP by running for the governorship of New York and polled a mere 14,651 votes.

After this unpromising start in politics he turned his activities to the trade-union front. His first attempt to penetrate existing labor unions came in 1893 when he captured District Assembly 49 of the Knights of Labor, a New York branch consisting mainly of Jewish garment workers,[17] and for about a year he used District Assembly 49 very effectively to exert socialist influence throughout the entire structure of the waning Knights.

But by 1895 the leadership had united to expel DeLeon from District Assembly 49.[18] This reverse coincided with another at the hands of Gompers and the AF of L. Gompers, whose family was of the same Dutch-Jewish stock as DeLeon's, never liked his Marxist rival. He continually accused him of changing his name from Loeb, and DeLeon lent some substance to this smear by maintaining an absurd pretense of being descended from a Spanish-American family of Roman Catholic grandees in Venezuela.[19]

This feud influenced the AF of L conventions of 1893 and 1894, when DeLeon led the socialist trades unionists in an effort to force the adoption of a socialist political program on the AF of L. This would have committed the Federation

16 *The People,* October 16, 1892.
17 Quint, *op. cit.,* 153–60.
18 *Ibid.,* 163.
19 Samuel Gompers, *Seventy Years of Life and Labor* (New York, 1948), 417; Quint, *op. cit.,* 142.

to "the collective ownership of the means of production, and distribution." Gompers and Strasser, opposed to a political program of any kind, fought this one with the utmost vigor and were able to insert a substitute motion calling for the "abolition of the monopoly system of land holding and the substitution therefor of a title of occupancy and use only." This smacked of Henry George's single tax, but grateful for anything to beat socialism the majority passed it.[20]

With one paragraph gone, the convention platform ruled that the entire program was now invalidated. In revenge the defeated socialists combined with the supporters of John McBride of the United Mineworkers to elect him A F of L president and unseat Samuel Gompers.[21] But even this substitute for victory proved short-lived. McBride's brief regime was marked by gross inefficiency and corruption; and at the 1895 convention the membership gratefully re-elected Gompers and routed the socialists. Wage conscious "pure and simple" trade unionists were now in complete control of the A F of L once more, and Gompers' position was never again seriously challenged.[22]

Defeated in both the Knights of Labor and the A F of L, the S L P switched from boring from within to establishing its own competitive union organization. The controversy over these two opposing policies continued for a decade or more, dividing the socialist movement as the Marxist-Lassallean debate had done in the previous decade. But for the time being DeLeon despaired of infiltration. Instead, on December 10, 1895, he called a series of meetings attended by his old comrades in District Assembly 49, the socialist-dominated Central Labor Federation of New York City, the Newark Central

[20] Commons and Associates, *op. cit.*, vol. ii, 509–14; Taft, *op. cit.*, 71–75.
[21] David J. Saposs, *Left Wing Unionism* (New York, 1926), 26.
[22] Taft, *op. cit.*, 73.

Labor Federation, the Brooklyn Socialist Labor Federation and the United Hebrew Trades.[23]

The result of these meetings was a new, militant, class conscious national labor organization, the Socialist Trade and Labor Alliance. From the very beginning DeLeon saw the ST & LA as the industrial wing of the SLP. Its purpose was, in his own words, to serve as "an ally and supplement of the SLP in contacting those masses who cannot be reached by . . . the party organization."[24] But the ST & LA never became an effective labor organization. At no time during its brief and tempestuous career could it claim more than 10,000 members, many of them only on paper and none outside the New York area. Most of the time the figure was far below this: by 1905 it was, on its own admission, down to 1500 members, and according to some estimates had only 600.[25]

Thus the ST & LA was never a serious threat to the AF of L. Its chief consequence was to worsen relations between the AF of L and the socialist movement. For all his dialectical skill DeLeon never really understood the American labor movement. His bitter, indiscriminate attacks on the AF of L as "labor fakers" and "labor lieutenants of the captains of industry,"[26] created a widening gap between his followers and the socialists in general, many of whom were themselves unsympathetic to the ST & LA. This mounting hostility from the Fabian wing of the SLP finally led to a split in the party itself. Many New York socialists, of whom Latvian-born Morris Hillquit was the most articulate, had opposed the whole idea of the ST & LA from the very beginning and felt that

23 Quint, *op. cit.*, 160–61.

24 *Proceedings of the Ninth Annual Convention of the SLP* (New York, 1896), 33.

25 Morris Hillquit, *History of Socialism in the United States* (New York, rev. ed., 1937), 337.

26 A phrase actually coined by Senator Mark Hanna, a Republican millionaire and an advocate of cooperation between management and labor.

DeLeon had imposed it on the SLP by trickery. For them, DeLeon's attempt to form dual unions was a profound tactical error. At all events, as one labor historian has written, "Its principal result . . . was (to coin a phrase) 'dual socialism.'"[27]

In 1898 the SLP dissidents, under Hillquit's able leadership, bolted the SLP and formed their own socialist group—the Rochester, or "Kangaroo" Convention, which three years later formed the core of the new Socialist Party of America. They believed that as socialism depended on union support, DeLeon's fierce antagonism for the AF of L meant it would never endorse socialist aims. Like German-born Victor Berger and his friend Max Hayes, they supported the type of evolutionary socialism Berger was to practice so successfully in Milwaukee during the next decade. For Berger led the Milwaukee socialists, closely allied with labor, to win control of the city administration with a policy of municipal socialism on Fabian lines.

By 1910 Berger had been elected to Congress, and by 1911 thirty-two other American cities, including Berkeley (California), Butte (Montana), and Flint and Jackson (Michigan) were socialist-controlled. Immediate reforms and vote-winning were highest on their list. This era of socialist expansion opened when, after many maneuvers,[28] Hillquit's "Kangaroos" joined hands with the Milwaukee Fabian socialists, the old western Social Democratic party, and the radical remnant of the Nationalist and Populist movements to form the Socialist Party of America in 1901.

The SPA symbolized a new socialist unity. Almost all the old dissenting groups, save DeLeon's small sect of Marxist purists in New York, were allied in the party. It embraced

[27] Pelling, *op. cit.*, 90.

[28] Hillquit, *op. cit.*, 319–94, contains a complete account of these complicated years seen from the eyes of a participant. David A. Shannon, *The Socialist Party of America* (New York, 1955), provides a modern summary.

evolutionists like Berger, Hayes, and Hillquit, visionary industrial unionists like Debs, rural readers of J. A. Wayland's very successful socialist paper *The Appeal to Reason,* and even direct-actionists in the rugged Western metal mines. Its basis was clearly far greater than DeLeon's SLP. In the coming years its growing power increasingly alarmed middle class Americans who had been outraged when a psychotic anarchist terrorist, Leon Czolgosz, acting alone, assassinated President William McKinley at the Pan-American exposition in Buffalo in 1901.

The SPA's rapid success was dramatic proof of the new party's appeal. In 1900 Debs polled less than 100,000 votes as the socialist candidate for President. By 1904 his vote had increased to 402,000, while party membership rose from 10,000 to 118,000 by 1910. In 1912 Debs polled more than 900,000 votes, or about 6 percent of the total popular vote, even running ahead of the Republican ticket in some states like Louisiana and Oklahoma, where his share was as high as 16 percent of the poll. With 135,000 members the SPA was six times larger than the largest British socialist party, the ILP.[29]

Many observers shared Wayland's view that "socialism is coming . . . like a prairie fire and nothing can stop it . . . you can feel it in the air, you can hear it in the wind . . . the next few years will give this country to the Socialist Party." President Theodore Roosevelt voiced the widespread alarm at this prospect when he described the growing threat as "far more ominous than any Populist or similar movement in time past." Nor was the growth of socialism confined to a rising presidential vote. Milwaukee and New York sent socialists to the House of Representatives, and progress within the labor movement was even more encouraging.

[29] Pelling, *op. cit.,* 89; Shannon, *op. cit.,* 78.

Thus, in the years before the First World War, socialists succeeded in dominating several important labor unions, including the Brewery and Bakery Workers, the Shingle Weavers, the Hat and Cap Makers, the International Ladies' Garment Workers, the Fur Workers, the Journeymen Tailors, the Metal Miners, and the International Association of Machinists. Even Gompers' own union, the Cigarmakers, elected the party secretary as a delegate to the AF of L conventions, while the International Typographical Union regularly sent a leading socialist there. Over half the United Mineworkers' delegates, and probably a third of the delegates at an average AF of L convention, were socialists at this time.[30]

The success of the SPA's moderate policy increasingly isolated its opponents in the socialist and labor movements. DeLeon's Socialist Labor Party was in decline, while its labor arm, the Socialist Trade and Labor Alliance, scarcely existed as a separate body. Opponents of the SPA's Fabian policy and advocates of militant industrial unionism began to look for a new forum. These militants found their new champion in the West, in the shape of the Western Federation of Miners.

The WFM was an organization of metal miners founded in Butte, Montana, in 1893. From the first it reflected the violent spirit of life in Western mining camps, where tough, uncompromising frontiersmen met the crude power of the employers in head-on collision. Almost every one of its many strikes ran the same gamut of court injunctions enforced by armed company guards, the calling out of state militia, imprisonment in bull-pens, beatings and deportation to other states.[31] For its

[30] David J. Saposs, *Communism in American Unions* (New York, 1959), 4–5.

[31] Vernon H. Jensen, *Heritage of Conflict* (Cornell, 1950), gives a detailed history of the WFM. The following relies heavily on this account. William D. Haywood, *Bill Haywood's Book* (New York, 1929), *passim,* is a vivid eye witness chronicle of these terrible events.

early battles, which soon became engagements in a permanent civil war, Gompers had managed to raise some limited financial support from the AF of L; and in 1896 the WFM joined the AF of L, sending Patrick Clifford and Edward Boyce, a militant Western advocate of industrial unionism who had just won control of the WFM to the AF of L convention to acknowledge their debt. Boyce was the most important single figure behind the union's policy at this time, until—as if fulfilling Western legend—he struck gold and retired to a more comfortable if less exciting life as a prosperous hotel proprietor in California,[32] leaving the dangerous business of labor leadership to more militant men like William D. (Big Bill) Haywood, Vincent St. John, and Charles H. Moyer, who all played leading roles in founding the IWW.

For them the class war was a self-evident fact which had little need for support from the works of Marx and Engels or the direct action tactics of European syndicalists. In the West men made their own laws. Even the few regulations governing industrial activity in the East were unknown. Hitting the boss hard on all possible occasions seemed the only practical means of curbing his otherwise almost absolute power over their life and labor. All this was a far cry from the "coffin society" activities of the AF of L—a term derived from the emphasis many unions placed on sickness and death benefits.

The already latent conflict in aim and method between the AF of L and the WFM soon became clearly visible. During a strike at Leadville, Colorado, in 1896–97, the metal miners' delegates to the AF of L again asked for financial aid.[33] Once more, as with the ARU during the Pullman strike, Gompers faced the problem of reconciling the demands of a

[32] Taft, *op. cit.*, 153; Haywood, *op. cit.*, 224.
[33] Boyce to Gompers, March 16, 1897. Quoted in Taft, *op. cit.*, 153–55. All letters quoted in this chapter are from the same source.

militant union with the cautious approach of his own craft unions.

Though the executive council of the AF of L's convention endorsed the strike, member unions contributed so little money that the WFM delegates left the convention indignant at what seemed to them a two-faced attitude. Fearing they might talk the WFM into leaving the AF of L, and anxious to retain the membership of such an influential union, Gompers hoped to be able to send a delegate to the WFM convention in March 1897 to explain his difficult position. The AF of L's policy was due more to lack of money and control over its affiliates, than lack of sympathy with the struggle on the part of the AF of L leadership. Gompers himself was not short of admiration for the WFM. "These men are engaged in an awful conflict," he told a colleague, "and the antagonism they have to contend with has brought their strength and courage into relief."[34]

However, a protracted correspondence—subsequently published as a pamphlet—between Gompers and Boyce did not remove the differences. Gompers denied that the AF of L had failed to support the miners' Leadville strike and warned against what he felt were the dangers of organizing the workers along sectional lines. Boyce replied by attacking Gompers' conservatism. "Sitting down in idleness until the capitalists starve us to death," he argued, was not the way to win battles. On this score, as on others, "the men of the West are one hundred years ahead of their brothers in the East." But there were easier ways of winning battles than through strikes, and Boyce urged Gompers "to get out and fight with the sword, or use the ballot box with intelligence"[35]: two courses of action that were the direct antithesis of Gompers' whole philosophy. Rec-

[34] Gompers to George A. Whitaker, March 6, 1897.
[35] Boyce to Gompers, March 16, 1897.

onciliation between the WFM and the AF of L was clearly impossible, and, in December 1897, the WFM withdrew from the American Federation of Labor.

An independent union once more, the WFM quickly set about organizing its own dual unionism. In May 1898 its executive board called a special conference of Western labor organizations at Salt Lake City. A majority (77 out of 121) of the delegates were metal miners, and from the meeting the Western Labor Union emerged. The WLU was Boyce's idea, to organize all labor west of the Mississippi "irrespective of occupation, nationality, creed, or color." In this it had only limited success. As one critical Californian labor leader put it, the Western Labor Union was little more than "the Western Federation of Miners under another name."[36]

Nevertheless, it gave the appearance of powerful support, and since the WFM itself had close to 30,000 members dual unionism was far from being a lost cause. Moreover, the schism in the house of labor had widened considerably now the WFM had established a rival to the AF of L. During the next seven years the WFM fought a series of bitter strikes at Coeur d'Alene, Salt Lake City, Telluride, Cripple Creek, Idaho Springs, and elsewhere. These strikes had many causes, but essentially they all formed part of the eight hour day movement. From these titanic struggles the WFM emerged unbowed, and sometimes victorious. More important, it greatly extended the appeal of militant industrial trades unionism.

Now firmly under the leadership of direct-actionists, the WFM received help from a veteran industrial unionist in 1902 when Debs abandoned his unsuccessful attempt to found a socialist colony.[37] Despite the failure of the Western Labor

[36] Walter MacArthur to Gompers, May 20, 1898.
[37] Quint, *op. cit.*, 280–318 describes this venture.

Union to get established, Debs was able to persuade the leaders of the WFM to extend its operations throughout the whole nation and change its name to the American Labor Union. Debs hoped the ALU would fulfill the hopes he had cherished for his own ill-fated American Railway Union; but from a practical point of view the ALU was no more successful than its predecessor had been.

Its real significance was that it drove a wedge between the WFM and the AF of L just as Gompers was trying to patch up their differences. The leaders of the WFM, Haywood, Moyer, and St. John, more militant than ever and determined to find a broad industrial basis for dual unionism, were rapidly moving into alliance with Debs of the railway workers, William E. Trautmann, editor of the Brewery Workers' newspaper, *Brauer Zeitung*, and Isaac Cowan, American representative of the Amalgamated Society of Engineers of Great Britain which had just been expelled from the AF of L because of jurisdictional disputes with boilermakers, machinists, and pattern makers. With other dissident leaders of the labor and socialist movements, like DeLeon, Ernest Untermann, another syndicalist writer, and Father Thomas J. Hagerty, the maverick Roman Catholic priest, a big black-bearded scholarly man, this group provided the industrial spearhead of the IWW. Hagerty, on six years unofficial leave of absence from his pastoral duties, was not only a good scholar but a good shot too. When railroad officials in Arizona objected to his activities among working men, he said to the messenger, "Tell the people who sent you here that I have a brace of Colts and can hit a dime at twenty paces."[38]

[38] Robert E. Doherty, 'Thomas J. Hagerty, The Church and Socialism,' *Labor History*, vol. 3, no. 1 (Winter, 1962), 41. Hagerty finished up in Chicago's skid row.

These men were the IWW's "founding fathers"; but the Wobblies had a mother too. This was "Mother" Jones, the fabulous figure from the Illinois coalfields. She was born Mary Harris on May 1, 1830, in Cork, and had come to America as a child to work on the railways. After the death of her iron-molder husband and four children in the yellow fever epidemic of 1867, in Memphis, Tennessee, she found a second purpose in life by devoting herself to the struggles of the coal-miners.

In those years she became a living legend. By 1905 she was the most famous and popular woman in American trades unionism. "Whenever trouble broke out against the miners," Haywood wrote, "Mother Jones went there. When a bridge was patrolled by soldiers she waded the river in winter. When trains were being watched the train crew smuggled her through." She organized "women's armies" during mining disputes to chase strike breakers with mops, brooms, and dishpans. "God! It's the old mother with her wild women!" the coal owners would groan when confronted with this formidable array.[39] She was still an active observer of the industrial scene as late as 1925, when she predicted, "The future is in labor's strong, rough hands." When she died on November 30, 1930, at the remarkable age of one hundred, she was buried alongside the Virdin union martyrs in the Miners' Cemetery at Mount Olive, Illinois.[40]

The failure of the long, bitter struggles of the Western Federation of Miners had emphasized their need for a new, militant supporting body. So the WFM was prominent at the so-called "secret" Chicago conference in January 1905 when

[39] Elizabeth Gurley Flynn, *I Speak My Own Piece* (New York, 1955), 80–81.

[40] Archie Green, "The Death of Mother Jones," *Labor History*, vol. 1, no. 3 (Winter, 1960), 68–80.

twenty-seven revolutionaries—including Haywood, Trautmann, Hagerty, Untermann, Mother Jones, and Frank Bohn, an organizer of the SLP and ST & LA—drafted an invitation to representatives of labor unions and socialist parties in both America and Europe to help found a revolutionary labor union movement on industrial lines. This Industrial Union Manifesto, or "January Manifesto" as it was known, called for a labor organization "embracing within itself the working class in approximately the same groups and departments and industries that workers would assume in the working class administration of the Cooperative Commonwealth . . ."

The new movement "must consist of one great industrial union embracing all industries, providing for craft autonomy locally, industrial autonomy internationally and working class unity generally."[41] Thus, although this conflict was not revealed for some years, the union's aims were irreconcilable, for local autonomy could often jeopardize working class solidarity. For the moment, however, the outcome of the January Manifesto was the founding conference of the Industrial Workers of the World, which met the following summer in Chicago.[42]

The 1904 Amsterdam Conference of the Second International, which DeLeon attended, had called for greater unity and internationalism among socialist groups. When the IWW's founders met in Chicago, the nation they looked to above all for inspiration and example was France. For it was in France, where trade union activity was permitted again in 1884 after the repression following the failure of the 1871 Paris Commune, that syndicalist methods of industrial organization and tactics were evolving.

[41] *Proceedings of the First IWW Convention* (Chicago, 1905), 5–6.
[42] Brissenden, *op. cit.*, 61–62; *The Launching of the IWW* (Berkeley, 1913), 46–49.

In Germany and Britain the new unions which had developed in the 1880s aimed at piecemeal improvements in wages and conditions. They also established close relations with the expanding political socialist parties. In France the new working class movement was influenced by the teachings of Pierre Joseph Proudhon, the leading anarchist writer of the 1850s. Workers in individual factories formed unions, or *syndicats,* which soon extended throughout whole industries.

In 1895 the *syndicats* formed their own confederation—the Confédération Générale du Travail. Within ten years, the CGT had accepted the ideas of Georges Sorel, whose influential book *Reflections on Violence* was published in 1906 shortly after the IWW was born. Sorel and other French thinkers, like Fernand Pelloutier, argued that the future of anarchism must be linked with the trade unions. Many anarchists, like Emma Goldman in the United States, rejected this idea, clinging instead to Bakunin's view of trade unions as a means by which the working class were tempted away from their true revolutionary destiny.[43]

Yet the Pelloutier policy immediately met with some success. The French syndicalist manifesto, the Charter of Amiens of 1906, combined agitation for immediate reforms with a long-term plan for the overthrow of capitalism. This was to start with a strike by individual unions, followed by a universal one-day strike, which would cause a general and complete stoppage everywhere, leading to a general strike and revolution. Many founders of the IWW, like Haywood, Hagerty, and Trautmann, were familiar with the Charter of Amiens, and warmly approved the French syndicalists' opposition to political parties and Parliament, which they described as "a sink of jobbery, corruption and compromise."

[43] Emma Goldman, 'Aims and Tactics of the Trade Union Movement,' *Mother Earth,* vol. i, no. 5 (July 1906), 27–32.

Like the French, Haywood and the others believed working class power would be won by direct action and the general strike, when the workers would seize their industries, lock out the employers and rule the state. As one of them explained, "The basic method and its revolutionary goal is the setting up of the trade union state to control industry and other social activities."[44] Yet while the French syndicalists believed in boring from within existing unions, the Wobblies wanted to create a dual union outside the structure of the AF of L. Moreover, while American syndicalists put great emphasis on industrial, as opposed to craft organization, this meant almost nothing to their European comrades, who generally regarded unionism as synonymous with organization on craft lines.

As the IWW founding convention opened, Czarist Russia was in the throes of revolution. While it deliberated, events took a new turn as the crew of the battleship *Potemkin* mutinied, an event immortalized by S. M. Eisenstein in his famous film. Working class victory in Russia seemed near. The founders of the IWW believed it would not be long before revolution swept them to power in the United States too.

It was no accident that the city of Chicago should have been the birthplace of the new revolutionary movement. Chicago was one of America's greatest centers of radicalism. The crusade for the eight hour day began there. So did the observance of International Labor Day on May 1, in memory of the Haymarket martyrs. The American Socialist Party had deep roots in Chicago, and the powerful AF of L teamsters and seafaring unions were organized there. Eventually, in 1919, the American Communist Party was to hatch in a West Side Wobbly Hall. In this tradition the IWW's founding convention opened at Brand's Hall, Chicago, on June 27, 1905.

44 William Z. Foster, quoted in John Strachey, *The Theory and Practice of Socialism* (London, 1934), 101.

3
INFANTILE DISORDERS

THE SYNDICALIST IDEA

If the workers took a notion
They could stop all speeding trains
Every ship upon the ocean
They can tie with mighty chains

Every wheel in the creation
Every mine and every mill;
Fleets and armies of the nation,
Will at their command stand still.

JOE HILL

The honor of delivering the opening address at the IWW's first conference went by general agreement to the hero of the Western metal miners, Big Bill Haywood. William Dudley Haywood, a huge figure of a man, with "a face like a scarred battlefield" as John Reed,[1] the Harvard-educated socialist journalist, described him seemed to personify the Wobbly spirit as he strode to the platform, seized a piece of board to use as a gavel and opened the convention with the words, "Fellow workers."

His experience was typical of many of the two hundred delegates. He was born in the Mormon settlement of Salt Lake City, Utah, in 1869 and grew up in the raw, frontier atmosphere of the West. Like another leading Wobbly, Frank Little, Haywood had some Indian blood. His father, an American of old stock, died in a mining camp when he was three, and thereafter he was brought up by his mother, a South African who came to the United States in adolescence.[2]

By the age of seven he was quite used to violence, bloodshed, and sudden death. "After all the talk of massacres and killings in Salt Lake City," he recalled in his autobiography[3] "I accepted it all as a natural part of life." About this time he accidentally stabbed himself in the right eye while making a

[1] Quoted by Charles A. Madison, *American Labor Leaders* (New York, 1962), 282.

[2] Haywood, *op. cit.*, 1. According to another Wobbly writer, Ralph Chaplin, this autobiography was ghosted for Haywood in Moscow shortly before his death by Louise Bryant, John Reed's common law wife, after Chaplin himself had refused the task.

[3] *Ibid.*, 12.

slingshot and was permanently blinded—a handicap that added to his burdens.

"Hardly a week passed," he remembered,[4] "without a fight with some boy or other, who would call me 'Dead-eye Dick' or 'Squint Eye' because of my blind eye." He added, significantly, "I used to like a fight." Haywood's natural pugnacity was tested when, at the age of nine, he started work in the mining camps to help support his widowed mother. Surviving this cruel test, he broke away from mining in his youth to start a new life as a homesteader in Nevada. He was happy among the cowboys with his teenage bride, Jane Minor. But his happiness was cut short when his land was taken by the government to make an Indian reservation.[5]

Haywood, who by then had two daughters and whose wife had become an invalid, was hard hit by this loss. Returning to the metal mines after his brief taste of independence he resented the fetters of "wage slavery" much more strongly. This resentment, a characteristic phenomenon in the West of the time, helps account for the rise of the IWW. The abolition of the wage system was a central tenet of syndicalist thought. But in America it had a different significance than in Europe. Most Western European countries had been bound to industrial capitalism, with its accompanying wage slavery, longer and more tightly than America. Here, across the great plains of the West, memories of the trapper and trader, the yeoman farmer, the rancher and prospector, were still very much alive, and already encrusted by a rich tradition of romantic myth. One common factor united all these trades and was spun through the web of legend surrounding them: sturdy independence. This, not the wage system, had opened up the frontier.

[4] *Ibid.*, 12.
[5] *Ibid.*, 51.

Haywood had lost this independence when the government took his land. But all over the West private enterprise based on individual endeavor was being replaced by the private enterprise of the finance corporation, the mining company and the lumber trust. Members of the Western Federation of Miners, which Haywood helped found in 1893, shared his indignation at the changes that had robbed them of their freedom.

In short, the protests made against the wage system in America at the turn of the century by the WFM and other bodies were much nearer the grass-roots level than similar protests in Europe. Few European working men could by that time remember any other system, or even clearly visualize an alternative. But the vision of a more decent life was still very vivid to many Americans living close to the frontier, where it was based on memories of the life they, like Haywood, had just lost.

The same experience held in Australia and New Zealand, where the frontier situation was also just being replaced by a wage system for the first time. Significantly, both countries developed a Wobbly movement much more akin to the American than the European model. The frontier, or rather its close, seemed to be producing a unique type of post-frontier syndicalism. And Chicago was the obvious center for a new union that would attract many migratory members. For a generation Chicago had been the Midwestern labor market for casual and seasonal workers and the most frequented crossroads in the United States. It still had traces of the "open town" life of the frontier.

With his quick mind and organizational gifts Haywood, who was also a powerful orator, soon provided a focus for these discontents. After helping to found the Western Federation of Miners he quickly won a reputation as a militant union man.

His political philosophy was forged in the crucibles of Colorado, where the WFM fought its bloodiest battles. Haywood saw nothing in common between the owners of the mining companies, with their private army of strike breakers, and the WFM. He believed passionately that "between these two classes a struggle must go on until the workers of the world organize as a class, take possession of the earth and the machinery of production, and abolish the wage system."[6]

So Haywood, as he addressed the founding conference of the IWW, thought he was looking at the movement that would accomplish this world-wide revolution. He hailed the meeting as "the Continental Congress of the working class,"[7] a proud boast which had little foundation in fact. But his claim that "there is no other organization . . . that has for its purpose the same object as that for which . . . you are called here together today"[8] was more accurate, even though the purpose was variously interpreted by his audience.

Haywood's own view was clear. "We are here today," he explained, "to confederate the workers . . . into a working class movement that shall have for its purpose the emancipation of the working class from the slave bondage of capitalism."[9] This was clearly not the purpose of the American Federation of Labor, despite its recent entry into politics with the policy of "rewarding friends and punishing enemies."

In 1905 the American Federation of Labor, stronger numerically than at any time in its history so far, still embraced only about 5 percent of the American working class.[10] The remaining 95 percent were unorganized and usually lacked any ef-

[6] *Preamble to the Constitution of the IWW.*
[7] *Proceedings of the First IWW Convention* (New York, 1905), 1.
[8] *Ibid.*
[9] *Ibid.*, 1–2.
[10] Commons and Associates, *op. cit.*, vol. iv, 13–19.

fective means of protecting their own interests in the labor market. The recent immigrants, often unskilled or semiskilled, speaking little or no English and completely unfamiliar with life in an industrialized society like the United States, were especially helpless. They were treated with suspicion and often open hostility by their more fortunate fellow workers who possessed skills and belonged to craft unions; frequently they seemed to justify this hostility by providing a floating pool of cheap labor and strike breakers.[11] But Haywood's opening words were addressed to these unorganized workers across the nation, rather than to his audience in Brand's Hall.

For by no stretch of even Haywood's imagination could these delegates be taken as representative of the American working class. Most of them came from unions that, for one reason or another, were at loggerheads with the A F of L. They were all radicals, and most of the leading personalities had been influenced by socialism of varying kinds, though this was often overlaid with syndicalism or anarchism. They shared a common conviction that the craft form of unionism, represented by the A F of L, should be replaced by industrial organization. The employers were organizing themselves on industrial lines by forming trusts and corporations, in the face of which craft unions seemed like powerless relics from a past era. The wage workers' answer to the trusts should be to organize industrially themselves. On this much there was general agreement. Beyond that the delegates seemed to lack any homogeneity.

Their unions represented a wide range of occupations.[12] More important, since the conference was called for the purpose of organizing along industrial lines, their structural differences were particularly bewildering. There were delegates

[11] Saposs, *op. cit.,* 111.
[12] At least forty were present. Brissenden, *Launching of the I W W, op. cit.,* 10–11, n., gives a complete list.

from industrial unions like the Western Federation of Miners; the multi-industrial American Labor Union; "internationals"—unions that organized in Canada too—like the United Metal Workers; the United Mineworkers of America, a non-federative industrial union; and state federations, like the Utah State Federation of labor. The American branch of the Amalgamated Society of Engineers of Great Britain was also present.

Despite this structural variety, differences in political ideology were of more immediate significance. The main division was between the Marxists, who belonged either to the left wing of the Socialist Party of America or to the Socialist Labor Party, and the anarchists and syndicalists. The SPA was not formally represented in the Chicago convention; indeed, its right wing had expressed strong disapproval of the new venture and the idea behind it when invited to attend the January convention in Chicago where the Industrial Union Manifesto, which convened the conference, had been drawn up in 1905. For example Victor Berger, leader of the Milwaukee socialist party, and Max Hayes of the Typographical Union disapproved strongly of the whole IWW venture from the start. Both were firm believers that militant, socialist trade unions should pursue a policy of boring from within the AF of L.

Hayes told a fellow trade unionist when the idea of the IWW was first being mooted, "This sounds to me as though we are going to have another Socialist Trade and Labor Alliance . . . it means another running fight between the socialists on one side and all other partisans on the other . . . I intend to *agitate on the inside* of the organizations now in existence."[13]

[13] Max Hayes' letter to W. L. Hall, secretary-treasurer of the United Brotherhood of Railway Employees, December 30, 1904, *Proceedings, op. cit.*, 99–100 (emphasis in original).

The left wing of the Socialist Party of America was represented by such diverse figures as Haywood himself; Debs, already twice a socialist candidate for President; and Algie Simons, holder of a Phi Beta Kappa key, who was editor of the *International Socialist Review*. Like the SPA, the Socialist Labor Party was not formally represented at the convention, but its leader, Daniel DeLeon, had brought fourteen delegates from the SLP's trade union wing, the Socialist Trade and Labor Alliance. Anarchists and syndicalists, like black-bearded Father Hagerty, Trautmann, editor of the *Brauer Zeitung*, and Lucy Parsons, widow of one of the Haymarket martyrs, formed a small but extremely influential faction.

These opposing groups, each led by strong personalities determined to get their way, held conflicting views about the policy socialists should adopt toward the labor movement. The right wing of the SPA argued that the only tactic not doomed to failure was infiltration. Berger, Hayes, and Simons all held this view, and of these only Simons attended the inaugural conference. Debs occupied an ideological position somewhere near the center of the SPA, still advocating independent, socialist unions with an industrial basis which would challenge the supremacy of the AF of L.

When Debs rose to speak at the IWW's first meeting he was framed by Mother Jones on one side and Lucy Parsons on the other.[14] Together they made a picture symbolic of the work the IWW had undertaken. Debs spoke in favor of compromise; but he was not entirely accurate in his assessment of the balance of power. "I believe it is possible," he said, "for such an organization as the Western Federation of Miners to be brought into harmonious relation with the Socialist Trade and Labor Alliance . . . for these elements to combine here

[14] Haywood, *op. cit.*, 183.

. . . and begin the work of forming a great economic or revolutionary organization of the working class so sorely needed for their emancipation."[15]

Voting at the convention was dominated by two organizations: the Western Federation of Miners, and its parent organization,[16] the American Labor Union. A little over 140,000 workers were represented at the convention. But of these over 90,000 merely sent observers, without voting rights. Unions whose representatives could vote claimed a total membership of some 51,000; thus the WFM and the ALU, who claimed 27,000 and 16,750 members respectively, could clearly dominate the proceedings.[17]

They failed to do so for several reasons. The leading personalities of the WFM were far from united about what sort of organization they wanted the IWW to be. Haywood, while still ready to enter the political arena, was veering toward the anarcho-syndicalism of Hagerty and Trautmann; but he had not forsaken the possibilities of political action entirely. Still, his ideas were sufficiently left wing to make Charles Moyer, a smelter man from South Dakota, somewhat uneasy. Moyer, who had become president when Boyce retired in 1902, was a strong, soft-spoken and gentle character with close family ties, whose experiences during the struggle for the eight hour day made him doubt the wisdom of constant strikes. By 1905 he held opinions closer to those of Debs than DeLeon or Haywood.

Moyer had been a close friend and comrade of Haywood

[15] *Proceedings, op. cit.,* 144.

[16] The ALU was in fact founded by the WFM in the hope that it would become a rival to the AF of L and a focus for dual unions within the United States—see chapter 1, above. However, the ALU never surpassed the WFM's membership.

[17] *Proceedings, op. cit.,* p. 611. There were also some individual delegates, representing no one but themselves. They included Debs, Mother Jones, and A. M. Simons. *Ibid.,* pp. 6, 54.

since the early days of the WFM. They had stood together in violent encounters with strike breakers during fierce Western mining disputes. But their friendship was near its close. As Haywood became more extremist, Moyer became more moderate. Ironically, their partnership collapsed when they came to face their greatest test: arrest and trial on a murder charge in 1906.

But at this stage neither man was assured of support from the rank and file members of the WFM. In any case, the WFM, with only four delegates, was seriously underrepresented when compared with the ST & LA's fourteen. Haywood and Moyer also represented the ALU, which tended to weaken their position because they had to worry about the reactions of two unions. By contrast Hagerty, the most articulate delegate from the ALU, and DeLeon had advantages not enjoyed by Haywood and Moyer. They had a clearer idea of what they wanted and fewer fears about the possible repercussions of their strategy on their own union members. Not surprisingly in these circumstances, the IWW emerged from the Brand's Hall meeting on a basis largely laid by Hagerty and DeLeon.

Though the WFM held an overwhelming majority of the votes, the main protagonists at this stage were really the ST & LA, led by DeLeon, and the American Labor Union (closely identified with the WFM), represented by Hagerty and Trautmann. Watching Debs closely as he spoke, DeLeon with his badger-gray whiskers and black-spotted chin represented a much more doctrinaire brand of American socialism. There were other contrasts between Debs and DeLeon too. One was a railway worker, the other a former university teacher; one was tolerant and willing to compromise, the other so inflexible that he had already earned the nickname "the Pope."

But on this occasion DeLeon was pleased with what Debs

had to say and later rose to agree with it warmly. In 1892, DeLeon had been convinced that the "ultimate, socialist revolution" would be won at the polls, when he had written, "Thanks to universal suffrage . . . the revolution will be achieved peacefully, in our day, by a mere expression of will at the ballot box."[18]

He saw labor unions as merely an instrument with which to organize this working class vote more effectively and tended to accept industrial unions simply as a means by which this could best be done. Trautmann and Hagerty and, to a lesser extent at this stage, Haywood, too, had as much scorn for the democratic ballot as they had for "pure and simple" trade unionism. Haywood lost faith in politics when socialists who captured state governments in 1906–7 were fraudulently counted out. Yet his attitude toward politics was sufficiently positive as late as 1906 for him to run for the governorship of Colorado, even though he was in jail. Moreover, he remained on the executive of the S P A, which emphasized political activity, until 1913.[19]

The anarcho-syndicalists saw industrial unions as a means of seizing power more effectively by expropriating the means of production in whole industries at a time.[20] The anarcho-syndicalists believed that "Political action leads to capitalism reformed. Direct action leads to socialism . . . All aboard for

18 *The People,* October 16, 1892.

19 Haywood, *op. cit.,* 202; Brissenden, *op. cit.,* 282 and n. For a full discussion of Haywood's attitude to politics, see chapter 6, below.

20 Hagerty's ideas can be read in the *Industrial Union Manifesto,* which he drafted in January 1905. Brissenden, *op. cit.,* appendix v, 46–49, reprints the 'secret' manifesto. See also Hagerty "On the Chicago Manifesto," *Weekly People,* February 18, 1905. Trautmann's most important work was "The United Brewery Workers and Industrial Organization," *A L U Journal,* September 3, 1903, and "Scabbing After Election," *Ibid.,* October 1904, "A Pickwickian Socialist," *Ibid.,* December 1904 and *Brauer Zeitung* and the *Voice of Labor,* 1903–5, *passim,* for anarcho-syndicalist ideas.

the IWW. Death to politics."[21] Haywood would not spurn political action entirely, though he increasingly emphasized direct action—the workers' assertion of economic power. But the anarcho-syndicalists and the syndicalists were willing to sink their differences in 1905 to get the one big industrial union started. DeLeon, for his part, seems to have been influenced increasingly by anarcho-syndicalist ideas in the years just before the founding convention.

This doctrinaire Marxist had started to republish in his paper, the *Daily People,* several articles by Trautmann which described the European syndicalist unions and the theory that these would provide the basis for government in the socialist commonwealth.[22] The articles also compared the potency of the general strike, in the hands of the working class, with the inadequacy of the ballot box. Further evidence of DeLeon's increasing interest in syndicalist ideas is shown by his reprinting of articles translated from the French syndicalist paper, *Le Mouvement Socialiste,* edited in Paris by Hubert Lagardelle.[23]

But DeLeon was far from accepting syndicalism completely. As late as the autumn of 1904 he was still dismissing the idea of the general strike as a "trifle" containing "a double error."[24] Nor had he yet endorsed the principle of industrial unionism, at least as Debs, in the center, or Hagerty, at the extreme left,

[21] E. J. Higgins 'Direct Action versus Impossibilism,' *Mother Earth,* vol. 11, vii no. 2 (April 1912), 39–46.

[22] See *The People,* January-March, 1905. DeLeon also received the *Brauer Zeitung* regularly at his office. Don K. McKee, 'Daniel DeLeon: a Reappraisal,' *Labor History,* vol. 1, no. 3 (Fall, 1960), 288, n.

[23] These reprints included Pablo Iglesias, 'Late Elections in Spain,' *The People,* July 2, 1899; Hubert Lagardelle, 'Truth about Millerand,' *Daily People,* June 4, 1901; 'In French Parliament: Debate on the Miners' Strike in France—Attitude of Parties,' *Daily People,* December 14, 1902 (anonymous, but apparently written by Emile Buré); and Robert Michels, 'Dangers of German Social Democracy,' *Weekly People,* April 8, 1905.

[24] Daniel DeLeon, *Flashlights of the Amsterdam Congress* (New York, 1929), 93, 96–97. Reports written for the *Daily People.*

understood that term. As he had shown in an address delivered at Newark, New Jersey, in April 1904[25] he still believed that revolution could be achieved *via* the ballot box. But in the last decade, the SLP's share of the votes cast for President had been declining ominously.

No doubt these electoral failures made him more attentive to the arguments of Trautmann and Hagerty that, in a revolutionary situation, the capitalists would use fraud to deprive the proletariat of their victory at the ballot box.[26] In such a situation, DeLeon was prepared to admit, direct action by the working class would be justified.[27] This was a different stand from that taken by the anarcho-syndicalists, who put all their faith in economic action. But this concession to direct action in certain circumstances was to prove the basis on which the IWW was founded.

DeLeon was one of the cleverest men at the founding convention, and also its ablest politician. His political ability, shown by his shrewd decision to bring a large ST & LA delegation with him, accounts for his influence on the early life of the IWW.[28] He was vitally concerned about launching a new trade union movement and securing his own place in it, because his political position was dwindling. The decline of the SLP was bad enough. But now the ST & LA was facing extinction.

With only 1500 accredited members[29] the ST & LA had

[25] Daniel DeLeon, *The Burning Question of Trades Unionism* (New York, 1947), *passim.*

[26] 'The United Brewery Workers and Industrial Organization,' *op. cit.*, and "Scabbing After Election," *op. cit.*

[27] 'The Seidenberg Spectre,' *Daily People* editorial, November 3, 1903, 4, and 'Events that are Approaching,' *Ibid.*, January 21, 1905, 4.

[28] The ST & LA delegation was 14 compared with 5 from the WFM. WFM membership was 27,000, ST & LA 1500. *Proceedings, op. cit.*, 611. See also n. 30, below.

[29] According to opponents, only 600. See Hillquit, *op. cit.*, 337.

little voting power; but DeLeon was able to use his skill in committee work to secure a policy statement that made concessions to his point of view. His only chance to save the ST & LA was to merge it with the new IWW. To achieve this he would have to accept the principle of industrial organization and anarcho-syndicalist direct action. Although there were signs, which have already been mentioned, that he had recently given both these theories more careful attention, he still believed strongly in political action.

But within the IWW political action might raise some awkward problems for DeLeon. The ST & LA was facing extinction and its political arm, the Socialist Labor Party, was in little better shape. Since 1899, when the SLP split into two factions, its fortunes had declined steadily. By contrast, SPA membership had risen steeply to 23,000 by 1905. In 1904 Debs netted 402,000 votes in his second run for President; the SLP candidate, a mere 31,000.[30] The lesson from these figures was clear. If the IWW were to affiliate with a political party it would be the SPA, not the SLP, that it joined.

This danger was made greater by the presence of several prominent left wing members of the SPA–Haywood, Hall, and Simons–at the founding convention. The ALU and other unions that sponsored the new organization had even officially adopted the SPA's program. Thus DeLeon's overriding aim at Chicago in 1905 was to prevent any such close political identification of the IWW with the SPA. He wanted to keep it unaffiliated and thus more easily dominate it himself on behalf of his own SLP.

[30] Hillquit, *op. cit.,* 338; McKee, *op. cit.,* 276. The SLP vote of 31,248 showed a decline from 34,191 in 1900 and 36,564 in 1896. By 1912, SPA membership had tripled; and Debs' poll in that year of over 900,000, represented 6 percent of the popular vote. See chapter 2, above, for SPA expansion in both state and city politics and in the AF of L.

The compromise that emerged from the conflict over political affiliation was a constitution that, while unmistakably anarcho-syndicalist in tone, still recognized the need for the IWW to agitate "on the political, as well as on the industrial field . . . without affiliation with any political party."[31] This celebrated "political clause," the root of so much controversy within the IWW and the reason for the schism of 1908, was entirely DeLeon's work.

"The Pope" probably had no detailed strategy in mind when he arrived at the convention. Hagerty's proposed draft of the preamble to the constitution included the statement that the proletariat should "take and hold that which they produce by their labor, through an economic organization of the working class." DeLeon claimed complete ignorance of this version until he was appointed to the constitution committee on the fifth day of the convention. Certainly his first major address, delivered on the third day, contained no mention of the idea that the workers' commonwealth would be achieved by seizure of industry through the trade union movement.[32] The main point of the speech was to emphasize the thesis contained in *The Burning Question of Trades Unionism* that the might of labor's economic arm should be used to back up the socialist ballot.

Hagerty's reaction to DeLeon's opening speech was prompt and unequivocal. He delivered a vigorous denunciation of DeLeonism. "Dropping pieces of paper into a hole in a box never did achieve emancipation for the working class, and to my thinking it never will," he argued.[33] The task confronting the IWW would be fulfilled, not through voting, but through

[31] *Preamble to the Constitution of the IWW*, as adopted at the first convention. Brissenden, *op. cit.*, appendix iv, 46.
[32] *Proceedings*, *op. cit.*, 149–52.
[33] *Ibid.*, 152–53.

the "capture of the tools of industry" by the economic movement of the working class.[34] As if to underline the antipolitical implication of this speech, it was seconded by Lucy Parsons, widow of one of America's most famous anarchists, who supported Hagerty's motion with an uncompromising speech. "My conception of the strike of the future," she explained, "is not to strike and go out and starve, but to strike and remain in and take possession of the necessary property of production. If anyone is to starve . . . let it be the capitalist class."[35] This syndicalist idea of the "sit-in strike" was used with great effect by the CIO in the 1930s.

Thus revealed to the convention at large, the dispute between politicians and direct actionists moved into the closed sessions of the constitutional committee, which met on the fifth and sixth days of the proceedings. Here the bargain was struck. The committee accepted DeLeon's amendment to Hagerty's proposed draft of the preamble. This amendment advocated political action, but specifically forbade the IWW to affiliate with any political party. In return, DeLeon accepted the idea that the IWW, as an industrial union, must be the means through which the working class would ultimately "take and hold that which they produce by their own labor."[36] The political clause, designed by DeLeon to avoid affiliation with the SPA and increase his own influence on the IWW, actually caused his expulsion three years later. But the syndicalist idea that trade unions should themselves seize power directly, which DeLeon originally accepted for tactical reasons at the first IWW convention, became, ironically, a permanent part of DeLeonism.

[34] *Ibid.*, 153.
[35] *Ibid.*, 170.
[36] *Preamble to the Constitution of the IWW*, Brissenden, *op. cit.*, 46.

At subsequent IWW conventions, and in the columns of the *Daily People,* DeLeon found himself having to defend the whole IWW preamble in order to ensure the adoption of the amendments he had added in committee. He defended his tactics by saying "the 'political clause' was a necessity . . . to switch the IWW movement right and counteract the pernicious effect of the 'pure and simple' political socialist schemers, who were poisoning the movement with their twaddle."[37]

Two speeches he made on the sixth day of the convention were a watershed in the early history of the IWW. In the first he championed the "take and hold" doctrine, propounded earlier by Hagerty in opposition to DeLeon's opening address. Working class power would be won "THROUGH AN ECONOMIC ORGANIZATION OF THE WORKING CLASS," DeLeon argued, because "it is out of the question to imagine that a political party can 'take and hold.'"[38] In the second speech, later the same day, DeLeon advocated the general strike for the first time in his life, knowing that failure to do so would risk losing the decisive votes of Haywood and the WFM.[39]

Clarence Smith of the ALU accurately gauged the true nature of the preamble when he complained from the floor, "It seems to me that this paragraph, the political clause of the preamble . . . represents a toadying to three different factions in this convention . . . to the man who does not believe in politics at all . . . to the socialist, and also to the anarchist . . ."[40] DeLeon later defended his amalgamation of anarchism and political Marxism, but made no effort to deny the truth of Smith's objections.[41] Despite this opposition from the

[37] *Weekly People,* February 10, 1906. A similar defense can be found in the *Weekly People,* October 30, 1909, and the *Weekly People,* April 13, 1912.
[38] *Proceedings, op. cit.,* 225–28, 231, (caps in original).
[39] *Ibid.,* 247–48.
[40] *Ibid.,* 229.
[41] *Ibid.,* 231.

floor, the DeLeon-Hagerty preamble passed. While technically committed to political activity, the IWW was unaffiliated with any party.

The early years of the Industrial Workers of the World saw little progress in the fields of unionization and job control: they were largely absorbed by internal faction fighting. In retrospect all this squabbling may seem of little importance. But in fact the debate between the Marxist wing of the movement, led by DeLeon, who believed in combining political with industrial working class agitation, and the antipolitical direct actionists, led by Haywood and St. John, was another stage in an argument that had divided revolutionary socialism for more than forty years since Marx and Bakunin had struggled for control of the First International.

The conflict appears unimportant now mainly because the Wobblies failed in their revolutionary aims. For this failure they have been cast into "the dustbin of history" as Trotsky put it. Yet the conflict between the Bolshevik and Menshevik wings of the Russian Social Democratic Party (in which Trotsky himself played a leading role) would, by the same token, seem unimportant now if the Russian Revolution of 1917 had failed.

Today the famous conference of the Russian Social Democrats, held in Brussels and London in 1903, at which the Bolshevik-Menshevik split first appeared, is rightly seen as one of the central events of the twentieth century. In 1905, with revolution raging in Russia, it seemed, as indeed it was, a conflict about who should lead that revolution. The Wobblies saw their schism as a conflict about who should lead the revolution in the United States, which they believed was close at hand. Today their hopes seem a little naive; but in 1905 they understandably felt nearer to power than a handful of obscure Russian exiles.

Besides temporarily settling these ideological differences, the organizing convention of the IWW organized very little. Its three industrial departments—mining, metal and machinery, and transportation—looked very formidable, but apart from the WFM, scarcely existed except on paper.[42] Indeed, at this stage, the WFM was virtually the only part of the IWW that had any real existence. Hagerty drew up a chart classifying the industrial population of the United States, which he intended as a basis for IWW organization drives. Gompers dubbed it "Father Hagerty's Wheel of Fortune,"[43] and indeed it bore little relation to practical possibility. The main problem facing the IWW, which Hagerty's chart did nothing to solve, was an acute shortage of money, organizers with ability or honesty, and, above all, members. If one ignores the massive contribution of the WFM, the Wobblies started life with 1100 members and $817.50.[44] In the following months little happened to improve the IWW's somewhat inauspicious start.

Before breaking up, the founding convention completed final business. Routine resolutions were passed condemning militarism, recommending the general strike, and adopting May 1 as the international holiday of the American working class. Membership, though restricted to wage workers, was made universally transferable: any union member coming to America from abroad was accepted into the IWW without the high initiation fees demanded by the AF of L. The delegates made a pilgrimage to the graves of the Haymarket martyrs in Waldheim Cemetery.[45] Lastly, the convention moved to elect its officers.

[42] Brissenden, *The IWW, op. cit.*, 113–14.
[43] *Ibid.*, appendix i, 350–51. The epithet was apparently coined by D. C. Coates, head of the ALU, and a founder member of the IWW, but used frequently by Gompers. Taft, *op. cit.*, 159.
[44] Brissenden, *The IWW, op. cit.*, 83–87; Fred Thompson, *The IWW: Its First Fifty Years* (Chicago, 1955), 23.
[45] Haywood, *op. cit.*, 186–87.

Characteristically, this step, which any other organization would have regarded as of central importance, was rushed through by the IWW in the most haphazard manner imaginable. Though DeLeon, an ex-university teacher, could look sufficiently like a wage worker to attend the IWW's convention, he was too little like one to run for office. Moreover, the non-affiliation provision precluded the election of the leader of the SLP. Similarly Debs, closely identified with the SPA, was disqualified and would have been unwilling to run in any case.

Charles Coates and Big Bill Haywood were both nominated, but declined to run because of official responsibilities with their own unions.[46] When Guy Miller nominated Haywood, he described him as a man who would not be afraid to go into the "bull-pens" if necessary, at which Mother Jones growled approvingly, "and lick the militia."[47] Almost by default, Charles O. Sherman of the United Metal Workers was unanimously elected first—and last—president of the IWW, with Trautmann as secretary-treasurer and a five-man General Executive Board.

After all the radical oratory during the convention the domination of the first GEB by conservative elements is remarkable. The Board members were Sherman and Trautmann, John Riordon and F. W. Cronin of the ALU; Frank McCabe of the United Brotherhood of Railway Employees; Charles Kirkpatrick of the Metal Workers; and Charles Moyer of the WFM.[48] Apart from Trautmann, none of the members was associated with the alliance between DeLeon and the anarcho-syndicalists which had dominated the rest of the meeting.

[46] *Ibid.*, 187. Coates was president of the ALU, Haywood an officer in the WFM.
[47] *Ibid.*, 190.
[48] *Proceedings, op. cit.*, 498–99.

Indeed, Sherman and several of the other men were closer to the right wing of the SPA than Debs. The failure of the radicals to take command in 1905 is all the more surprising because the GEB had been invested with considerable power. The entire responsibility for conducting the union's affairs between conventions was placed in its hands. The Board was given full power to issue charters; levy special strike funds; and supervise and control the union's official journal as well as select its editor.[49] The manner in which the GEB used these powers during 1905–6 caused the first of the IWW's many internal battles.

It took place in almost comic opera circumstances during the second convention. Originally scheduled for May 1906, the meeting was postponed after the arrest of Moyer, Haywood, and a black-listed miner-shopkeeper, George Pettibone, who were all charged with the murder of Frank Steunenberg, the former Governor of Idaho. It was held finally during September and October in Chicago.[50] Sherman's lavish personal spending of union funds, Trautmann's apparent incompetence and heavy drinking, and the dictatorial inefficiency of the GEB created some strong opposition during the year.[51] This opposition was given powerful ideological undertones by DeLeon. Since neither Hagerty nor Debs was present at the convention, and Haywood was in jail, DeLeon had a great opportunity to try to capture the IWW. His attempt was vigorously combated by president Sherman and the entire GEB, with the exception of Trautmann who supported DeLeon.

The dispute began with a protracted wrangle over the seat-

[49] *Ibid.*, 455, 499–500.

[50] *Daily People*, May 26, 1906; Thompson, *op. cit.*, 26.

[51] For evidence of Sherman's extravagance and Trautmann's conviviality, see *Proceedings of the Fifteenth Annual Convention of the WFM* (1907), 539, 581 and especially the statements of Rawling and Moyer. See also *Proceedings of the Second IWW Convention* (Chicago, 1906).

ing of certain delegates who were known DeLeon supporters. Sherman not only refused to accept the DeLeon delegation's credentials, but appointed his own credentials committee without allowing the convention to scrutinize *its* credentials first.[52] This dispute continued while the conference moved from the KP Hall on Halsted and Adams streets to Brand's Hall, a larger building on North Clark Street more suited to a noisy convention.[53]

After more than a week of wrangling DeLeon's delegation was seated; but no sooner had he won this victory than a new danger threatened. The dispute over seating had lasted so long that the DeLeon delegates, lacking means of subsistence, began to talk about leaving. DeLeon, fearful that his supporters would melt away, moved that an expense allowance of $1.50 a day be paid delegates and accused Sherman angrily of trying to intimidate the opposition, which was undoubtedly correct. "We believed we could starve them out," Sherman explained,[54] "by obstructive tactics, but at the end of the tenth day DeLeon had a resolution passed that they all be allowed $1.50 per day as salary and expenses while attending the convention. This was more money than any of them had earned in their lives and they were ready to stay with him until Christmas." DeLeon's motion passed by 380½ votes to 251, and $450 was spent from union funds in clear violation of article VI of the provisional constitution, which said that delegates must pay their own expenses.

At this stage Vincent St. John of the WFM joined forces with DeLeon and Trautmann in their bid to remove Sherman from office. On October 4, after three weeks of steadily mounting tempers and defeats for the GEB, Sherman decided to put

52 *Proceedings, op. cit.,* 5–7, and Jensen, *op. cit.,* 173 and n.
53 *Proceedings, op. cit.,* and Jensen, *op. cit.,* 173–74.
54 *Chicago Record-Herald,* October 7, 1906.

syndicalist principle into practice and "take and hold" the IWW headquarters at 146 West Madison Street. The DeLeon-Trautmann-St. John faction may have violated the constitution in their attempts to overthrow what they felt was a corrupt and inefficient leadership; but Sherman and his comrades scarcely cut a heroic dash by hiding in the union offices and guarding themselves with burly detectives.

St. John, in a piece of individual direct action, tried to storm the offices with Frank Heslewood. They climbed to the fifth floor on Madison Street and challenged two agents from the Mooney-Bohlen Detective Agency, who shouted down to them, "You fellows can't come in here." St. John asked, "What is the reason we can't come in here? We're members and officers of this organization and this is our office and we have a right in here." One of the detectives retorted, "It's none of your goddam business," and when St. John asked to be shown his authority the same agent hit him over the head with a blackjack.[55] After this scuffle St. John and Heslewood decided discretion was the better part of valor and left just in time to avoid arrest by a twenty-one-man police riot squad called in by a jumpy Sherman.

St. John's next move was to take the whole matter to Clarence S. Darrow, the celebrated attorney—an ironic example of revolutionaries calling in the "judicial lackeys of the bourgeoisie." St. John accused Sherman of trying to use office equipment and IWW equipment to stage a phony referendum in his own favor. Darrow instituted a court action to unseat Sherman legally, but before the court could decide—incidentally, in favor of the DeLeon-Trautmann-St. John faction—Sherman had lost control of the union, although the Sher-

[55] Jensen, *op. cit.*, 177.

man faction stayed on at West Madison for several months after the DeLeon group had set up shop at 212 Bush Temple.[56] Thus the coalition of doctrinaires and direct actionists, which had dominated most of the proceedings at the first convention, gained complete control of the IWW at the second. But their victory was hollow. Within a year it led to the withdrawal of the WFM.

After ten years of bitter fighting many WFM members were wondering whether a union that struck less and concluded more contracts with the employers might be more valuable. They were unconvinced of the value of direct action and even more doubtful about the intentions of Daniel DeLeon. Moyer, for example, advocated dealing with the employer "in a straightforward, businesslike manner, supporting our position with facts . . . if the application of sound judgment, based on experience, takes us backward then I am prepared to shoulder any responsibility that may attach to me."[57] Two other industrial unions, the Brewery Workers and the United Mineworkers, had refused to join the IWW but had still won shorter hours and higher wages for their members. Yet Moyer's policy depended on employers accepting the fact that their employees had a right to form trade unions, which few employers at the time were willing to concede.

Many WFM members disapproved of both the behavior of the DeLeon group at the second IWW convention and the convention tactics of one of their own leaders, Vincent St. John. This was revealed almost immediately by the reaction of the editor of the *Miners' Magazine*, J. M. O'Neill. "The acts of the convention are null and void," he wrote. "The constitution was brazenly and flagrantly violated . . . and the

[56] Thompson, *op. cit.*, 27.
[57] *Proceedings of the Sixteenth Convention of the WFM* (1908), 16–18.

convention practically degenerated into a mob."[58] In O'Neill's view, the second convention was part of "a conspiracy that contemplated the resurrection . . . of a political corpse"[59]—by which he meant the Socialist Labor Party. Within the WFM two groups quickly formed, one led by St. John, which backed the Wobblies, and the other headed by O'Neill, wishing to leave the IWW. The conflict was long and bitter. It lasted almost two years and drove a rift between Moyer and Haywood during their imprisonment and trial in Idaho on charges of assassinating Governor Steunenberg.[60]

Its violence can perhaps be judged from the fact that St. John was shot by another member of the WFM, Paddy Mulloney, and permanently crippled in the hand.[61] The decisive stage in this fight was reached during the WFM's marathon convention in June 1907, which lasted two months and was the longest the union ever held.[62] St. John was backed by Frank Heslewood, his companion when he stormed the IWW headquarters in 1906, Al Ryan, Percy Rawling, and John Riordon. St. John summed up his view of the issues at stake when he remarked that "the fate of the Western Federation of Miners as a progressive organization . . . hangs in the balance here."[63]

Much of the controversy turned on whether St. John's group had violated the IWW's constitution when they deposed Sherman. In the midst of it one speaker recalled that Trautmann had shouted, "To hell with the constitution!" during the pro-

58 *Miners' Magazine,* October 4, 1905, 6. October 11, 7, 11. See also November 1, 8–10, November 8, 4–9, November 15, 7–9, November 22, 7–11. Quoted in Jensen, *op. cit.,* 177.
59 *Ibid.,* October 11, 7–11.
60 Haywood, *op. cit.,* 190–222, *passim,* esp. 216–17.
61 *Ibid.,* 225, Flynn, *op. cit.,* 84.
62 Jensen, *op. cit.,* 178–96, gives an excellent account.
63 *Proceedings of the Fifteenth Convention of the WFM* (1907), *op. cit.,* 525.

ceedings.[64] It would be hard to find a clearer illustration of the temperamental gulf that separated the left wing extremists from the moderates in the socialist and labor movements of the time or of the quarrel Moyer had with Haywood in their prison cell. In the circumstances of 1907 this gulf proved unbridgeable. The St. John forces managed to stall until the following summer. But in July 1908 the WFM officially severed all ties with the IWW.[65]

The struggle within the WFM had been embittered by the trial of Moyer and Haywood at Boise, for the moderates begrudged giving money to defend men they regarded as hotheads. Frank Steunenberg, the Democratic Governor of Idaho from 1897–1901, an honorary member of the Boise Typographical Union and a prosperous sheepman, was murdered on December 30, 1905, outside his home in Caldwell, Idaho. He opened his garden gate and triggered a bomb someone had planted in the snow. Mortally wounded, he was carried to his house crying, "Who shot me?"[66]

Although he was a former union man, Steunenberg had adopted a very tough line toward labor unions in general and the WFM in particular during his term of office.[67] So when the murder took place, the popular presumption was that union members had killed the ex-Governor in revenge. The assassination created a wave of anger throughout the state. Citizens committees raised a $25,000 reward, to which Governor Frank R. Gooding added a further $5000.[68] In January 1906, Harry

[64] *Ibid.*, 340–41, and see a letter from Moyer, 584–86. Jensen, *op. cit.*, 182, points out that St. John and Al Ryan insisted that Trautmann's actual words were "if the constitution is to be used as a shield for fakers and grafters, then to hell with the constitution."

[65] *Miners' Magazine*, July 23, 1908, 5–7; July 30, 1908, 5; *Proceedings* (1908), 21–23. Quoted by Jensen, *op. cit.*, 197.

[66] Jensen *op. cit.*, 197.

[67] *Ibid.*, 72–87.

[68] *Ibid.*, 198–99.

Orchard, whose real name was Albert E. Horsley, a little, round-faced, affable and friendly man, was living in Caldwell under the name of Thomas Hogan and passing himself off as a sheepman. Orchard confessed to the killing and implicated Moyer, Haywood, and Pettibone.[69]

In fact, the whole affair of Orchard's confession was probably a clumsy effort to frame the WFM leadership, made by an "inner circle" of WFM officials or, more likely, by the mineowners.[70] Many motives have been advanced for Orchard killing Steunenberg, the most convincing being revenge. As Governor of Idaho, Steunenberg had driven Orchard out of Coeur d'Alene in 1899, depriving him of a one-sixteenth interest in the Hercules Mine which would have made him a millionaire.[71] Orchard's confession and testimony were prepared for him by the head of the Denver Pinkerton Detective Agency, James McParland, the notorious key witness at the Molly Maguires trial in 1875, whose suspect evidence sent ten Pennsylvania miners to their death.

The three union men were kidnaped by Pinkerton agents in Denver, Colorado, and smuggled by special train to Boise, Idaho, where they were locked in the prison death house. The WFM, which was the IWW's only important source of money and members at this time, launched a campaign to raise $10,000 for the defense fund and helped rouse the entire American labor movement to support the three prisoners. With the money they raised, the WFM hired Clarence Darrow, the most celebrated trial lawyer of his day, for the defense. Darrow was suffering from an attack of mastoiditis so severe that

69 Jensen, *op. cit.,* 197–218, and Haywood, *op. cit.,* for a full account. Orchard told his own story in 'Confession and Autobiography,' *McClure's Magazine,* November, 1906, where he admitted earlier attempts on Steunenberg's life.

70 Jensen, *op. cit.,* 210.

71 *Ibid.,* 211.

it almost killed him.[72] Nevertheless, he prepared a brilliant case in the stuffy, crowded court where the trial was held.[73]

The Boise trial captured the attention of the entire nation when it began in May 1907. Workers everywhere were shocked by the brazen kidnaping of the defendants. *The Appeal to Reason,* J. A. Wayland's very successful socialist paper, brought out a special edition of three million copies to spread the protest. Debs wrote a front page editorial entitled *Arouse, Ye Slaves.* In Canada, Frank Heslewood armed several hundred men and was ready to march on Boise to free the prisoners until Frank Bohn, an IWW organizer, stopped him.[74] Darrow was not happy about these efforts to turn the trial into a revolutionary crusade. Although he was himself a socialist, he refused to allow Debs to report the trial.

His relations were already bad with Haywood, who suspected he had refused Debs' help because he wanted all the limelight himself. During the trial they grew even worse. Darrow developed a great dislike for Haywood, but he nevertheless believed him innocent.[75] On the other hand, an experienced labor lawyer who attended the trial, Judge O. N. Hilton, thought that while Moyer and Pettibone were completely innocent, Haywood might not have been on all counts.[76] Darrow's courtroom strategy was to defend Haywood first, believing that if he could secure his acquittal the other two men would go free. He destroyed McParland's testimony and then called

[72] Irving Stone, *Clarence Darrow for the Defense* (New York, 1941), 193–94; Clarence Darrow, *The Story of My Life* (New York, 1932), 157–59.

[73] David H. Grover, *Debaters and Dynamiters* (Oregon State University, 1964), tells the detailed story of the trial. The full transcript is on microfilm at the Industrial and Labour Relations School Library at Cornell University.

[74] Conversation with Frank Bohn, January 28–29, 1966.

[75] Jensen, *op. cit.*, 215.

[76] *Ibid.*, 204, n.

eighty-seven witnesses on Haywood's behalf, including Edward Boyce, an old comrade from the early days of the WFM, who came out of retirement in California and withstood fierce cross-examination.

The prosecution was conducted by William E. Borah, the junior United States Senator from Idaho, a leonine-headed politician who later became one of the nation's most distinguished legislators. Shortly before the assassination, however, Borah and others—including Steunenberg himself—had been indicted on charges of having been engaged in timber frauds, and although they were acquitted the episode probably weakened the impression he made on the jury.[77] Darrow's strategy proved correct. By concentrating on the defense of Haywood, who was a thousand miles away when Steunenberg died, he made things easier for the other two defendants.

But not before a long struggle in the juryroom. One juryman, Samuel D. Gilman, stuck out for conviction until the foreman, convinced of Haywood's innocence, wore him down.[78] Gilman returned, gray-faced and ashen, with the other jurors and returned a solemn verdict of not guilty. Moyer was acquitted too and Pettibone went free; Orchard alone was convicted, largely from his own testimony, and sentenced to life imprisonment.[79] Although Judge Fremont Wood's pointed remarks when sentencing Orchard revealed his belief that the others were guilty, the Wobblies had won the first of many courtroom battles.

It was a costly victory. It helped the WFM moderates persuade the union to defect, so dealing the IWW a shattering blow. The trial also exacted a personal as well as a po-

[77] *Ibid.*, 198 and n.; Portland *Oregonian,* October 1–8, 1907.
[78] Haywood, *op. cit.,* 216–17.
[79] Jensen, *op. cit.,* 217. Orchard died in jail in 1954.

litical price: it ruined the friendship of years between Moyer and Haywood. The Idaho experience finally converted Moyer to moderation, while driving Haywood to greater extremes. Darrow, who championed the cause of trade unions, agreed with Moyer and was thinking of the future of the labor movement when he urged Haywood to return to the life of a rancher in the hills after he had secured his acquittal.[80]

The conflicting attitudes of the two defendants were revealed in an apocryphal tale of a verbal exchange between them in the Boise death house. Haywood, as usual, was making things difficult for men in authority, causing trouble and bringing reprisals from the guards on other prisoners. "Put an ice pack on your head," Moyer told him. "Get it from under your feet first," was Haywood's rejoinder.[81] The trial had convinced Moyer that direct action was folly, and personal considerations supported his political conversion. His family ties were much stronger than Haywood's, and he was anxious to avoid another term in jail.

His sensibility contrasted with Haywood's growing ruthlessness in personal relations. Haywood had already broken with Moyer; victory in court did not reconcile him to its architect, Clarence Darrow; and when his co-defendant, George Pettibone, died within a year, Haywood could not find time to go to his funeral. He did not even go to his wife's funeral ten years later; but by then what had begun as a love match with Jane Minor had long since grown cold.

She had never recovered properly from the ordeal of bearing children in the primitive conditions of the West. An invalid for much of her life, she turned in despair to faith healing, which drove her unsympathetic husband to spending even less time

[80] Haywood, *op. cit.,* 218; Stone, *op. cit.,* 233–34.
[81] A story I owe to my father, George Renshaw.

at home. He saw little of his wife and three daughters after 1900 and started drinking heavily, a habit he broke only when he became convinced that Moyer and his other opponents in the WFM were trying to get him drunk for political reasons.[82] In a dramatic bid to give up drinking he deliberately smashed a bottle of Canadian Scotch between the carriages of a railway train, but by then he was already exhibiting symptoms of an illness which, though never properly diagnosed, may well have been diabetes, which often causes a craving for drink.[83]

Against this background the IWW convened in Chicago on September 21, 1908, for its most decisive convention to date.[84] Just before the defection of the WFM, Haywood, who had been doubling as organizer and lecturer for both organizations, was suddenly released by the Federation.[85] This enabled him to devote his great energies and talents to saving the IWW from the threat of imminent extinction. Like his comrade St. John, Haywood blamed the loss of the WFM directly on Daniel DeLeon. He knew how much ill-feeling and bitterness DeLeon's tactics had created, and how little his intentions, or those of his Socialist Labor Party, were trusted. St. John, shot in the hand by an opponent in the WFM, had good reason to deplore this bitterness. Accordingly, both men agreed that the first step to save the IWW must be the immediate expulsion of both the SLP and its leader.

When Haywood and St. John arrived at the 1908 conven-

82 Haywood, *op. cit.,* 228–29.
83 Haywood, *op. cit.,* 228–29.
84 *Industrial Union Bulletin,* October 10, 1908, 2. The *Bulletin* published the proceedings of the fourth IWW convention. The third convention, held in Chicago in 1907, was dominated by DeLeon and passed off quietly. Rudolf Katz 'With DeLeon since '89,' *Weekly People,* November 20, 1915, 2. See also Vincent St. John, *The IWW: History, Structure and Methods* (Chicago, 1917), 7.
85 *Miners' Magazine,* April 23, 1908, 1. The notice releasing Haywood was signed by the WFM's vice-president, Charles Mahoney, a leading protagonist in the WFM's dispute with the IWW.

tion, they took care to bring with them a large delegation from Seattle, Spokane, Portland, Los Angeles, and the Pacific Coast. Many were former members of the WFM who wished to remain loyal to the idea of revolutionary industrial unionism. Only one of the twenty-six delegates controlling seventy votes was a woman—a teenager named Elizabeth Gurley Flynn, who was destined to win the same sort of reputation as Mother Jones.[86] She boasted six generations of Irish rebels in her family and kinship with George Bernard Shaw on her mother's side. She was a soapbox orator in New York City at seventeen, and during her years with the IWW became known as "the red flame" and "the Joan of Arc of the working class."

According to the *Industrial Union Bulletin* this was the first convention composed of "purely wage workers." For the first time the West was furnishing "genuine rebels—the red-blooded stiffs," or the "overalls brigade" and the "bummery element" as these migratory workers, who stole rides on freight trains to reach Chicago, were popularly known. The first action of this strongly proletarian convention was to elect St. John its permanent chairman and debar DeLeon from participating in the proceedings[87] on the grounds that he was not a wage worker and therefore ineligible for membership. His credentials were challenged on the grounds that he represented a Store and Office Workers Union, instead of the Printing and Publishing local which, as editor of *The People,* he should have joined.[88] It was an ironic reversal of the GEB's tactics of 1906, because this time Trautmann, who had stood by DeLeon in his struggle with Sherman, was using them against DeLeon.

Rising to speak, despite his opponents' cries of "I'd like to

86 *Industrial Union Bulletin,* October 10, 1908; Brissenden, *op. cit.,* 221.
87 *Ibid.*
88 Thompson, *op. cit.,* 39.

get a punch at the Pope,"[89] DeLeon made a spirited defense of his position and policy. But the title under which his speech was later republished, *The Intellectual Against the Worker*,[90] shows the extent to which he had antagonized and drifted out of touch with the working class membership. It also revealed how rapidly the coalition he had formed with the direct-actionists in 1905 was breaking up under the pressure of events. For four days the convention wrangled angrily over DeLeon's credentials. Eventually the convention ruled that he could not be seated.[91]

The IWW had removed the influence of the SLP. But this was not enough. It had to ensure that no more political influence would ever penetrate its syndicalist ranks. DeLeon's "political clause" in the preamble to the constitution had been designed to increase the political influence of the SLP over the new organization, under the pretense of excluding political influence entirely. Now St. John and Haywood had seen through this pretense, and their next move was to strike out the political clause completely.[92] After three years of flirting with politics, the IWW had returned to its basically antipolitical attitude of direct action on the industrial front.

Expelled from the Chicago convention, DeLeon took his supporters to Paterson, New Jersey, and founded his own IWW, which eventually set up headquarters in Detroit.[93] The Detroit IWW confined its activities to DeLeonite propaganda and agitation on what it called "the civilized plane," but its influence was negligible. Like the old ST & LA, its membership over-

[89] *Proceedings, op. cit.*, 438.
[90] *Industrial Union Bulletin*, October 10, 1908.
[91] *Ibid.*, October 17.
[92] *Ibid.*, November 7, 1908.
[93] *Ibid.*, December 12 and March 6, 1909. See also the *Weekly People*, November 7, 1908.

lapped with that of the SLP; and when DeLeon died in 1914 it changed its name to the Workers' International Industrial Union before expiring completely in 1925.[94] Meanwhile, all that remained for the syndicalists in Chicago in 1908 was to institutionalize their victory, which they did by electing St. John secretary-treasurer, Trautmann general organizer and a GEB consisting of Cole, Miller, Ettor, Whitehead, and a Negro waterfront worker named Gains.[95] Henceforth this group led the IWW with a policy of revolutionary overthrow of the capitalism and abolition of the wage system.

St. John, the thirty-four-year-old-son of a Wells Fargo express rider, born in Kentucky of Irish and Dutch ancestry, was rapidly becoming one of the most notable leaders of the IWW. Detectives hired by the Mine Owners Association reported that "St. John has given the Mine Owners of Colorado more trouble in the past years than any twenty men . . . If left undisturbed, he would have the entire district organized in another year."[96] Known as "the Saint" he was perhaps the best-loved of all IWW leaders. In the 1890s he ruined his lungs when he helped rescue dozens of men from a smoke-filled mine in Telluride, Colorado, after a disaster. On his death in 1929, Joseph Ettor, another prominent IWW organizer, wrote "When the true story of labor's efforts across the past thirty years . . . is written, the Saint must be at the heart of it."[97]

So by 1908 the IWW had settled its internal differences. The uneasy alliance of 1905 between industrial unionists like Moyer and Debs, Marxist politicians like DeLeon, syndicalists agitators like Haywood and St. John, and antipolitical anarcho-syndicalists like Father Hagerty inevitably broke up within a

[94] Brissenden, *The IWW, op. cit.*, 218–20. Thompson, *op. cit.*, 39–40.
[95] *Industrial Union Bulletin, op. cit.*, March 6, 1909.
[96] Joyce L. Kornbluh, ed., *Rebel Voices* (Ann Arbor, 1964), 43.
[97] *Industrial Solidarity,* July 17, 1929; Flynn, *op. cit.*, 85–87.

few years. Moyer and Debs left a union they believed to be dangerously extremist; DeLeon was expelled; Hagerty drifted away because no post could be found in a revolutionary union for a Catholic priest. The syndicalists alone were now in control. Not only had they triumphed in the internal faction fights, they had survived an attempt by the Idaho mineowners to break them at the Boise trial. Haywood and St. John were the leaders, and their lieutenants included such notable figures as Gurley Flynn and Joseph Ettor. They had now to grapple with the task of establishing the IWW as a revolutionary union.

4

GOLDFIELD, McKEES ROCKS, AND FREE SPEECH

THE PREACHER AND THE SLAVE

(Tune: "Sweet By and By")

Long-haired preachers come out every night
Try to tell you what's wrong and what's right;
But when asked how 'bout something to eat
They will answer with voices so sweet:

(CHORUS)

You will eat, bye and bye,
In that glorious land above the sky;
Work and pray, live on hay,
You'll get pie in the sky when you die.

JOE HILL, *IWW Songbook*

By September 1907 about two hundred locals of the IWW had been chartered.[1] However, the turnover of members was very high. In the previous year 118 charters had been issued to branches, making the number of locals chartered since the foundation 928.[2] Membership had fallen to about 6000 and the financial situation was not healthy: in 1906–7 the union received roughly $30,000 but spent over $31,500.[3] With the defection of the Western Federation of Miners in 1908 the IWW found itself close to extinction. Some of the locals it formed, like the Stogie Workers of Cleveland, Ohio, the Hotel and Restaurant Workers of Goldfield, Nevada, and the Window Washers of Chicago[4] proved short-lived, as did the Bronco Busters and Range Riders Union founded by Haywood himself in 1905 at Denver during a rodeo,[5] to organize the cowboys.

Harry Brennan, a champion rodeo rider, was president of the BBRR; the secretary was Tom Minor, Haywood's father-in-law. The union won an agreement for riding in contests with wages fixed at $5 a day for bronco busting and $50 a month for range riding on the ranch. Haywood became acting secretary while they looked for a proper headquarters and Minor found a permanent address. But the Bronco Busters were soon headed for the last round up.

However, there were glimpses of light for the IWW in the

1 *Proceedings of the Third Convention of the IWW* (Chicago, 1907); *Industrial Union Bulletin*, August 10, 1907.
2 *Industrial Union Bulletin*, September 14, 1907.
3 *Proceedings*, *op. cit.*, 2.
4 *Proceedings of the Second Convention of the IWW* (Chicago, 1906), 106.
5 Haywood, *op. cit.*, 190–92.

gloom. The Saw Mill and Lumber Workers of Lake Charles, Louisiana, proved to be the basis of some remarkably stable unions in that state, and migratory workers, the homeless hobos who had taken charge of the 1908 convention, were coming to dominate the movement.

For two years during this early period of uncertain growth the IWW made its greatest impact at Goldfield, Nevada. Goldfield is a ghost town today. But in 1905, with a population of 30,000, it was at the height of a gold boom, bursting with all the lusty growth and vigor of boom town life. Here, amid the raw, energetic mining camps, the IWW tried out its new brand of revolutionary industrial unionism. The years 1906–7 saw several hard-fought disputes between the mineowners, on one side, and the Western Federation of Miners and the IWW on the other.

When the IWW first arrived in Goldfield in 1906 the WFM was already strongly entrenched there, while the AF of L was weak, embracing only the carpenters and typographical workers.[6] The IWW lost no time in staking out their claim. "We proceeded," an organizer wrote,[7] "without force, without intimidation, without deportations, and without murder, to organize all wage workers in the community . . . In the organization were miners, engineers, clerks, stenographers, teamsters, dishwashers, waiters—all sorts of what are called common laborers." This concept fitted exactly the Wobbly idea of one big industrial union of wage-earners with equality for all. It did not appeal to the members of AF of L craft unions, like the carpenters and printers, and the conflict of interest between craft unionists and IWW dual unionists led almost at once to jurisdictional strife between the two groups.

[6] Brissenden, *The IWW, op. cit.,* 123.
[7] *Industrial Union Bulletin,* March 30, 1907. Quoted by Jensen, *op. cit.,* from which most newspaper quotations in the next few pages are drawn.

The trouble started when the IWW decided to boycott the two local newspapers, the *Goldfield Sun* and the *Tonopah Sun,* partly because of the violent anti-IWW propaganda they published, but also because the printers had refused to join the town workers in the one big union. The newsboys stopped selling the papers, and after a few days the boycott seemed to be working. It worked even more effectively when Local 77 of the IWW decided to merge with Local 220 of the WFM.[8] The miners were in a great majority in the area, and the employers were not yet ready to meet them in open conflict. The motto, "an injury to one is an injury to all," which the IWW had coined at its inaugural conference, contrasted sharply with the more cautious slogan of the Knights of Labor, "an injury to one is the *concern* of all." It gained its first notable victory with this merger between two locals of the IWW and the WFM.[9] Faced with this united front the newspaper owners sold out, and the new proprietors merged the two journals and changed the name to the *Goldfield Daily Tribune*. The *Tribune* adopted a more friendly attitude to the IWW and reinstated all the striking members, including the newsboys.

Almost immediately another strike developed. Local 77 of the IWW included the messenger boys of the Western Union telegraph agency, who struck for a pay rise to $20 a day. Although the IWW supported the strike, they felt less secure than they had been when challenging the newspaper tycoons. They settled almost at once for $5 a day and the men returned to work. Over almost as soon as it started, this strike was nevertheless indicative of the militant spirit that swept Goldfield after the arrival of the IWW.

[8] *Industrial Union Bulletin,* April 6, 1907; *Proceedings, Fifteenth Annual Convention of the WFM* (1907), 33.

[9] *Industrial Union Bulletin,* April 6, 1907; Brissenden, *The IWW, op. cit.,* 193.

In another dispute, Local 220 of the WFM demanded a $5 a day minimum for all kinds of mine work. Between 1200 and 1500 men were idle, and the employers were forced to concede $5 for skilled workers and $4.50 for unskilled men. Elsewhere in Goldfield the IWW and the WFM won an eight hour day with wages of $3–$5 and full board for all restaurant workers and hotel employees, a ten hour day with wages of $5 for clerks, and an eight hour day with $6 wages for bartenders.[10] The pay of railway employees in the Goldfield region was forced up by the IWW from $1.75 for a ten hour day to $4.50 for an eight hour day.[11]

Despite these undoubted successes, the efforts of the IWW were resisted, not only by the employers, but by some of the workers themselves. The AF of L carpenters were in Goldfield building an arena for the 1908 Nelsons-Gans world lightweight boxing championship fight, in which Battling Nelson took Joe Gans' title with a 17th-round knockout. They resented the miners who were pressing them to join forces with the IWW and the WFM, and retaliated by boycotting work on the miners' union hospital then under construction.

These jurisdictional conflicts were often as bitterly fought as the conflicts between management and labor. In one, the Socialist Labor Party's candidate for president, M. R. Preston, killed a restaurant keeper, Tony Silva, while on picket duty during a strike.[12] The evidence seems to indicate that Preston shot in self-defense, but feelings in Goldfield ran very high as a result of Silva's death.[13] Preston, convicted of second degree murder, was jailed for twenty-five years, but released on parole in 1914 after seven years of agitation by the IWW. In another

[10] *Weekly People,* April 6, 1907.
[11] *Industrial Worker,* January 29, 1910.
[12] *Weekly People,* July 18, 1908.
[13] Flynn, *op. cit.,* 133.

clash Vincent St. John was wounded by a WFM member, Paddy Mulloney.

The violence in Nevada brought swift reaction from Washington. A full Congressional investigation of the Goldfield situation placed much of the responsibility on the shoulders of the pusillanimous Democratic Governor of Nevada, John Sparks.[14] President Theodore Roosevelt accused him of "failing to call the legislature together because, in your judgment, the legislature would not call upon the Government of the United States for the use of troops . . . The State Government certainly does not appear to have made any serious effort to do its duty by the effective enforcement of its police functions."[15] The Federal commissioners also reported that the mine operators were afraid of carrying out their policy of reducing wages and blacklisting all WFM members unless they had the protection of Federal troops. "They accordingly laid a plan to secure such troops," the commissioners reported,[16] "and then put that program into effect."

Governor Sparks responded promptly to these criticisms, and the Nevada legislature passed a state police bill.[17] The Goldfield Mine Owners Association adopted the open shop to stop unions organizing in and around their mines. The workers angrily denounced the "state militia [as] inimical to the interests of state sovereignty [and] . . . a relic of antedeluvian, fossilized, fiendish, barbarism . . . We raise our voices in protest [against] creating the organization of legalized, uniformed murderers . . . under the disguise of state militia."[18]

The Nevada state militia, denounced so savagely by the

[14] *Labor Troubles in Goldfield, Nevada, 60th Congress, 1st. Session* (Washington D.C., 1908), 11.
[15] *Ibid.*, 13.
[16] *Ibid.*, 24–26.
[17] *Industrial Union Bulletin*, March 1907.
[18] *Ibid.*, 25.

IWW, quickly restored law and order to Goldfield, which meant in effect that the mineowners were able to break up the Wobbly organization there. The IWW's position was further undermined by a sudden, sharp economic recession. In October 1907 severe financial panic hit the United States. Money dried up, and the mineowners promised to pay the men by checks issued against ores in transit, to which the men agreed. In November the Consolidated Mines Company gave notice that henceforth it would pay its workers half in legal tender and half in the scrip of John S. Cook and Company. Again the unions agreed. But when a few weeks later the employers said cash payments would have to be suspended altogether, they tried the patience of their workers once too often. The unions met and insisted on full payment in legal tender.[19]

The meeting could not save them or the owners. The panic routed the remnants of the IWW in Goldfield. Indeed, it almost wiped out the organization throughout the country. An IWW official wrote, "Its locals dissolved by the dozens and the general headquarters at Chicago was only maintained by terrific sacrifice and determination."[20] The *Industrial Union Bulletin,* founded as the IWW weekly, was forced to appear fortnightly and then to suspend publication altogether.

Yet despite this ultimate failure, St. John looked back on the Goldfield period as the halcyon days of the IWW. "Under the IWW sway in Goldfield," he wrote,[21] "the minimum wage for all kinds of labor was $4.50 a day and the eight hour day was universal. The highest point of efficiency for any labor organization was reached by the IWW and the WFM in Goldfield, Nevada. No committee was ever sent to

19 *Miners' Magazine,* January 16, 1908.
20 *Solidarity,* February 25, 1911.
21 Vincent St. John, *The IWW: History, Structure and Methods* (Chicago, 1917), 18 (emphasis in original).

any employers. The unions adopted the wage scales and regulated hours. The secretary posted the same on a bulletin board outside the union hall, and it was the LAW. The employers were forced to come and see the union committees."

After the failure of the Goldfield locals and the defection of the Western Federation of Miners in 1908, the future of the new industrial unionism looked black. Eugene Debs' campaign as socialist candidate for President in 1908, featuring a "Red Special" railroad campaign train, revived the movement for a time. But on the industrial front the panic of 1907 had given way to calm like the calm of the grave. However, just when the IWW seemed on the verge of dying out, it suddenly flared into life. The spark that set the tinder burning again was a dispute at McKees Rocks, Pennsylvania.

Here the Pressed Steel Car Company, a subsidiary of United States Steel, ran what amounted to a company town. The labor force, predominantly immigrant workers, was not organized to resist the all-powerful employers. But when the company announced a new wage system, which depended entirely on piecework, they became confused and angry. Under this new system wage rates were not fixed: a worker's wages depended on the output of his workmates. Many of the immigrants, who spoke little or no English, did not understand this method of fixing pay; and before long this exploded the powder keg of their many other grievances.

In July the men formed a committee of forty which asked the management to explain the new wages rates. The forty men were sacked peremptorily, and the strike began at once. McKees Rocks quickly became an armed camp, with special deputies and two hundred state police on duty facing 6000 determined strikers.[22] In an atmosphere reminiscent of the

22 Robert L. Tyler, 'The IWW and the West,' *American Quarterly* vol. xii, no. 2, part 1 (Summer, 1960), 179.

violent struggles of the WFM a decade earlier, a Czech-born striker named Steven Horvath was killed in a clash with company guards. The funeral was turned into a political demonstration, which revealed a significant difference between this strike and those led in the West by the WFM. The graveside eulogies were delivered in fifteen different languages—a sign that the IWW was gaining support among the immigrant workers on the Eastern seaboard.

The violence at McKees Rocks dragged on for another two months, during which time the strikers remained completely solid, although seventy-six of them were seriously injured. In August, the IWW's general organizer, William Trautmann, appeared on the scene, conducted public meetings and established a permanent IWW local. A week later the conflict reached a new peak of intensity with a pitched battle between strikers and state troopers in which eleven people were killed. An added touch of barbarity came when arrested strikers were dragged down the streets behind the troopers' horses. Not surprisingly, the Russian-born workers dubbed the police "Cossacks"—a name that stuck to them afterwards in much IWW propaganda.[23]

By now public sentiment in the Pittsburgh area had swung completely around in favor of the strikers. Before long the Pressed Steel Car Company capitulated and granted their demand for a return to the old system of fixed wage rates.[24] The IWW had won a famous victory.

The McKees Rocks episode attracted most attention, but the Wobblies were also active elsewhere that year. Other strikes involved the lumberjacks at Somers and Kalispell in

[23] *Ibid.*, 180.

[24] R. D. Smith, "Phases of the McKees Rocks Strike," *Survey*, xxiii (October 2, 1909), 38.

Montana, and Eureka, California, who struck against wage cuts, the sheet and tin plate workers at New Castle and Shenango, Pennsylvania, and the farm laborers at Waterville, Washington.[25]

Trautmann, the secretary-treasurer of the IWW, blamed these "constant irritative strikes" for the failure of two-thirds of the IWW membership to pay their dues.[26] Because these disputes involved about half the union's members in one year, they could not afford to pay union dues while they were on strike, or jobless and blacklisted if the strike failed. Trautmann was already showing signs of the disenchantment with the antipolitical, industrial action of the IWW majority wing that was to take him back before long into Daniel DeLeon's Detroit wing of the IWW, which advocated industrial action combined with political affiliation to the Socialist Labor Party and penetration of the AF of L. By 1923 Trautmann had become an advocate of works councils and supported Woodrow Wilson's concept of shop democracy and Walter Rathenau's *New Society*.

Despite Trautmann's pessimism, the IWW was showing unmistakable signs of growth. The McKees Rocks strike was the first indication of a new spirit of militancy sweeping through the hitherto unorganized Eastern immigrant manufacturing workers. The IWW offered them advice, direction, and leadership where no established labor organization had cared to act, and its efforts to organize these workers were reflected in the type of organizer active within the IWW at this time.

For example, Joseph J. Ettor, a twenty-four-year-old IWW General Executive Board member working at McKees Rocks, could speak English, Italian, and Polish fluently, as well as a

25 Brissenden, *The IWW, op. cit.*, appendix viii, 368.
26 *Industrial Union Bulletin*, October 24, 1908.

little Hungarian and Yiddish. Ettor, born in Brooklyn but raised on the West Coast, was already a veteran IWW official who had worked the West Coast shipyards, mining camps, and lumber forests. An IWW comrade once described him as "a short, stocky Italian . . . with a thick shock of hair upon which a small hat sits rather jauntily. He wears a flannel shirt and a large bow for a tie . . . He has a kindly, boyish face . . . an apparently unlimited supply of physical vitality, and a voice that is strong and resonant."[27] Within a few years Ettor was to become one of the most prominent Wobblies. He was a strike leader with the Brooklyn shoeworkers in 1910–11, was jailed during the 1912 textile strike at Lawrence, Massachusetts, and later organized the Western Union messenger boys of New York City in 1912, and the Minnesota metal miners in 1916.

From 1909–12 the union concentrated on the West, using the new tactics of the "free speech fight." As early as 1906 there had been a minor clash between Wobblies delivering propaganda speeches and local police. But not until 1909 did these free speech fights achieve the proportions of a national epidemic. Wobbly leaders campaigned for the right to agitate on street corners, not so much to defend a constitutional principle (though some believed one was at stake), nor even to attract free publicity (though the fights soon hit the headlines) but to make the world more fully aware of the miserable conditions in which migratory workers lived and labored.

Just how bad conditions were can perhaps be judged from eye witness accounts. The whole of the West Coast was worked by a labor force of migratory workers. Some 3,500,000 of the 10,250,000 unskilled workers in the United States in 1910

[27] Justus Ebert, *Trial of a New Society* (Cleveland, 1913), 68–71.

were migratory. Lumberjacks, construction workers, agricultural laborers and miners, they traveled from job to job, working ten or twelve hours a day for a few days here and a few days there, living in primitive camps. An IWW organizer, J. T. (Red) Doran, said, "Camps were insanitary, abominable places . . . Many times there was not any hay, much less mattresses. The grub . . . was mighty poor, to say the least. Sanitary conditions were poor, little or no provision was made for bathing and dirty filthy animal life [was] in abundance; animal life you had to pack with you."[28]

"Camp conditions were basically unchanged from fifty years before," Al Parkin, another migratory worker, wrote.[29] "Food was poor, crudely prepared, dished up in tin utensils. Living quarters were still of the traditional pattern—crudely built bunkhouses with rude double-deck bunks, infested with bedbugs and sometime lice. There was no washhouses or dryhouses, no recreation facilities. Men still packed their own blankets between camps."

These bindle stiffs, carrying their blankets or bindles from camp to camp, were a familiar sight in California and Washington. Most of them did not stay long in one job, and when a job was completed thousands were laid off. So there was always a large army of unemployed men, floating from job to job or looking for work. They had no families. Most of them did not belong to any church. They did not stay long enough in any one town to register and vote. Constantly moving and working in miserable conditions, these voteless and economically weak workers saw direct action, as advocated by the

[28] Evidence and cross-examination of J. T. (Red) Doran in the case of U.S. v. William D. Haywood.

[29] Al Parkin, "A Brief History of Trade Unionism in British Columbia's Lumber Industry," *B. C. Lumber Worker,* 1948. Quoted by H. A. Logan, *Trade Unions in Canada* (Toronto, 1948), 280.

IWW, as their only weapon against the system that oppressed them. According to the report of a Federal Commission into conditions in the lumber industry at the time, one lumber operator recognized the IWW as "the cry of the oppressed . . . it is misery articulate."

In the hands of this floating army, the "free speech fight" was a formidable weapon—indeed, it was the IWW's most significant contribution to the syndicalist armory. In the lumber camps of the Northwest, the fields of California, the fruit- and wheat-producing areas on both sides of the Rocky Mountains, in the Pacific Coast industries and elsewhere thousands of migratory workers, who had no reason to feel any obligation to capitalism or the established order of things, were ready to fight them with the first weapon at hand.

Unrest among these migratory workers had first boiled over into open rebellion in 1894 when General Jacob Coxey had led a bedraggled army of jobless migratory workers and bankrupt farmers across the Midwest to Washington, D.C., demanding social justice. The threat of Coxey's Army passed once the panic of 1893 had subsided. Migratory workers were too individualistic to join any one organization for long—as the IWW was to discover. The few who had any feeling of class consciousness and solidarity came into their own only when a tightening of the labor market sent a new feeling of insecurity sweeping through the land.

It was this sense of insecurity that helped to launch the IWW, and it also helped other movements of itinerant workers. Chief among them was the International Itinerant Migratory Workers' Union, or the Hobos of America Inc., led by Jeff Davis. The most conspicuous figure in this organization was Dr. Ben L. Reitman, an anarchist who was also the lover of Emma Goldman, America's most notorious woman anarchist. Emma

Goldman was a remarkable woman who, throughout a long career, kept her anarchist convictions with such passionate sincerity that she came to personify American anarchism. Reitman, a small, bearded, quiet-spoken intellectual, was prominent in the migratory society of Chicago in the years before 1914. Another "king of the hobos" was James Eads How, the son of a wealthy St. Louis contractor, who organized the International Welfare Association, which claimed 300,000 members in 1914.

The IWW free speech fighters often met in the "slave market" sections of big cities, where migratory workers gathered between jobs and were fleeced by employment offices and labor sharks, who often charged as much as $2 for placing men in work. The seditious, unpatriotic, and threatening tone of their speeches, as well as its effect on their audiences, alarmed commercial circles. Businessmen soon persuaded the city fathers to pass ordinances banning IWW speakers from the streets.

In answer to this challenge IWW organizers summoned footloose Wobblies from all over the country. Jumping rides on freight trains, riding the rails in boxcars, they would throng to the chosen town, asserting their right to freedom of speech, and assemble on improvised soapbox platforms at street corners everywhere. They would quickly be arrested. Before long the jails were dangerously full of high-spirited men and women. Crowded prisons, congested legal timetables, and the high cost of paying extra police and feeding extra prisoners often drove desperate officials to scrap the anti-IWW ordinances. Then the whole process would start all over again.

Reviewing the free speech fights, an observer of the labor movement wrote,[30] "It was one of those strange situations which crop up suddenly and are hard to understand. Some

[30] San Francisco *Call,* March 2, 1911, quoted by Kornbluh, *op. cit.,* 96. Quotations from other newspapers in this chapter are from the same source.

thousands of men, whose business it was to work with their hands, tramping and stealing rides, suffering hardships and facing dangers—to get into jail. And to get into one particular jail in a town of which they have never heard the name before, in which they have no direct interest."

Between 1907 and 1916 the IWW conducted about thirty major free speech fights of up to six months duration, mostly in the Far West, at such places as Missoula, Montana; Spokane, Washington; or Fresno and San Diego, California. All of them centered on the IWW's right to recruit members at street meetings. One of the most notable took place at Fresno in 1910, where a new local of unskilled fruit workers had been organized in the San Joaquin Valley by Frank Little, a tough, able, half-Indian IWW veteran of the Missoula and Spokane free speech struggles, who seven years later was lynched by employers' vigilantes at Butte, Montana.

Trouble broke out when a contractor, finding it hard to attract labor to build a much-needed irrigation dam for the fruit region on the low wages he was offering, told the Fresno police chief that the labor shortage was being deliberately created by Wobbly agitators. Soon the police started breaking up the IWW's open air meetings and arresting members on vagrancy charges. Little himself was one of the first to be sentenced. Given twenty-eight days in jail on bread and water he telegraphed IWW headquarters in Chicago for help.[31]

Aid came quickly and in a practical manner. In Portland, Oregon, over 150 Wobblies answered Little's call, stealing rides on trains as far as the California state line where they jumped off to avoid railway police. They walked the remaining 300 miles to Fresno, crossing the Siskiyou Mountains in a snow

[31] *Industrial Worker,* May 1910.

Arturo Giovannitti, the Italian-born IWW who was acquitted of murder during the Lawrence strike.

Changing the guard at a silk mill during the Lawrence strike of 1912.

Members of AWO 400 make a decision.

storm. Other members came from all over the country to help fill the Fresno jails. A hundred unemployed workers left St. Louis, more than 1500 miles to the east, and marched on Fresno, hoping to raise another thousand demonstrators en route.[32] In Denver, over 500 miles away, plans were made to recruit 5000 Colorado workers to march on Fresno in the spring.[33]

Before long Fresno's prison cells were filled to overflowing with militant Wobblies, lecturing their guards on the class struggle and singing their now famous songs of class conflict. Punished with a bread and water diet, they staged a soapbox demonstration through the bars. The prison governor, fearful of mutiny, called out the fire department, who turned their high pressure hoses on the rebellious prisoners. Shielding themselves with mattresses the men refused to be cowed, and a truce was only reached when the icy water had risen knee-deep over the entire cell block.

Conditions were just as bad in the women's cells. Elizabeth Gurley Flynn, the heroine of many free speech battles, has given a vivid description of her ordeal. She found that one prison, in Spokane, was used by police and jailers as a brothel, where the unfortunate inmates were forced into prostitution.[34] When she made this revelation public it caused widespread concern and sympathy for the Wobbly cause. Progressive opinion also protested when the *Industrial Worker,* an IWW newspaper, was confiscated in Spokane.

With the official policy of repression in ruins, the news that thousands more free speech volunteers were on their way to Fresno forced the mayor to repeal his ban on public speaking

[32] St. Louis *Globe-Democrat,* September 6, 1910.
[33] Denver *Post,* February 1911.
[34] Elizabeth Gurley Flynn, *I Speak My Own Piece* (New York, 1955), 98–99.

in the streets on March 9, 1911. Released in small groups every few hours the prisoners made their way to Wobbly headquarters, collected their traveling packs, and set off on the trail looking for work. On the way they coined a new couplet to one of the best-known Wobbly refrains, *Hallelujah, I'm a Bum:*

Springtime has come and I'm just out of jail
Without any money, without any bail.

The local press bitterly criticized the city fathers for capitulating to the free speech fighters. "For men who come here with the express purpose of creating trouble," one leader writer declared,[35] "a whipping post and a cat-o-nine-tails well seasoned in salt water is none too harsh a punishment." Other newspapers were no more restrained. When a Free Speech League, 2000 strong and uniting a wide variety of militants, including anarchists, syndicalists, socialists, single-taxers and some A F of L members, was formed in San Diego in 1912, the San Diego *Tribune* urged that all demonstrators should be shot down or hanged.[36] Over 5000 people took part in the demonstrations, fire hoses were used regularly to clear the streets, and by the summer hundreds of arrests had been made.

Feelings on both sides at San Diego were greatly exacerbated by the dynamiting of the Los Angeles *Times* building, with the loss of twenty-one lives, in the spring of 1911. The newspaper was owned and edited by Harrison Gray Otis, a diehard opponent of trade unions, who first called the IWW "the Wobblies" in print. At the time of the catastrophe, Los Angeles trade unions were engaged in a general strike to enforce the closed shop throughout the city, while the *Times* led the fight to continue the open shop.

[35] Fresno *Herald and Democrat,* October 1910.
[36] San Diego *Tribune,* March 4, 1912.

Police investigations showed that the building had not been blown up: fire, which suffocated most of the men who died, had started when a small charge of dynamite exploded in an alley beneath the press room. They also showed that the IWW had had nothing to do with the incident. A few days before the disaster three men had taken some dynamite from a quarry in San Francisco and sailed off across the bay in a small boat. Later the police found dynamite at the headquarters of the Structural Iron Workers in Indianapolis and more explosives in a safe-deposit box and at a farm, both rented in that city by Joseph J. McNamara, the secretary of the union.

The police arrested him and his younger brother, James B. McNamara, an active member of the Typographical Union, who had been living in San Francisco when the dynamite was stolen. They also arrested Ortie McManigal, who turned state's evidence and implicated the McNamaras. Anti-union feeling, always powerful in California, reached a new peak of intensity with these arrests. The press, not surprisingly since a fellow newspaper had been damaged, led the attack on "that hobo gang which calls itself 'the Industrial Workers of the World.'"[37]

The IWW's reaction to the arrests was to call for an immediate general strike demanding their release.[38] At their annual convention in 1912 the IWW passed a resolution declaring that the McNamara case "demonstrated beyond doubt that no legal safeguard can be invoked to protect any member of the working class who incurs the enmity of the employers by standing between them and the unlimited exploitation of the workers."[39] Later they maintained the explosion had been caused by a defective boiler.[40] The IWW also accused the

[37] San Francisco *Chronicle,* May 2, 1911.
[38] *Industrial Worker,* May 11, 1911.
[39] *On the Firing Line* (Spokane, 1912), 7–9.
[40] Thompson, *op. cit.,* 87.

American Federation of Labor of not helping the defendants because "the moral support guaranteed these members of the working class was practically *nil* so far as the American Federation of Labor was concerned."

These harsh words were unjustified. The Structural Iron Workers, of which Joseph McNamara was secretary, was affiliated to the A F of L, which hired Clarence Darrow to defend him and his brother.[41] He found them to be "pleasant, prepossessing young men"; but they had given him a case that even a courtroom genius like Darrow found difficult. In addition to McManigal's confession, James McNamara had made a statement[42] admitting that he placed a small charge of dynamite outside the *Times* office and prepared it for detonation. His intention, he claimed, was not to destroy the building but simply to scare the open shop *Times* employees and others in the city who worked non-union shops. The charge by itself had not been large enough to blow up the building. But he had unwittingly placed it near some barrels of ink, which vaporized and caused the fatal fire.

Darrow could see only one way out: by pleading guilty the McNamara brothers would escape the death penalty to which Darrow was unalterably opposed in principle. At a long, emotional series of meetings in the jail house he eventually persuaded the defendants to take this course. Helped by the trial judge, Cyrus F. McNutt; LeCompte Davis, a confidant of John D. Fredericks, the State's attorney; and his friends Lincoln Steffens and Fremont Older, Darrow pointed to the number of indictments (twenty-one in all), the depth of feeling and the evidence the State could call.

Darrow had no important evidence in rebuttal and could not

[41] Darrow, *op. cit.*, 172–191 gives his version of this celebrated case.
[42] *Ibid.*, 182.

risk putting James McNamara on the stand because the State would destroy him on cross-examination with what he had already told the State's attorney about his part in planting the dynamite. Darrow kept his plan secret, and the guilty pleas caused a sensation. He has described the dramatic scene in the crowded courtroom and his own feelings as James McNamara was given a life sentence, and his older brother fifteen years instead of the ten agreed earlier by the State.

Outside the court and across the nation the effect was even more stunning. The labor movement's campaign to free the "political prisoners" was cut off in full cry. Job Harriman, a defense attorney in the case and socialist candidate for mayor of Los Angeles, was crushed by his Republican opponent in a wave of triumphant anti-Red sentiment. More was to follow. Darrow himself was indicted on two charges of conspiring to tamper with the jury in the case, but found not guilty on the more serious charge, while the other was dismissed after the jury failed to agree.[43]

Of course, the IWW suffered most in the aftermath of the McNamara case. Though the brothers were not Wobblies, the IWW was widely believed to advocate dynamiting. Anti-union feeling, greatly strengthened by the outcome of the trial, quickly turned against the IWW as the most militant pro-labor movement. The San Diego free speech fight, which began as a protest against a city ordinance banning demonstrations during the McNamara trial, was still in progress. Angered at the failure of the authorities to crush the IWW, local businessmen took the advice of the Californian press and formed their own vigilante committees.

These vigilantes terrorized community leaders sympathetic to the free speech campaign, like the editor of the San Diego

[43] *Ibid.*, 183, 186–91.

Herald, who was kidnaped and then beaten up outside city limits.[44] They meted out the same savage treatment to IWW members. In a sworn affidavit one of their victims, John Stone, testified how he and another organizer, Joseph Marko, were arrested, grilled by the police for ten hours, and then handed over to a gang of thugs, who drove them out of town, beat them up and finally shot at them as they limped away.[45] Emma Goldman described similar events in her fascinating autobiography.[46] Her lover, Dr. Ben Reitman was stripped naked by a mob, branded with the letters IWW, and then tarred and feathered.

Such vigilante reprisals became so widespread that California's Republican Governor, Hiram W. Johnson, who was by no means sympathetic to the IWW, ordered Colonel Harris Weinstock to investigate them. Despite obstruction by city officials, Weinstock reported that local businessmen had encouraged and supported the beatings, in which police had openly joined.[47] The Wobblies, Weinstock emphasized, resorted to passive resistance. Governor Johnson supported his commissioner's findings; but no action was taken and the clashes continued.

The free speech fights reached their bloody climax with the "Everett massacre" on November 5, 1916. After a six-month struggle to establish free speech in this Washington lumber town, following the usual pattern of vigilante violence and passive resistance from the Wobblies, a party of nearly 300 IWW members set sail from Seattle across Puget Sound to Everett in two steamboats, the *Verona* and the *Calista.* They

[44] Kornbluh, *op. cit.,* 96.
[45] *Solidarity,* April 13, 1912.
[46] Emma Goldman, *Living My Life* (New York, 1935), vol. i, 494.
[47] Los Angeles *Citizen,* May 24, 1912; Commons and Associates, *op. cit.,* vol. iv, 494.

were in high spirits, singing ballads and verses from the IWW songbook, and confident the demonstration would be a success.

As they tried to land, the *Verona* was met with a fusilade of shots from the quay, where armed vigilantes and policemen were lined up to prevent them from landing. In the ensuing fray five workers and two vigilantes were killed, with over fifty wounded on both sides and seven missing. The IWW dead were Felix Baron, a Frenchman; Hugo Gerlat, a German; Gustav Johnson, a Swede; John Looney, an Irishman; and Abraham Rabinowitz, a Russian Jew. The water turned crimson, and corpses were washed ashore for days afterward.[48]

The *Verona* sailed back to Seattle and warned the second ship to return to harbor. At the Seattle docks nearly all the passengers of both ships were detained and seventy-four Wobblies arrested, charged with the murder of the two vigilantes and removed to Everett jail. The AF of L backed the IWW's defense committee and a prominent West Coast attorney, George F. Vanderveer, who later acted for the IWW in the great Chicago trial of 1918, conducted the defense, helped by Fred Moore, the IWW's own attorney who had won acquittal for Ettor, Giovannitti, and Caruso in 1912.

A leading Washington Wobbly, hard-jawed Tom Tracy, was put on trial first, alone. After a two-month hearing the defense demonstrated that no one could tell who fired the first shot and that the vigilantes who died, milling around the pier, were likely to have been shot by their own side. Tracy was acquitted, and the other seventy-three defendants were freed. Throughout the trial a defense committee, uniting AF of L and IWW Locals, played an active part, helped by the work of a gifted

[48] Walker C. Smith, *The Everett Massacre* (Chicago, 1917), gives a full account of this incident. See also two articles by Anna Louise Strong in the *Industrial Worker*, November 2, 1946.

young English-born organizer and agitator named Charles Ashleigh and his comrade Herbert Mahler. Ashleigh was in charge of defense publicity, and the Everett massacre ended as a notable propaganda victory for the IWW.[49]

The free speech fights had shown the power that could be wielded by demonstrations and passive resistance. But they also laid the IWW open to bloody reprisals and soon became a wasting asset. Moreover, they neglected the more important work of building up strong locals in industry. Many observers, some of them in the labor movement, regarded the IWW as little better than a rabble and its members as no better than work-shy tramps. But they were much more than a rabble or a mob. They were usually decent working men, more perceptive and spirited than most, who revolted against intolerable working and living conditions; migrants unable to find permanent jobs using the only weapons they had at hand to assert the dignity of their labor.

The words "hobo," "tramp," and "bum," all more or less terms of abuse denoting an idle, shiftless way of life, were bandied about freely in descriptions of the IWW. The union's own song, which became almost its signature tune, was *Hallelujah, I'm a Bum*. In fact the terms were not synonymous. Ben Reitman, the anarchist intellectual who suffered at the hands of the San Diego vigilantes, drew a neat distinction between the three modes of life these terms encompassed. "The hobo works and wanders," he explained,[50] "the tramp dreams and wanders, the bum drinks and wanders."

[49] Ashleigh's novel, *Rambling Kid* (London, 1930), which contains some autobiographical material, has much authentic Wobbly atmosphere and is one of the best fictional accounts of the IWW. The author came to the United States from England as a young man in 1911, after walking across South America. A defendant at the Chicago trial of 1918 he was imprisoned at Leavenworth and deported in 1923.

[50] Nels Anderson, *The Hobo* (Chicago, 1923), 87.

By 1912, apart from the demonstrations during the McNamara trial, the free speech movement among the migratory workers of the West was a spent force. The Wobbly revolt had not died down, however, but changed its direction. When it flared up again it was among the Eastern immigrant workers in the textile mills of Lawrence, Massachusetts.

5

LAWRENCE AND PATERSON

SOLIDARITY FOREVER!

(Tune: "John Brown's Body")

It is we who plowed the prairies; built the cities
where they trade;
Dug the mines and built the workshops; endless miles
of railroad laid.
Now we stand outcast and starving, 'mid the wonders
we have made
But the union makes us strong.

(CHORUS)

Solidarity forever!
Solidarity forever!
Solidarity forever!
For the union makes us strong.

RALPH CHAPLIN

The textile workers' strike at Lawrence, Massachusetts, in 1912 was the crest of the IWW's power. It turned wage cuts into wage increases for 30,000 workers. But its implications went far beyond this. It came at a time when the socialist revolution seemed near, for it coincided with the climax of years of labor unrest in other countries. In Britain, on Clydeside and in the South Wales mining valleys, syndicalist agitators led several long and bitter disputes, while in Dublin Jim Larkin's transport workers staged an eight month strike. Big Bill Haywood, who was an outstanding figure during the Lawrence strike, had actually crossed the Atlantic in 1911 to put his experience and advice at the disposal of his British comrades and made a lasting impression in South Wales. In other English-speaking lands, like Canada, Australia, New Zealand, and South Africa, 1912 was a year of industrial turmoil. Even in the United States, Eugene Debs polled nearly one million votes as Socialist candidate for President. Encouraged by all these activities, the IWW went about its work at Lawrence with a will, and during the nine week strike it suddenly found its feet as a militant, industrial union.

"Lawrence was not an ordinary strike," one observer noted.[1] "It was a social revolution *in parvo*." Lawrence was a major center in a belt of textile mills that stretched along the banks of the Merrimack River at Manchester and Nashua, in New Hampshire, and Lowell and Lawrence in Massachusetts. Most of the mills were owned by the American Woolen Company, one of the most powerful of the textile trusts, whose president,

[1] Brissenden, *op. cit.*, 293.

William N. Wood, the son of a poor Portuguese fisherman from the Azores, had taken the quickest route out of poverty by marrying the boss's daughter and then used his own brains and ability to become one of the nation's industrial giants.

Lawrence was a town of first- or second-generation immigrants, like Wood. It had a population of nearly 86,000, of whom at least 60,000 depended on mill wages. Some 30,000 men and women worked long, aching hours in the grim mills of Lawrence. The plight of such immigrant textile workers, who lived and labored in dismal, dangerous and unsanitary conditions, had been brought home to the public in a dramatic way in March 1911, when nearly 150 workers, mostly women and girls, died in the notorious Triangle Shirtwaist Factory fire in New York City, suffocating in an attic behind doors bolted to exclude union organizers, or dashed to death on the pavements in a vain effort to escape the flames.[2]

January was always a bad month at Lawrence. The 1891 Pemberton disaster, when a mill collapsed killing eighty-eight workers and maiming hundreds more, the typhoid epidemic in the same year, and all the strikes—1882, 1894, 1902—had occurred between New Year and April.[3] January 1912, cold, damp, and dark, followed the pattern. The strike began suddenly on January 11, the first payday of the year. The issue was a pay cut. The highest paid workers, the weavers, were earning between $6 and $10.50 a week, while the spinners, carders, and spoolers averaged $6 to $7.

These were virtually starvation rates,[4] but a law reducing the hours of women and children under eighteen from 56 to 54

[2] Donald B. Cole, *Immigrant City: Lawrence, Massachusetts, 1845–1921* (North Carolina, 1963), 116; Arthur M. Schlesinger, *The Crisis of the Old Order* (Cambridge, 1957), 96.

[3] Cole, *op. cit.*, 179.

[4] *Report on the Strike of Textile Workers in Lawrence, Mass.*, 62nd Congress, 2nd session (Washington, D.C., 1913), 9.

a week had just passed the state legislature in the face of stern opposition from the Wool Trust. Now the employers cut wages by 32 cents a week—and 32 cents bought ten loaves of bread. As the pay envelopes were issued the cry "Short pay! Short pay!" rang round the mills. Workers swarmed into the streets in spontaneous protest and adopted the battle cry "Better to starve fighting them than to starve working!" Within twenty-four hours Lawrence was in the grip of a general strike.

Lawrence Local 20 of the IWW, formed in 1906, which had only about three hundred paid-up members, was overwhelmed by events and wired Joseph Ettor, a member of the GEB, for help. Ettor, an experienced IWW organizer and a fine orator in both English and Italian, went straight to Lawrence from New York City, taking with him his twenty-seven-year-old Italian-born friend, Arturo Giovannitti, a poet and agitator who edited the Italian labor paper *Il Proletario*.

They were soon followed by Gurley Flynn, James P. Thompson, who had acted as an IWW organizer in Lawrence before, and Big Bill Haywood. January 15 was the crucial day of the strike. Initial enthusiasm was wearing thin in the cold weather and strikers were talking about returning to work. Then some 15,000 workers, demonstrating outside the Prospect Mill, were met by militiamen with fire hoses. The shock of the icy water in subzero temperatures united the workers again and probably saved the strike from ignominious collapse.[5] Like the charge by armed police at Tonypandy, South Wales, in a mining strike in 1910, it was something thousands of workers never forgot.

A crowd of 15,000 strikers greeted Haywood at the station when he arrived on January 21 and escorted him to Lawrence Common, where he spoke urging solidarity. Ettor had already

[5] Cole, *op. cit.,* 180 and n.

selected interpreters to help organize the strike and called mass meetings among the many nationalities to try to elect strike committees from as many mills, departments, and racial groups as possible. The IWW leaders preached direct action, passive resistance, and solidarity. With nearly 1500 militiamen, plus police and state troopers in town, Lawrence was fast becoming an armed camp, and in the many clashes between guards and strikers such solidarity was vital. Yet it was never really obtained. The really interesting thing about the Lawrence strike was the way the workers responded on an ethnic basis. When they struck it was as if the great American melting pot had suddenly boiled over, for they represented at least twenty-five different nationalities.[6] The largest groups were the 7000 Italians, 6000 Germans, 5000 French-Canadians and an equal number of English-speaking Canadians, 2500 Poles, 2000 Lithuanians, 1100 Franco-Belgians, and 1000 Russians, Greeks, Letts, Turks, and Poles.[7]

The Belgians, Italians, Germans, and English all had, for the most part, some previous experience of trade unions. The Belgian weavers even wore the *sabots* of their homeland, from which, in the historic traditions of direct action, the word sabotage may have been derived when their forefathers threw clogs into the machines. Gurley Flynn, the "red flame," who played a prominent part in the strike, estimated that only 8 percent of the strikers were born in the United States.[8] Lawrence was the leading Irish center north of Boston and a sixth of its foreign-born inhabitants came from Britain, a percentage exceeded by only one other city in the United States. On the other hand, its French-Canadians were so nu-

[6] Flynn, *op. cit.*, 119; Thompson, *op. cit.*, 55.
[7] Flynn, *op. cit.*, 117.
[8] *Ibid.*, 132.

merous that a convention of Canadian societies from as far away as Montreal and Chicago had met there in 1887. Next to Boston, Lawrence was the largest German city in Massachusetts, and it had more Syrians than any American city save New York.[9]

For the most part, old-stock immigrants disapproved of the strike. No Irish representatives served on strike committees, and no Irish organization paraded with the IWW on Memorial Day. City hall, on the other hand, was full of Irishmen, like Judge Mahoney, Assistant Marshal John J. Sullivan, John Breen, head of the school board, and Mayor Scanlon, who supposedly hired detectives from the Sherman Agency to spy on the strikers.[10]

These men illustrated how immigrants could become more conservative as they became more firmly entrenched in American society and had more to conserve. Father O'Reilly, the Irish Catholic priest in Lawrence, who passively supported the millowners in 1912 and attacked the IWW for misleading ignorant foreigners, had himself criticized the corporations in the strike of 1894, while John Breen's father had fought the employers in the strike of 1882.

Post-Civil War immigrants were apathetic about the strike: the French-Canadians and non-socialist Germans, for example, joined it only halfway through. The German-language newspaper, *Anzeiger und Post,* expressed sympathy with "willing and peaceful strikers," but not with what it called "the rough criminal fellows" who used violence to intimidate those who wished to remain at work. At the very end only four hundred Germans had joined the IWW Local. The English workers had a branch of Local 20, but English scabs and blacklegs were

[9] Cole, *op. cit.,* 12 and n.
[10] *Ibid.,* 184–85.

common, although one Englishman, Thomas Halliday, served on the strike committee.[11]

The Franco-Belgians, with their *sabots* and syndicalist traditions, were always among the most violent elements in the strike committees. They had played a prominent part in earlier Wobbly and anarchist activities in Lawrence, and at the outbreak of the strike, two-thirds of the IWW's membership was in the Franco-Belgian branch of IWW Local 20. Their leader, Cyrille Detollenaere, had been close to Ettor and the IWW since 1905. The Franco-Belgian workers not only lent their cooperative hall to the IWW for use as a strike headquarters, they also advocated that scabs should be thrown into the river—a suggestion that came to nothing.[12]

Three important Syrians served on strike committees. They were Farris Marad, a dyer and tailor who also acted as special policeman and court interpreter; James Brox, a grocer; and a Dr. Hajjar. Brox had joined the IWW the year before and invited Ettor to speak at the Syrian church. The Polish community lent the IWW their Chabis Hall, and also rioted and threw ice at the soldiers. Polish barbers refused to shave men who remained at work. The Portuguese allowed the IWW to use their hall, but were cautious, while the Lithuanians were divided, with one group supporting the IWW, while another, mostly Catholics, opposed them.[13]

The Italians became the backbone of the strike and provided an important part of the local leadership. Indeed, observers often believed the strike was a purely Italian affair. But, just as with the Irish a generation before, the Italian community was split into businessmen and workers who found themselves on opposite sides. The Italian Catholic priest, Fa-

[11] *Ibid.*, 187–88.
[12] *Solidarity*, July 22, 1911.
[13] Cole, *op. cit.*, 188–89.

ther Milanese, was rumored to have received $50,000 from Wood to get his flock back to work.[14] Though a leading member of the Italian community, Fabrizio Pitoccheli, or "Peter Kelley"[15] as he was known, put up bail bond when Haywood was arrested, the Italian church and business groups in general were closer to the Irish and French-Canadians than the Italian strikers.

In one of the clashes between pickets and police a woman striker, named Anna LoPezzi,[16] was killed. Tension quickly reached breaking point. Colonel Sweetzer, the commander of the militia, tried to prevent the IWW making political capital from the incident by banning a mass funeral. Yet his own actions could hardly have failed to provoke the strikers. He gave orders of "Shoot to kill. We are not looking for peace now"[17] and told his men not to salute the Stars and Stripes when carried by the IWW. His militiamen, mostly native-born business and professional people, or young bloods out for a bit of excitement, were very like the vigilantes who broke up IWW free speech fights in the West. They were not averse to riding into picket lines on horseback, swinging clubs and lunging with bayonets at the crowds, which often included women and children.

True, the amount of violence they used has probably become exaggerated in the folk memory of Lawrence, just as it has been at Tonypandy. Compared with the Homestead Strike in Pennsylvania in 1892, when thirty-four people were killed,

[14] *Ibid.*, 187–88.

[15] When an immigrant 'got on' in Lawrence, like Pitoccheli, he often took an Irish name—more evidence of the dominant position of the Irish as social arbiters.

[16] Several different spellings of this name exist. I have followed that used in the latest study of Lawrence by Cole, *op. cit.*, 182, 184. Variants include LoPizzo and LaPizza.

[17] Flynn, *op. cit.*, 119.

Lawrence was a placid affair. Yet the fact remains that poor immigrants who had risked everything to find a better life in America were being forced back to intolerable conditions with guns, bayonets, and clubs. For a generation and more, many hungry people all over the world had looked at Lawrence with hope. Now they were being beaten down.

Moreover, the attitude of the militia was often recklessly irresponsible, to judge from one of their officers, who recalled: "Our company of militia went down to Lawrence during the first days of the strike. Most of them had to leave Harvard to do it, but they rather enjoyed going down there to have their fling at these people."[18] In another of these attacks an eighteen-year-old Syrian boy, John Rami, was stabbed to death from behind.

Faced with this mounting violence, some of the strikers began to talk of returning to work, but the militants used the threat of reprisals to keep them out and warn off strike breakers hired by the wool manufacturers. Business and commercial interests in Lawrence also made efforts to try to discredit the IWW, partly by blaming them for the violence, but also by deliberately trying to frame them.

Some twenty-eight sticks of dynamite were found in three places in the city, one of them where Ettor received his letters. Far from being the work of "blood-stained anarchists" it was planted by a businessman, John Breen of the school board, the son of a former mayor. Arrested on January 29, Breen was released on $1000 bail before being tried and convicted. He was fined a mere $500.[19] Later, Wood, the head of the Wool Trust, Frederick H. Atteaux, a Boston businessman, and D. J. Collins were tried for complicity in the dynamite conspiracy.

[18] *Outlook*, October 1912.

[19] *Hearings on the Lawrence Strike* (Washington, Government Printing Office, 1912), 39.

Although both Breen and the man who sold him the dynamite, Ernest Pittman, implicated him, Wood was acquitted. The jury failed to agree about Atteaux, and found Collins guilty.[20]

Middle class Americans were not slow to blame the IWW for fomenting trouble. Yet in the dynamiting scandal few could question the comment of the Progressive magazine *Outlook* on the trial. "Two things are perfectly plain," it wrote. "There was an attempt to discredit the strikers by making it appear that they and their sympathizers were harboring dynamite . . . and that large sums of money were paid by the millowners to Atteaux without an accounting to show for what purpose that money would be spent."[21]

On January 30, the day after Breen's arrest on the dynamiting charge, the IWW suffered a heavy blow. The police charged a striker, Joseph Caruso, with the murder of Anna LoPezzi on the picket line, and held two IWW strike leaders, Ettor and Giovannitti, as accessories because they had advocated picketing. The Socialist Party leader, Eugene Debs, telegraphed the three prisoners: CONGRATULATIONS. VICTORY IS IN SIGHT. THE WORKING CLASS WILL BACK YOU UP TO A FINISH IN YOUR FIGHT AGAINST PEONAGE AND STARVATION. THE SLAVE-PENS OF LAWRENCE, UNDER THE PROTECTION OF AMERICA'S COSSACKS, ARE A DISGRACE TO AMERICAN MANHOOD AND A CRIME AGAINST CIVILIZATION.[22]

Ettor, Giovannitti, and Caruso were kept in prison for five months without trial. During this time the IWW launched a campaign for them, and formed a defense committee headed by Haywood, Trautmann, Gurley Flynn, and Frank Heslewood. The union hired a team of lawyers led by their regular attorney, Fred H. Moore, from Spokane, who later appeared for

20 *Ibid.*, 44.
21 *Outlook*, June 21, 1913.
22 Flynn, *op. cit.*, 118.

the union in the Everett massacre trial and the great IWW trial at Chicago in 1918. Carlo Tresca, Gurley Flynn's anarchist lover, was also prominent in the campaign to free the three men. Tresca, an Italian-born writer who came to the United States in 1904, lived with Gurley for thirteen years. Later he became a leader of the Anti-Fascist Alliance and was mysteriously assassinated on the street in New York City in 1943.

In the Northeast, the IWW conducted a series of sympathy strikes. Finally, the three men were brought to trial at Salem, Massachusetts, scene of the notorious witchcraft trials of 1692 when nineteen victims were hanged for alleged sorcery. The prisoners appeared each day fettered together in an iron cage. The detectives hired by the employers testified that Giovannitti had urged strikers to "sleep in the daytime and prowl around like wild beasts at night," but admitted under Moore's cross-examination that this speech was in Italian and they had no written report.[23]

The trial lasted several weeks.[24] Caruso, who was charged with the actual murder, denied he was ever a member of the IWW, but emphasized his determination to join it as soon as he was free. Moore, an able attorney who was prone to nervous attacks which kept him out of court, conducted the defense skillfully, and all three of his clients were acquitted. On their return to Lawrence they were given a tumultuous reception.

While the struggle to save Ettor, Giovannitti, and Caruso was in progress, events at Lawrence itself moved to a conclusion. The strikers were in good heart. Ray Stannard Baker, the young Progressive journalist, captured their mood in one of his reports from Lawrence. "It was the first strike I ever saw which sang," he wrote.[25] "I shall not soon forget the curious life,

[23] Samuel Yellin, *American Labor Troubles* (New York, 1936), 183.
[24] Ebert, *op. cit.*, tells the full story of the strike from an IWW viewpoint.
[25] *The American Magazine*, May 1912.

the strange, sudden fire of the mingled nationalities at the strike meetings when they broke into song."

Often these songs were in the strikers' native tongue, mostly Italian. But the lyrics which Wobbly folk poets like Ralph Chaplin, T-Bone Slim, Covington Hall, Charles Ashleigh, and Joe Hill wrote to popular melodies and hymn tunes were becoming increasingly familiar to strikers through the IWW's *Little Red Songbook*. As one writer has observed, "One of the few radical movements ever to possess a sense of humor . . . the IWW was also a revolution with a singing voice."[26]

For example, the most popular song during the Lawrence strike was Joe Hill's gibe at John Golden, conservative head of the United Textile Workers, the AF of L craft union in the city. When the strike broke out Golden had ordered his members to stay at work and ridiculed the IWW because it had only 287 members at Lawrence. Hill's song *A Little Talk with Golden* set to the hymn tune "A Little Talk with Jesus," was a sharp attack on the sort of business unionism men like Golden and Gompers favored. Its first verse ran:

In Lawrence, when the starving masses struck for more to eat,
And wooden-headed Wood he tried the strikers to defeat,
To Sammy Gompers wrote and asked him what he thought,
And this is just the answer that the mail man brought:

(CHORUS)

A little talk with Golden makes it right, all right;
He'll settle any strike, if there is coin in sight,
Just take him out to dine and ev'ry thing is fine
A little talk with Golden makes it right, all right.

[26] Walter B. Rideout, *The Radical Novel in the United States* (Harvard, 1956), 93.

This barb struck home, and the cry "A little talk with Golden makes it right, *all right!*" became the strikers' catch-phrase. Members of the UTW were quickly infected with the spirit of solidarity sweeping Lawrence and the highly skilled weavers and loom fixers struck in sympathy.

The dispute was attracting other revolutionary groups, too, mostly socialists or anarchists, who tried to wrest the leadership away from the IWW. An anarchist group from Boston paraded a banner *ARISE! SLAVES OF THE WORLD! NO GOD! NO MASTER! ONE FOR ALL AND ALL FOR ONE.* Such propaganda not only gave the police a pretext for breaking up the demonstration; more seriously, it alienated the predominantly Roman Catholic labor force at Lawrence and lent impetus to Father O'Reilly's argument that the IWW was misleading his flock.

A few days later the same banner appeared in Quincy, where it caused a riot. The IWW leadership was enraged, but lacked the power to end this anarchist intervention. "That banner was worth a million dollars to the employers," Gurley Flynn noted angrily, "and may have been a deliberate act of provocation. Some of us believed that it was."[27] Employers commonly used *agents provocateurs* to break strikes and discredit strikers, and the case of Frederick Sumner Boyd at Paterson in 1913 may have been another example.

The reaction of middle class Progressives to this new development was revealed in an editorial in the magazine *Survey,* which was by no means unsympathetic to the strikers. "Are we to expect that instead of playing the game respectably . . . the laborers are to listen to . . . such strange doctrines as those of 'direct action,' 'sabotage,' 'syndicalism,' 'the general strike,' and 'violence?'" the magazine asked.[28] "We think that our

[27] Flynn, *op. cit.,* 139.
[28] *Survey,* xxviii, no. 1, April 6, 1912.

whole current morality as to the sacredness of property and even of life itself is involved in it."

Survey was right: the IWW *was* challenging the whole basis of middle class morality. The Lawrence strike also enabled the union to parade the idea of the general strike. In his first speech at Lawrence Common, Big Bill Haywood had argued "If we prevail on other workers who handle your goods to help you by going out on strike, we will tie up the railroads, put the city in darkness and starve the soldiers out."[29]

As the strike progressed, the agitation for a general strike grew more vigorous, reaching its peak after the arrest of Ettor, Giovannitti, and Caruso. The seventh IWW convention in 1912 heard the General Executive Board threaten that unless these "fellow workers are acquitted the industries of this country will feel the power of the workers expressed in a general tie up in all industries."[30] In addition the *Industrial Worker* ran a special "Boycott Lawrence" number, which carried the message "Railroad men: Lose their cars for them! Telegraphers: Lose their messages for them! Expressmen: Lose their packages for them! . . . Against the bludgeon of *Industrial Despotism* bring the silent might of the *Industrial Democracy!*"[31]

Yet, ironically, the IWW's most potent strike weapon—the evacuation of children—was forced on them by necessity. The 1912 winter in Lawrence was severe even by New England standards. The sacrifices the strikers had to bear were made all the harder by the bitter weather. Despite antagonism from AF of L leaders, who were fearful of the IWW's threat to

[29] Mary E. Marcy, 'The Battle for Bread at Lawrence,' *International Socialist Review*, vol. xii, March 1912, 538.

[30] 'On the Firing Line,' a pamphlet republished in the *Industrial Worker*, October 24, 1912.

[31] *Industrial Worker*, March 21, 1912.

craft unionism, the rank and file of other labor unions raised $11,000 to help the strikers, the Socialist Party contributed $40,000, and other IWW locals raised $16,000.[32] Though Federal investigators at Lawrence reported that "these relief funds come from all sections of the country and average $1000 a day"[33] they worked out at around 33 cents per striker per day.

Families could hardly keep body and soul together on this money. Despite the efforts of the Franco-Belgian cooperative bakery, who fed the strikers for nine weeks, and the organizers of the IWW's eleven soup kitchens, children especially began to suffer privation in subzero temperatures. The strike committee accordingly decided to send them away from Lawrence, and on February 17 the first group of 150 children left to stay with sympathetic families in New York City and Barre, Vermont. The committee in charge of the evacuation was headed by Mrs. Margaret Sanger, chairman of the women's committee of the Socialist Party, who later became a pioneer advocate of contraception. She and her helpers escorted the children during the train journey, and on arrival at Grand Central Station in New York they were met by a crowd of 5000. For the first time outsiders could see for themselves the plight of the strikers at Lawrence.

Many wept as they saw the obvious signs of poverty and suffering these half-starved children had endured. Newspapers that had attacked the IWW suddenly turned the full blast of their criticism on the wool trusts. Famous journalists, like Ray Stannard Baker, Mary Heaton Vorse, and Mrs. Fremont Older, went to Lawrence, were shocked by what

[32] L. H. Marcy and F. S. Boyd, 'One Big Union Wins,' *International Socialist Review*, vol. xii, April 1912, 624.
[33] *Federal Report, op. cit.*, 66.

they saw in this desperately poor and struggling city, and reported their shock to the nation at large.

The propaganda value of the evacuation was not lost on the IWW. Nor was it lost on the management and the city fathers, who after the strike launched a campaign to redeem Lawrence's reputation in the eyes of the rest of America which set the tone of city life for a decade.[34] Just how badly Lawrence needed redemption was shown on February 24, 1912, when the forces of law and order took action. Forty strikers' children bound for foster homes in Philadelphia were separated from their parents at the Lawrence railway station by 200 policemen armed with clubs. Their mothers were unceremoniously rounded up and arrested on charges of "neglect" and "improper guardianship."

Senator Miles Poindexter, a Progressive Republican elected with IWW support in the state of Washington two years before, protested against this brutal attack and the imprisonment of pregnant women, nursing mothers, and children. His attempt to secure an immediate Senate hearing was blocked by another Republican, Henry Cabot Lodge, the senior Senator from Massachusetts. But national opinion was indignant. William Dean Howells, the seventy-five-year-old doyen of New England literary figures said, "It is an outrage—who could think it anything else?" Senator William E. Borah of Idaho, a Republican who had prosecuted Haywood at the Boise trial in 1907, described police prevention of the evacuation as "an invasion of constitutional privilege," while Samuel Gompers, though hostile to the IWW, denounced the police attack as "a crime."

Frederick W. Lehmann, the United States Solicitor General, asked, "What right did they have to do that? It is the right of

[34] Cole, *op. cit.*, 195.

any parent to send his children anywhere if he is guided by parental foresight and is acting for their welfare." Almost alone in his criticism of the strikers, John Golden, head of the UTW, said the evacuation "was a desperate means to raise money for an unjustifiable strike."[35] In fact, the evacuation had been a desperate step which, unexpectedly, helped raise money and win middle class support. But it did much more than this. The police had patently exceeded their authority, and public opinion swung firmly round behind the strikers.

William Allen White, editor of a Kansas newspaper, the Emporia *Star*, spoke (as so often) for Main Street, USA, when he wrote "the strikers were justified and there was no excuse for the violence by police and military." Years later he told Elizabeth Flynn that he never saw more heart-rending sights than in Lawrence.[36] Newspapers demanded a Congressional investigation, which soon took place. The Cleveland *News*, for example, pilloried "an industry, enjoying tariffs of 40 percent to 150 percent as protection against the pauper labor of Europe, which pays only $6 to $8 per week for skilled American workers."

On March 1, the employers capitulated. The American Woolen Company announced 7½ percent wage increases in thirty-three cities. On March 6, 125,000 workers in cotton and woolen mills in six states had their pay increased by from 5 percent to 7 percent. Finally, on March 20, the American Woolen Company, the Atlantic Mill, and other main textile employers agreed to raise rates of pay by from 5 percent to 20 percent, with better overtime rates and no victimization of strikers.[37] Though the increases were partly offset by a speed-up on the machines, the Wobblies had won.

[35] All quotations from Flynn, *op. cit.*, 128–29.
[36] *Ibid.*, 129.
[37] Brissenden, *op. cit.*, 292–93; Flynn, *op. cit.*, 131.

The victory at Lawrence created a wave of militancy among New England textile workers. Membership of the IWW's Local 20, a derisory 200 or so in 1911, leaped to some 14,000 the following year. In other New England textile towns fresh strikes were quickly settled by the Wool Trust on terms highly favorable to the workers. But this fillip proved short-lived. At Lawrence the IWW had taken control of a spontaneous protest by the workers, just as they had at McKees Rocks in 1909. Their lack of firm organizational structure and control prevented them from consolidating their position or resisting employers' efforts to whittle away the workers' gains. When Wobbly leaders realized why they had failed to take root at Lawrence they began a dispute about organization which lasted for many years.[38]

By 1914 IWW membership at Lawrence had dwindled to around 400, while the speed-up in production had eroded the recent pay awards. Despite these set-backs, IWW spirits were buoyant after the Lawrence strike. Less than a year later the union became involved in a second major strike in Paterson, New Jersey, another textile town. Though not as varied ethnically as Lawrence, Paterson was a cosmopolitan community with workers of Italian, German, Irish, and other national origins.[39] Their attitude toward the dispute followed the same pattern as at Lawrence. The older stock Irish, who ran city hall and the police department, were hostile to the strike, the post-Civil War Germans and French-Canadians were mostly divided and apathetic, while the newest immigrants, Slavs, Poles, and Italians, were the most militant.

Paterson had a reputation as a "hot-bed" of anarchism. Luigi

[38] For a full discussion, see chapter 6, below.

[39] Herbert C. Gutman, "Industrial Invasion of the Village Green," *Transaction,* vol. 3, no. 4 (May-June 1966), 19–24 sketches the growth of Paterson.

Galleani, the editor of an anarchist paper which served an old-established anarchist movement there, had led a strike a few years before; Enrico Malatesta, a leading Italian anarchist, was shot at in the city; and one Bresci, who assassinated Umberto I, the King of Italy, at Monza in 1900, hailed from Paterson. Known as the "Lyons of America," Paterson was a silk-weaving city with a population of 123,000, fifteen miles from New York. More than one-third of its 73,000 workers held jobs in the silk industry, and there was a tradition of unionism stretching back to the National Labor Union and the Knights of Labor.

The IWW had established a local there in 1907. Operatives who were now in charge of four looms each, instead of two or three as before, were incensed when the management fired their negotiating committee, which had tried to discuss the elimination, or modification, of the four-loom system. On January 27, 1913, some 800 workers at the Doherty Silk Mill walked out in protest against the firings. Within a month the strike had hit the whole town. When IWW leaders arrived in February 1913, fresh from the Lawrence triumph, they were eagerly greeted by the strikers, but resisted by the employers as "outside agitators."[40] With over 25,000 workers idle and 300 mills closed the employers were understandably in a fighting mood.

Accordingly, on February 25 the police arrested three IWW organizers, Gurley Flynn, her lover Carlo Tresca, and Patrick L. Quinlan, of the Socialist Party, at a mass meeting. Mayor Andrew F. McBride defended the arrests by maintaining that Paterson was invoking "the ancient right of cities to rid themselves of undesirables"[41] but it was difficult to prove

[40] New York *Tribune,* February 26, 1913.
[41] *Ibid.,* February 28.

anything against the trio at this stage and they were released on six months' bail.[42]

Average rates of pay at Paterson were similar to wages at Lawrence. Men made $10.59 a week, women $7.17, girls under 16 $1.85. The speed-up meant operatives had to work four hours for each three they had worked before at the same rate.[43] Union members demanded an end to victimization of their fellow unionists. Management had practiced these "tactical dismissals" since the speed-up, which gave them an excuse by calling for increased output but a decreased labor force. The IWW urged a universal eight hour day for hard silk or ribbon weavers, dyers and dyers' helpers, a $12 minimum, a $1 increase for hard silk weavers, and payment of a schedule agreed nearly twenty years before for ribbon weavers. They also insisted on an end to the victimization of union members which management had practiced since a speed-up that called for a decreased labor force and increased output.

These demands were summarily rejected, and the 25,000 strikers decided to stay out. The strike lasted throughout the summer, with the same violent scenes that had become familiar at Lawrence. This time the police and militia were even more numerous. They arrested hundreds of strikers in the first few weeks on charges of unlawful assembly and incitement to riot. In clashes between pickets and guards two Italian workers were killed.

Some of the "outside agitators" arrested at the start of the strike were dealt with harshly. Patrick Quinlan, who arrived with Tresca and Gurley Flynn, was sentenced to from two to seven years, while the editor of a New Jersey socialist newspaper, the Passaic *Issue,* was jailed for from one to fifteen years.

[42] Flynn, *op. cit.,* 143–44.
[43] *Ibid.,* 140.

Though Flynn and Tresca were acquitted, spirits were dropping as the strike dragged on through the hot summer. Some socialists advocated a shop-by-shop settlement, which they believed the employers could be persuaded to accept, but the IWW strenuously opposed these tactics and continued to press for a universal agreement.

Flagging enthusiasm was revived by a propaganda move which made Paterson one of the most celebrated strikes of this century: the Paterson pageant.[44] John Reed, the burly, curly-haired twenty-four-year-old Harvard-educated radical journalist from Oregon was reporting the strike for *Metropolitan Magazine*, then edited by former President Theodore Roosevelt. He was arrested, and while in jail thought of staging a pageant, which would dramatize the issues at stake and spread the workers' case across the nation. Helped by his many New York friends like Walter Lippmann, Edmund Hunt, Hutchins Hapgood, Mabel Dodge, and other writers, artists and actors from Greenwich Village, Reed hired the old Madison Square Garden and staged the huge show.

Yet this was far from being a professional affair. More than a thousand strikers took part, and Reed himself, a born publicist whose early promise was cut short when he died in a typhus epidemic in Soviet Russia in 1921, directed. Throughout the performance the letters IWW blazed in red lights above the central stage. The pageant unfolded the story of the strike from the first walk out at the Doherty Silk Mill. While massed choirs sang the funeral march Reed had composed for the dead Italian strikers, huge red carnations were piled onto the burial casket, as they had been at the funeral in Paterson itself.

44 *Ibid.*, 154–56 gives a vivid eye witness description of the pageant; Kornbluh, *op. cit.*, 401, 413–14 has a full bibliography.

Fifteen thousand spectators watched enthralled as the pageant described the great struggle. The lights of the mills on a cold winter morning, the piercing call of the factory whistle, the endless clatter of the looms—the production captured all this and more. In the pageant the workers sang *The Marseillaise,* battled with the police, and buried their dead with solemn splendor. "These scenes unrolled with a poignant realism that no one who saw them will ever forget," wrote one newspaper reporter. "For a few electric moments there was a terrible unity between all those people," Mabel Dodge recalled. "They were one: the workers who had come to show their comrades what was happening . . . and the workers who had come to see it." In short, the Paterson pageant was perhaps the supreme example of the kind of dramatic propaganda gesture at which the Wobblies excelled.

The pageant was also notable because its program cover, which depicted a workman springing from a background of chimneys, became another symbol of IWW activity. Designed by a nonpolitical Harvard friend of Reed's, it appeared year after year on dozens of IWW pamphlets. During the strike the IWW once again arranged for the evacuation of the strikers' children, but on an even bigger scale than at Lawrence and in the certain knowledge that it would prove a potent propaganda weapon. Once more, the sight of these poor, forlorn, and hungry children, badly clothed and clutching their few pitiful belongings, created a wave of sympathy for the strikers. During the pageant, the evacuation scene, which followed speeches by Gurley Flynn and Carlo Tresca, brought the show to a climax. The production ended with a fighting speech from Haywood, emphasizing what the silk workers were struggling for, and a rousing chorus of *The Internationale* sung by the entire audience.

Fifteen thousand people paid to see the Paterson pageant. It was a tremendous propaganda success, and also had undoubted artistic merit. Rarely do strikers get the chance to put their case across so clearly and dramatically to the nation at large. The pageant was acclaimed as a fine production and a new form of drama. Yet it apparently lost money, and there was bad feeling about the accounting.[45] More serious, it took many strikers away from their proper place on the picket line and created petty jealousies in Paterson between those who took part and those who stayed behind.[46]

Once again, as during the Lawrence strike, the IWW was blamed for the verbal excesses of volunteer speakers, mainly anarchists, who urged violence and sabotage. One of them, Frederick Sumner Boyd, antagonized many strikers with his violent attacks on the American flag. The employers retaliated by making patriotic appeals to the workers. Recent immigrants, anxious to prove their claim to be American beyond all question, were especially susceptible to this kind of appeal.

Boyd was arrested on a charge of advocating the destruction of property and sentenced to from two to seven years in jail. He was released after signing a petition for pardon in which he renounced all sabotage and "subversive ideas" and immediately disappeared from the labor scene, raising doubts in the minds of Elizabeth Gurley Flynn and others about whether he was just an irresponsible extremist or an *agent provocateur*.[47]

In the end the 1913 strike at Paterson failed, like so many other textile strikes. By July funds were running out, hunger was increasing and more pickets were being arrested. By the end some 1300 had been jailed, but not one of them was

[45] Interview with Benjamin Kaminsky, an eye witness of the Paterson strike, January 17, 1966.

[46] Flynn, *op. cit.*, 156.

[47] *Ibid.*, 148–49.

armed.[48] The companies offered to deal with the strikers shop-by-shop, an offer that some of the socialists had been willing to accept for months but that the IWW had resisted because they wanted every work shop to be covered by one industry-wide agreement.

This lack of unity, and the failing spirits of the strikers themselves, ruined the IWW's hopes. The strikers, united for nearly five months, splintered into some 300 separate work shop units. Powerless once more in the face of the employers' united front, they were forced back to work on much the same terms that had driven them out in February.[49] The speed-up went on, IWW members were victimized and fired, and the IWW itself was discredited in Paterson. The 1913 strike was just one in a long series of disputes at Paterson, but it was the only time the textile workers followed the lead of the Industrial Workers of the World.

Lawrence and Paterson were epic struggles. They rank beside Haymarket, Homestead, and the Pullman boycott in the legends of the American labor movement. But they left the IWW pretty much where it had been before. The Wobblies rarely maintained deep-rooted union organization. Indeed, they were often suspicious of authority even within their own union. They had abolished the office of president in 1906, replacing it with collective leadership by the General Executive Board. Strikes like those at Goldfield or McKees Rocks, and the free speech fights, had all been run on the basis of collective leadership.

"Who is your leader?" the Wobblies were asked after the Everett massacre. "Immediate and unmistakable was the answer," recorded an eye witness.[50] "We are all leaders." This sort

[48] Leo Mannheimer, *The Independent,* May 29, 1913.
[49] Kornbluh, *op. cit.,* 203–4.
[50] Smith, *op. cit.,* 88.

of collective leadership was also the rule at Lawrence and Paterson, where IWW members were advisors as much as leaders.[51] Yet the decline of Wobbly influence in both Lawrence and Paterson after the strikes seemed to show that collective leadership was not suited to Eastern conditions, where masses of partly assimilated immigrant workers needed firm direction to unite for industrial action on a permanent basis. Collective leadership worked better among the more fully assimilated migratory workers in the West. Now the IWW became involved in a protracted wrangle over union organization, decentralization and the rival claims of Easterners and Westerners.

[51] Donald M. Barnes, *The Ideology of the Industrial Workers of the World, 1905–21* (unpublished doctoral dissertation, University of Washington, 1962), 41 and n.

6

DUAL UNIONISM AND DECENTRALIZATION

HARVEST WAR SONG

(Tune: "It's a Long, Long Way to Tipperary")

We are coming home John Farmer; we are coming
back to stay.
For nigh on fifty years or more, we've gathered
up your hay.
We have slept out in your hayfields, we have heard
your morning shout;
We've heard you wondering "where in hell's them
pesky go-abouts?"

(CHORUS)

It's a long way, now understand me; it's a long
way to town;
It's a long way across the prairie, and to hell
with Farmer John.
Here goes for better wages, and hours must come
down;
For we're out for a winter's stake this summer,
and we want no scabs around.

PAT BRENNAN, *IWW Songbook*

With the strikes at Lawrence and Paterson the IWW had reached a new peak of activity. Free speech fights were being fought in the West, the union was active in the Midwest and the South, and was also organizing other East Coast industries. At Akron, Ohio, while the Paterson dispute was still in progress, the IWW led a six week strike of Firestone rubber workers who stopped work when piece rates were cut by 35 percent.[1] Bad and insanitary working conditions, industrial poisoning from the rubber processes, and the speed-up created by a new working system were additional grievances. The IWW managed to prevent the 35 percent wage cut, but failed to establish the principle of collective bargaining, so that the strike was only half a victory.[2]

The rubber industry remained unorganized until the 1930s, despite the fact that John L. Lewis, one of the founders of the CIO during the New Deal era, was AF of L organizer at Akron in 1913. But the Wobblies had sown the seeds of industrial unionism which ripened a generation later, just as they did at Detroit. The first industrial union for automobile workers, a predecessor of the United Auto Workers, was launched in 1913 in the motorcar city by Frank Bohn, one of the founding members of the IWW, who had organized among the lumber men of California, Washington, and Oregon.[3]

The immediate gains, however, were few. At Akron and

[1] Thompson, *op. cit.*, 70–71; *Solidarity*, February 1911 and *International Socialist Review*, May 1913.
[2] Thompson, *op. cit.*, 73–74.
[3] Private letter from Bohn to author.

Detroit, as at Lawrence and Paterson, IWW influence vanished within a year. The IWW found it lacked funds to keep permanent, full-time organizers in the field who could bring the message of industrial unionism to the many-tongued labor force. There was some small progress: in the pine forests of Louisiana mixed locals of lumber workers united both white and Negro loggers in the same branches, a courageous policy in a region where, decades later, racial integration and labor unions were both still regarded as anathema. In some states, like Mississippi, there were twice as many Negroes as whites in 1910. They were a massive majority of unskilled laborers, and in states like Louisiana, Texas, and Arkansas, where the IWW was prominent from 1910–13, they joined in great numbers.

These mixed locals led several successful strikes in 1912 and 1913, and even made some small but significant interventions into politics, as for example, in Vernon and Winn parishes, Louisiana, in the heart of the Southern pine region where the lumberjacks and hillbillies gave Eugene Debs 5249 votes for President in 1912—more than President Taft polled. Despite its avowed antipolitical policy, the IWW was largely responsible for this political surprise in the old South where socialism had made virtually no progress. The Wobblies had intervened during a violent dispute which had occurred in the lumber industry in 1911–12.

The trouble had begun in 1910 when the Brotherhood of Timberworkers was founded to organize lumber men in the forests of Louisiana, Arkansas, and Texas. The use of Negroes as scabs and strike breakers complicated the IWW's attitude. However, during the next few years, the Brotherhood enrolled some 35,000 members, half of them Negroes. At its annual convention, in May 1912, the Brotherhood joined the IWW as the Southern District of the Forest and Lumber Workers'

Union, when Haywood made a rousing speech in favor of complete racial equality.[4]

After this convention the Brotherhood demanded fortnightly payment of wages at the Galloway Lumber Company's mills at Grabow, Louisiana. The company replied with a lockout which shut down forty-six mills and hit the whole Louisiana lumber industry. The outstanding feature of the dispute from the IWW's point of view was that Negroes and whites struck together and remained solid throughout the dispute. A special strike issue of *Solidarity* carried a long statement issued by the strikers at Merryville, Louisiana, which illustrates this theme of racial integration and working class unity.[5]

The presidential election of 1912, in which the Democratic candidate, Woodrow Wilson, defeated the two candidates of the divided Republican party, President William Howard Taft, and the Progressive Theodore Roosevelt, occurred at the height of this industrial trouble. Haywood campaigned actively for Debs, who had been a founding member of the IWW, and in this mood of class conflict the socialist vote skyrocketed at Vernon and Winn—showing that American syndicalists could drop their antipolitical policy when it suited them. By 1916 labor conditions had become quieter, and the socialist vote there slumped to a mere 249.[6]

By then IWW elements in the SPA had been expelled and Haywood himself recalled from the National Executive Committee. Trouble which had been brewing between right and left wing elements came to a head at the party's 1912 convention. Under the banner "the syndicalists must go" the right

[4] Sterling D. Spero and Abram D. Harris, *The Black Worker* (New York, 1931), 331 and n; testimony of Haywood in US v. William D. Haywood et al. 11, 129–30.
[5] *Solidarity*, September 28, 1912.
[6] Vernon H. Jensen, *Lumber and Labor* (New York, 1945), 87–94.

drew up a motion, proposed by Victor Berger, that anyone who advocated "violence, sabotage, and crime" should be denied party membership. The motion was clearly aimed at the IWW, and Haywood sprang to the union's defense. "I feel I can go to the working class," he said, "to the eight million women and children, the four million black men—the men who have no votes—to organize the only power that is left to them: their industrial power."

But Haywood's oratory was to no avail. Berger's motion was carried by a majority of more than 2 to 1—and the SPA expelled its IWW members. By February of the following year Haywood himself had been recalled from the NEC, so bringing to a head the feelings of disgruntlement with the SPA he had long felt at not being named the party candidate for President. This crisis marked a watershed for both the socialists and the IWW. After 1913 American socialism turned its back finally on syndicalism and extremism. Many of its more radical supporters in the Midwest and the Southwest shared Haywood's disillusion and membership fell from 135,000 to 78,000 between 1912–13, though it picked up again later.

The IWW, for its part, committed itself equally firmly to an antipolitical policy after the SPA's 1912 convention. Moreover, Haywood was now free to devote all his great energies to organizing industrially for the IWW. There was an even more significant implication behind the events of 1912–13. The SPA's antisabotage clause foreshadowed the criminal syndicalism laws which antilabor state governments were soon to enact in the years ahead to try to smash the influence of the IWW. Ironically, they were given a lead in this by the moderate left.[7]

[7] Philip S. Foner, *A History of the Labor Movement in the United States*, vol. iv, *The Industrial Workers of the World 1905–17* (New York, 1965), 403–14.

The IWW's total failure to establish permanent industrial unions at Lawrence, Paterson, Akron, or Detroit precipitated another important policy conflict. What was the purpose of the IWW? Was it merely a means of spreading revolutionary propaganda through free speech fights and wildcat strikes? Or was it to be a genuine industrial union grappling with the enormous problems of organizing the unorganized, the foreign-born, the unskilled, and semiskilled? If the IWW existed simply as a platform for soapbox orators in the Far West it could manage with a minimum of control. If it existed to found revolutionary industrial unions, as its pioneers had foreseen in 1905, it would have to accept more internal discipline.

The problem sprang in part from the contrasting philosophies of the anarchists and syndicalist factions of the movement. Anarchists like Carlo Tresca and James Rowan resisted any sort of political control in principle. They were decentralizers. In opposition to this the syndicalists, like Haywood, Ettor, Elizabeth Flynn and the majority of the General Executive Board, were centralizers who favored greater control from headquarters to prevent the IWW dissipating its energy on fruitless free speech fights and propaganda battles.

From 1910 onward two distinct factions of the movement began to emerge: the footloose, migratory workers of the lumber camps, mines and wheat fields of the South and West; and the IWW of the immigrant workers in the great East Coast industries. Each faction became identified with a different policy. The Easterners generally favored greater centralization in the IWW organization and more control of union activities from the center. The Westerners usually believed in less control and more autonomy for local branches. Ettor, born on the East Coast, raised on the West, active in both areas, was one of the Wobblies who bridged this growing division within the ranks.

In fact, the two factions represented a cleavage in the working class revolutionary movement that went back at least as far as the clash between Marx and Bakunin during the First International in the 1860s, if not to the earlier conflicts in the 1840s and 1850s between Marx, on one side, and Herzen and Proudhon on the other. The decentralizers were really the heirs of anarchists like Herzen, Proudhon, and Bakunin, who thought that all organizations, even working class ones, were evil and corrupt. The centralizers, on the other hand, inherited Marx's belief in firm leadership and organization as the basis of successful revolution.

The conflict between the two wings involved the whole question of the structure of the IWW, the proper distribution of functions and the relative merits of authoritarian state socialism *versus* "voluntary socialism." The Eastern wing of the IWW opposed affiliation to any political party—though one of its leaders, Haywood, served on the Executive Committee of the SPA until February 1913.

The Eastern wing's beliefs were really syndicalist. They saw the IWW as the nucleus for dual unions which would make an effective challenge to the AF of L's claims to represent organized labor. The decentralizers were really anarcho-syndicalists, opposing executive control from the center of the IWW just as they opposed capitalist control from the center of industry. On the whole the struggle, as it had developed by 1913, was between the Western membership, individualistic and anarchistic, and the Eastern membership, more used to union discipline and sympathetic to state socialism.

The American syndicalists wanted the IWW to follow the example of their French comrades, who had gained control of the Confédération Générale du Travail and were using it as a militant union to win higher wages, shorter hours, and better conditions. However, the syndicalist centralizers themselves were split into two camps. The IWW was a dual union. Its founders expected it to compete with the AF of L craft unions for the leadership of organized labor, and eventually to replace the craft principle by the industrial. But the success of the French syndicalists, in sharp contrast to the failure of their American counterparts, seemed to show that it would be wiser for the IWW to try to capture the AF of L, as the French syndicalists had captured the CGT. Thus in the United States a conflict between borers from within and dual unionists overlapped the battle between centralizers and decentralizers.

Syndicalists of all kinds, both borers from within and dual unionists, agreed that if the IWW wished to make any progress among the industrial workers of the East Coast and Great Lakes region it must abandon its revolutionary gestures and anarchist impulses and get down to bread-and-butter questions, dealing with problems on the shop floor, meeting management on a day-to-day basis and trying to negotiate for better conditions.

In short, the IWW would have to copy some of the unexciting but effective tactics used by the hated and despised AF of L craft unions. Spontaneous organizations might work among the migratory lumberjacks, miners, maritime construction workers and harvest hands of the West. Indeed, they might be the only method of organizing casual workers whose trades were so varied they could be fitted only into "mixed" locals of general workers rather than industrial ones.

But spontaneity was useless in towns like Lawrence, Paterson, Akron, and Detroit, as the Wobblies had learned to their cost. Permanent organizers and locals were needed simply to communicate with the immigrant masses, most of whom spoke little or no English. The IWW had to learn to speak to them in their own language. The size of this task can be gauged from the fact that in some steel works, rubber plants, or car factories men from twenty or thirty different nationalities worked side by side.

The IWW also had to bridge the gulf between white workers and black. How was the union to do this? By aiming at building its own industrial unions the Wobblies anticipated the efforts of the Congress of Industrial Organizations by a whole generation. But the CIO's task was made easier by the fact that, in the 1930s, it was organizing the English-speaking children of this last great wave of immigrants.

In the 1910s the immigrants were unorganized, and the IWW was wondering whether they were also unorganizable. Against this general background the question "Why don't the IWW grow?" emerged persistently at IWW conventions. First asked in print in 1911 by William Z. Foster, a young IWW organizer on the brink of a lifetime of revolutionary activity which was to take him to leadership of the American Communist Party, it led to a major conflict over organization and leadership within IWW ranks. Foster had returned from a European trip convinced that the IWW's belief in the efficacy of dual unions was misguided. In an article in the *Industrial Worker*,[8] he argued that the IWW should disband so that its members could capture the AF of L, just as the French syndicalists had captured the CGT.

Foster's views were shared by others. Trautmann, an important protagonist in the IWW faction fights of 1906 and 1908, also became convinced of the impotence of dual unions, and by 1913 had quit the Chicago IWW to join DeLeon's Detroit faction. These two Americans were supported

[8] *Industrial Worker*, November 2, 1911.

by James Connolly, the Clydeside Irishman who later won martyrdom during the Easter rebel rising in Dublin on April 24, 1916, and Tom Mann, an English engineer who had become the "dockers' champion" in 1889. Connolly, who lived and worked in the United States from 1903–10, was strongly influenced by the Wobblies during his stay. When he returned home he helped organize the 1911 Singer strike in Glasgow and wrote an early British study of industrial unionism. Called *Socialism Made Easy,* this closely followed the ideas on which Daniel DeLeon had founded his breakaway faction of the IWW at Detroit.

Connolly, like Foster, believed that the IWW should dissolve itself and start boring from within the AF of L. Tom Mann, a key figure in the development of links between syndicalist movements in Britain, Europe, South Africa, Australia, New Zealand, and America, undertook continuous propaganda and organizing tours all round the world between 1910 and 1913. His visits to France and the United States convinced him that dual unions like the IWW were a waste of effort and that the French syndicalists were right.

When Mann arrived in America in 1913 he told advocates of dual unions, "If the fine energy exhibited by the IWW were put into the existing trade union movement . . . the results would be fiftyfold greater than they are now" and he urged them to discard the idea of forming dual unions to compete with the AF of L for members.[9] Foster agreed, arguing that "Among syndicalists the sentiment is strong, and growing ceaselessly, that the tactics followed by the IWW are bad, and that endeavors should be made inside the AF of L; that it is in the existing unions that the syndicalists must struggle . . ."[10]

[9] *International Socialist Review,* January 1914, vol. xiv, 394.
[10] *The Syndicalist,* March 1913.

The advocates of dual unionism got the better of this argument by showing that Mann's policy of infiltrating the AF of L was impractical. Haywood declared that it was virtually impossible for an unskilled worker to join the AF of L because of "a vicious system of apprenticeship, exorbitant fees"[11] and so on, while Ettor rebutted Mann and Foster by accusing them of trying to save the Federation. "We don't want to save the Federation any more than to save the nation," he wrote.[12] "We aim at destroying it."

American syndicalists avidly read French syndicalist writers like Lagardelle himself, Emile Pouget and their intellectual ally Georges Sorel, while personal contacts, like Haywood's meeting with CGT leaders at the International Labor and Socialist Congress in Copenhagen in May 1911, further helped to spread their ideas. In August of the same year, Foster was sent as IWW representative to the International Labor Secretariat's seventh annual conference in Budapest. He was not admitted because only the CGT supported his claims before the conference credentials committee. James Duncan, the AF of L's delegate at Budapest, described one incident in his fight for recognition. "During the discussion," Duncan said, "Foster lost control of his temper. He even threatened assault . . . ocular demonstration of what an IWW really is!"[13]

The French syndicalists, so much admired by IWW intellectuals, had made the policy of boring from within pay dividends. Yet they, too, were divided over the vexed question of centralization. The IWW's centralization dispute coincided with a similar conflict in the syndicalist ranks of the French CGT, which Foster, one of the advocates of dissolution, had

[11] *International Socialist Review,* March 1914, vol. xiv, 546.
[12] *The New Review,* May 1914, 283.
[13] *International Socialist Review,* vol. xii, October 1911.

been able to observe at first hand. The CGT, at this point, was itself split into "red" and "yellow" groups representing revolutionary and more conservative factions.[14] Hubert Lagardelle, the French syndicalist, commented: "The present crisis compels a general revision of the facts and ideas of syndicalism. After a glorious beginning we find ourselves faced with that which is generally the result of forced marches in complete exhaustion."

Lagardelle's view was echoed by the IWW centralizers, like Ettor and Haywood, who had become convinced that the IWW must adopt a more disciplined policy. The IWW's early activity had been sporadic, flaring up suddenly but dying down just as quickly, leaving no trace of a permanent organization behind. A contemporary observer of the IWW noted that "no one uses the word 'organization' oftener and practices it less."[15] In fact these organizational issues had their roots in the contrary goals the movement had sought from the very outset. The Industrial Union Manifesto of January 1905, which launched the IWW, had called for a new movement that "must consist of one great industrial union embracing all industries—providing for craft autonomy locally, industrial autonomy internationally and working class unity generally."[16]

In theory all power should be placed in the hands of a collective membership. In practice the union's aims were often irreconcilable. International industrial autonomy and natural working class solidarity, or local autonomy, might prove to be contradictory aims.[17] Should IWW members come out in sympathy when workers in the same industry in another country

[14] Brissenden, *op. cit.*, 274 and n.
[15] John G. Brooks, *American Syndicalism* (New York, 1913), 175.
[16] See above, chapter 2; Justus Ebert, *The IWW in Theory and Practice* (Chicago, 1914), 122.
[17] Barnes, *op. cit.*, 72.

went on strike? Or should they concern themselves with local, that is, American, autonomy? Similarly, local autonomy often jeopardized working class solidarity. At Goldfield in 1907, for example, the industrial solidarity of the AF of L carpenters union had proved stronger than the working class solidarity urged by the WFM and the IWW, so that the strikers had returned to work.[18]

The centralizers held that "a purely democratic working class federation is impossible."[19] The eventual leader of the decentralizers, James Rowan, who became known as the "Jesus of Nazareth of the lumberjacks of the Northwest," believed that "branch, i.e. local, autonomy will inspire enthusiasm and initiative within the ranks of the IWW, and at the same time promote good feelings among the branches, the industrial unions, and throughout the organization as a whole."[20]

This debate between centralizers and decentralizers, which was also in large measure a dispute between the union's Eastern and Western wings, grew in part from the contrasts between members in the East and the West. In 1912, at Lawrence, 86 percent of the population was either foreign-born or had foreign parents.[21] At Paterson the proportion of foreign-born workers was about 66 percent; and over 90 percent of this foreign-born group remained in IWW locals after the strike had failed.[22] By contrast only 42 percent of the migratory workers in states like California were foreign-born.[23] Judging from these figures there was an important ethnic difference between the two factions.

Yet other factors were perhaps equally important. The IWW

[18] See chapter 4, above.
[19] Gambs, *op. cit.*, 124.
[20] James Rowan, *More Power to You* (Los Angeles, n.d.), 41.
[21] Barnes, *op. cit.*, 26–27 and n.
[22] *Ibid.*, 26.
[23] *Ibid.*, 27.

was not simply a movement expressing political, economic, and social discontent. It helped channel the feelings of cultural alienation felt by the most oppressed sections of the working class. Thus the cultural distinction between patterns of working class life in East and West was of major significance in the centralization dispute.

Just as significant was the fact that Western Wobblies were mostly footloose, young unmarried men: 60 percent of them were under the age of thirty.[24] By contrast Easterners had family ties, church affiliations, and other social contracts and obligations. This could have made them easier to organize permanently. But the fact that they spoke so many different languages made it virtually impossible to reach the workers in Eastern mass-production industries until their American-educated children came of age in the 1930s. In the 1910s foreign-born migratory workers were forced by the restless nature of their lives to become assimilated much earlier than Eastern factory workers. They learned English more quickly than their counterparts in places like Lawrence and Paterson, who too often remained huddled together in the security of their own nationality group.

What united Easterners and Westerners, and made them more ready to accept the IWW's antipolitical brand of propaganda, was the fact that neither had the right to vote in any significant numbers, the immigrants because they were so recently off the ship, the migratory workers because they moved about too often to qualify. The Western wing of the IWW had set the pace from the very beginning. Men like Haywood and St. John who controlled the union, believed in centralization. But they were Westerners by birth and upbringing, who sym-

[24] Philip S. Foner, *History of the American Labor Movement,* unpublished lecture course at United Auto Workers' library, Detroit, part. iv, 14.

pathized with the Westerner's outlook on life and his natural suspicion of planning and organization. Moreover, until Lawrence, the IWW had made its greatest impact in the West, with the Goldfield strikes and the free speech fights. But free speech struggles had outlived their usefulness by 1912.

In the West the centralization dispute, like other episodes in IWW history, had its melodramatic moments. One of these involved St. John, who as secretary-treasurer ran IWW headquarters in Chicago with quiet efficiency during all the arguing. In 1913 he sent Charles Ashleigh, who spoke fluent Spanish, to discipline two Arizona locals in a Spanish-speaking region. These locals were so little under central control that they even printed their own dues stamps and kept the dues. Ashleigh, a prominent West Coast agitator and publicist, was working as an IWW organizer-at-large when he was summoned to St. John's Chicago office.

"The Saint" had a picture of Ashleigh, taken when he had walked alone across Argentina a few years before, with a gun in his belt. "Can you use it?" he asked. "Yes," Ashleigh replied, a little uncertainly, whereupon St. John handed him a Colt .45 and told him to take a train down to Arizona and deal with the decentralizers. "I didn't have to shoot any of them," Ashleigh recalled long afterward.[25] The two locals responded to reason and returned to the fold.

This sort of local anarchy and refusal to accept GEB control was perhaps inevitable so long as the IWW tried to organize migratory workers with no fixed home, who roamed the West looking for work on farms, in lumber camps and mines. Yet at Lawrence and Paterson IWW organizers had a chance to put down firm roots among workers in major East Coast in-

[25] Conversation with author, November 19, 1965.

dustries. They failed. Despite the theory of collective leadership, which had been tried at Lawrence, membership fell from 10,000 in 1913 to some 400 in the following year during the pre-war depression.[26] At Paterson the story was the same. While the footloose Western Wobblies pressed for more autonomy and less control from the center, the General Executive Board believed that more, not less, centralization was the only way the IWW could overcome its appallingly rapid turnover in membership, which averaged 133 percent a year at this period.

The Lawrence and Paterson disputes had shown that if the IWW was to grow it must transform itself from a purely propaganda and guerrilla body into an ordinary union, with all the responsibilities and compromises a permanent mass membership would impose. Reporting the IWW's annual convention in 1911, which first debated the centralization issue, B. H. Williams, the editor of the union newspaper *Solidarity*, explained: "We see in the West individualism . . . that scoffs at . . . group initiative by general officers and executive boards and conceives . . . of 'direct action' in all things through the 'rank and file.' Hence the proposal . . . for minimizing the general administration."[27] In the East, Williams added, workers in large industrial centers needed a centralized union.

Frank Bohn, one of the signatories of the January manifesto that launched the IWW in 1905, was scathing in his criticism of the Western decentralizers, describing them as "spittoon philosophers." He asked "Is this chair-warming sect now the leading element in the IWW? Is it in the majority? If it is, the IWW is not dying. It is dead."[28] Soon Bohn had resigned his

[26] Kornbluh, *op. cit.*, 163; Thompson, *op. cit.*, 89.
[27] *International Socialist Review*, vol. xii, November 1911.
[28] *International Socialist Review*, vol. xii, July 1911.

post as a Wobbly organizer in protest against the power the decentralizers were exerting. At the sixth convention the decentralizers made a serious challenge to the general administration's authority over members. Several amendments, most of them prepared by Rocky Mountain and Pacific Coast locals, tried to minimize the GEB's power, but after much debate they were all defeated.[29]

Yet Frank Bohn need not have worried. In 1914 the centralizers won. At the IWW's ninth annual convention, in September of that year, their victory was clearly revealed. The convention agreed that mere propaganda tactics, such as free speech fights, or marching hungry unemployed workers to city halls where there was nothing to eat anyway, were foolish. Instead, the convention decided, the unemployed should be organized on union principles to find work and resist efforts by the employers to use them as strike breakers and blacklegs.[30] More important, the convention took steps to consolidate the start that had been made in 1913 to organize the migratory farm workers in the Midwestern grain belt.

Working conditions for the so-called "harvest stiffs" were quite as bad as they were in the lumber industry. Men, women, and children worked together ten and twelve hours a day in the fields in temperatures that reached 100 degrees and more. The camps where they lived were small, infested with lice, and insanitary. Sleeping arrangements were rough, while the food was poor and badly served. This bedraggled army of harvest hands was further exploited by unscrupulous employment sharks and had to pay from one to three dollars to be hired for work, which often proved nonexistent when they reached the site.

Work was irregular, even during the harvest, and pay never

[29] *Ibid.*, 300–02.
[30] Thompson, *op. cit.*, 89.

more than $2.50 a day. At harvest time, Midwestern farmers needed to hire migratory workers from centers like Kansas City, Omaha, Minneapolis, and more distant places. Farmers with one hundred acres might want five to seven extra hands to help bring in the crop. On average, a harvest hand might hope for only seven or fourteen days work on one farm, before having to move on. As the harvest ripened simultaneously over a wide area, he had to travel North and West quickly, usually riding the rails. In this situation the amount a laborer could earn was very uncertain. After the grain harvest, the hired hands would often go corn husking in Iowa or Nebraska, potato picking in Minnesota, or return to the oil fields or the woods of the South and Far West. Others, luckier or more hopeful, dreamed of saving a stake from the grain-harvest months large enough to see them through the winter without work.[31]

The Wheatland hop riot of 1913 dramatized the awful conditions migratory farm workers endured. Thousands of workers took part in a riot, which started as a peaceful meeting, and two I W W organizers, Hermann Suhr and Blackie Ford, were jailed for life for second degree murder after the district attorney, the deputy sheriff, and two workers were killed in the disturbances. Aware of the militant feeling created by such incidents the I W W in Kansas City organized Local 61 of the Agricultural Workers' Union to channel the radical groundswell they sensed was running among migratory workers. It aimed at winning wages of $4 a day, and quickly won a raise to $3. Its job was to organize harvest workers in the vast American wheat belt, which stretched from the Mexican border into Canada. Yet the huge task of looking after the interests of thousands of job

[31] Philip Taft, "The I W W in the Grain Belt," *Labor History*, vol. 1, no. i (Fall, 1960), 55–56.

hunters riding between work in railway boxcars, huddled in hobo "jungles" or idling on Main Street proved too much for Local 61.

During the IWW's 1914 convention Frank Little, a militant member of the GEB, had argued that "some means should be taken for concerted and efficient action in the harvest fields next year."[32] Ironically, the method chosen owed much to the decentralizers' policy of collective leadership. In the Agricultural Workers Organization 400, which the IWW formed to replace Local 61, organizers were known as job delegates. They were responsible to a recruiting, or industrial union, but this body equipped them with membership cards, dues stamps and the like and the job delegates themselves were expected actually to organize at the point of production.[33]

The Agricultural Workers Organization 400 opened its headquarters in Kansas City, Missouri, in April 1915. Its general secretary was a big, blond, German-Swiss named Walter Nef, who rarely talked politics but was one of the most efficient organizers the IWW ever had.[34] Moving the union headquarters to Minneapolis, Nef had helped increase the AWO's membership to 18,000 by the end of 1916,[35] and under Nef's leadership the AWO persuaded the IWW to change direction. It aimed at organizing the farm laborers and harvest hands across the entire Midwest. Its mobile job delegates followed the harvest from springtime on the Mexican border to autumn in the Canadian prairies, using the fact that strikes called just as the harvest was ripening could ruin farmers if they refused to settle quickly.

There was no denying that these new-style Wobbly unions

[32] *Solidarity,* March 10, 1914.
[33] *Proceedings of the Tenth Convention of the IWW* (Chicago, 1916), 41.
[34] Conversation with Ashleigh, November 19, 1965.
[35] Flynn, *op. cit.,* 189; Thompson, *op. cit.,* 95.

won wage scales which eliminated the differential—often as much as 100 percent—between pay rates on the fringe of the wheat belt and at the center. Their work schedules called for an end to the ten hour day, or sunrise to sunset routine, which was common throughout the grain belt and in the lumber forests. But while functioning like any other union, by striking bargains and negotiating agreements, the AWO and its imitators in other industries used typical Wobbly tactics too.

Thus, when members rode the rails, they refused to share their boxcar with migratory workers who were not members. In this situation the IWW's red membership card was a passport to free travel, and as the AWO grew it proved a most effective aid to recruitment, especially when railway police and even railway bandits showed signs of respecting the red card too.[36] Of course, this situation was not without its dangers. Some train robbers found it useful or necessary to join the IWW to obtain the red membership card for use on the railway lines. "There was a criminal element in the IWW," Ashleigh has admitted, giving details of some of the criminal activities he knew about at firsthand.[37] Yet in America this criminal element, which moved in when the IWW began to make money, was never welcomed by the union, as it was in the Australian IWW.

In Australia anarchists and syndicalists justified their disastrous policy of welcoming criminals with open arms by quoting Bakunin's belief that criminals were simply one more class in revolt against bourgeois capitalism. The AWO never went so far as this but it was not averse to using strong-arm methods, often in self-defense against union breakers hired by farmers, to force harvest workers to join the IWW. Organizers and

[36] Taft, *op. cit.,* 60–62.
[37] Conversation with author, November 19, 1965.

their followers, sometimes armed with clubs, pickhandles, and even guns, virtually took over some freight trains entering the harvest fields during seasonal recruiting campaigns.

Soon the AWO's organizers claimed they had established an 800-mile picket line "from Kansas to Aberdeen, South Dakota. The longest picket line . . . simply represented an effort to keep non-union men off the job."[38] Forrest Edwards, who was elected secretary of the AWO in 1916, defended his organizers' use of force. "Some say the methods are too severe. In fact, this seems to be the general opinion of the old-time IWW men. This new blood is putting over stuff and getting away with it so that the old Wobbly seems amazed at it.[39]

Thus, despite the modified use of the principle of collective leadership, which seemed to have failed so signally at Lawrence and Paterson, the AWO was soon functioning as a genuine labor union, not just as a propaganda outfit. So the AWO marked a significant breakthrough for the IWW. For the first time it began to put down roots as an industrial union. At the tenth IWW convention in 1916 the AWO, with seven delegates holding 252 of the 335 votes, was easily the most powerful force. Its campaign in the harvest fields had boosted membership and increased the IWW's income from a mere $9000 in 1915 to nearly $50,000 in the following year. In that same year the GEB issued 116 charters, a record for a twelve-month period.[40]

The success of the AWO's organizing drives clearly inspired other industrial sections of the IWW to greater efforts. Perhaps 300 delegates worked the job delegate system in the AWO alone, and Haywood, at the Chicago trial, reckoned that by 1917 the IWW had "5000 delegates organizing in the

38 *Solidarity,* August 19, 1916.
39 *Ibid.*
40 *Proceedings, op. cit.,* 106–7.

field."[41] Membership rose to the 100,000 mark and remained steady. Income increased fivefold. And more money meant better organization, more filing clerks and typists, better equipment for dealing with the administrative side of union work. More important, it stimulated a change in IWW policy which can clearly be traced in IWW newspapers and propaganda. *Solidarity* spoke for almost everybody connected with the Wobblies when it noted, with some surprise and a trace of regret for the heroic days of yore, that "the tenth convention is remarkable as denoting decline of the 'soapboxer' as a dominant element."[42]

This abandonment of the soapbox had an important influence on the leadership of the IWW. Since returning to Chicago in 1907 after being shot at Goldfield, St. John—a tough, quiet, rather obscure little man—had wrestled with the IWW's financial crises and wearisome office details as secretary-treasurer. The victory of the mainly Eastern centralizers did not really please a man whose heart was in the West, and he clashed with Haywood, who was jealous of the hold St. John had on the affections of the rank and file membership.

Describing his 1913 interview with St. John about the decentralizing Arizona locals, Ashleigh recalled years afterward, "This couldn't have happened just that way a year or two later. There would have been a formal letter . . . and he would have left it up to me how I discreetly brought about the decentralization affair with the branch committee, after I'd chatted with some rank and filers and found support and so on. No question of a gun. I think that's one reason at least why the Saint faded out."[43] At all events, St. John had a sudden urge to return to the wide open spaces in 1914 and went back

[41] Barnes, *op. cit.*, 41 and n.
[42] *Solidarity*, December 2, 1916.
[43] Private letter from Ashleigh to author.

to prospecting in Jicarilla, New Mexico, where the clean air helped his old lung complaint.

Haywood, who was elected secretary-treasurer in St. John's place in 1914, saw that while the centralizers had won the battle for control of the IWW, the AWO's job delegate system of recruiting new members marked a partial return to the decentralizers' theory of collective leadership. At the tenth annual convention he voiced his misgivings about the AWO's activities, arguing that it was more like a mass organization than an industrial union. He also urged the AWO to abstain from recruiting non-agricultural workers,[44] another example of the local autonomy planned for the IWW since 1905 conflicting with the working class solidarity the IWW existed to defend.

The dispute over centralization blew up again at the convention over the vexed question of direct action. Though the centralizers supported direct action, they felt it should be used with caution. They strongly opposed the view, advocated by Frank Little and other extreme decentralizers, that it should include wrecking and sabotage as well as go-slows and strikes. In the IWW pamphlet on sabotage, Gurley Flynn defined it as "the withdrawal of efficiency . . . either to slacken up and interfere with the quantity, or to botch in your skill and interfere with the quality, of capitalist production . . . Sabotage is not physical violence, sabotage is an internal, industrial process . . . it is simply another form of coercion."[45]

Yet tough elements in the AWO interpreted "coercion" as meaning smashing harvesters and other farm machinery or equipment, and even burning grain in the fields: the blazing crops of Zane Grey's viciously anti-IWW novel *Desert of*

44 *Proceedings, op. cit.*, 4–5.
45 Flynn, *Sabotage, op. cit.*, 5.

Wheat were not entirely fiction. This sort of direct action was dangerous on many counts. It gave labor spies a better chance of inciting Wobblies to violence, and thus discrediting the IWW; and it laid the union open to bloody reprisals, of which there were many in the immediate years ahead. Accordingly, the GEB withdrew Gurley Flynn's pamphlet *Sabotage* and also deleted Joe Hill's *Ta-Ra-Ra-Boom-De-Ay*, a poem about wrecking harvesters, from the IWW's *Little Red Songbook*.

Yet despite these doubts and inconsistencies, the example set by the AWO inspired the IWW to start organizing many different types of worker—the lumber men, the road construction and building hands, the metal miners and the shoreside and seagoing maritime workers. Within the IWW itself "mixed" locals—which united in one local men who had worked in different industries—grew increasingly popular. This was mainly because in a single year a Western migratory worker might vary his employment from logging, to building or agriculture and then to mining. Then his IWW membership was transferable without fees and was honored by locals everywhere.

Moreover, industrial growth in the West was not sufficient to ensure enough members to justify separate industrial locals, except in mining and lumbering, the region's two big industries. So three factors—limited industrial development, dependence on recruitment from migratory workers, and the universal transfer system of membership—gave permanence to mixed locals.

A move was made to replace them, however, by a General Recruiting Union at the 1916 convention. The debate about mixed locals showed that the decentralizers' old doubts were only a little below the surface, while, for its part, the GEB was still worried about its authority over the union as a whole. The idea behind the proposal was that recruits would join the

GRU and then be transferred to whichever industrial union was appropriate to their line of work. This policy would undoubtedly have tended to create more centralized control over IWW affairs. Still, nothing could alter the fact that in many areas no industrial unions existed, and none could be formed. So mixed ones flourished, and the proposal came to nothing.[46]

In Cleveland, Ohio, George Hardy, another British-born Wobbly, was busy recruiting Great Lakes seamen. Equally significant, the IWW was able to use its foothold among deep-sea sailors to spread its message to ports across the world in South America, Australia, Great Britain, and other countries. The Negro longshoremen of Philadelphia, Baltimore, and Norfolk remained the hard core of the IWW's Marine Transport Workers membership throughout these years. During its active life, from 1905 to about 1924, the IWW issued about a million membership cards, of which about 100,000 were to Negroes.[47]

On the Philadelphia waterfront, a group of dockers who had been active in the labor movement for fifteen years, half of them Negroes and the rest mostly Irish, Poles, and Lithuanians, had applied for an IWW charter in May 1913 and struck to gain recognition from the employers. Initially, the men had no organizational support, but before long the Marine Transport Workers section of the IWW and the International Longshoreman's Association of the AF of L appeared on the scene. The workers voted to join the IWW at a mass meeting, and formed Local 8 of the Marine Transport Workers.[48] At this stage the IWW was still opposed to making agreements with employers, but the Philadelphia longshoremen were able to sign a con-

[46] *Proceedings, op. cit.,* 106; Leslie H. Marcy, 'The Tenth Annual IWW Convention,' *International Socialist Review,* xvii, November 1916, 406.
[47] Spero and Harris, *op. cit.,* 331 and n; Gambs, *op. cit.,* 167.
[48] Spero and Harris, *op. cit.,* 334–36.

tract and carried out their side of the bargain. The MTW ran the Philadelphia longshore force for eight years, until 1921, and won recognition from both deep-sea and coastal shipping interests, despite the control the AF of L Longshoreman's Association gained in other harbors around the country, where it was encouraged by a government fearful of growing IWW influence.[49] For example, during the First World War the AF of L tried to break the IWW's hold in Philadelphia, using T. V. O'Connor, chairman of the United States Shipping Board, who was a former president of the International Longshoreman's Association.

Despite this hostility, the IWW remained firmly entrenched in Philadelphia, and its members worked in such strategically important centers as the Du Pont arms works and the United States Navy Yards, without jeopardizing the nation's war effort. The IWW's control of the Philadelphia waterfront ended only with the so-called "Philadelphia situation" of 1921, when difficulties over transferability and initiation fees were brought to a head by the Communists and caused Local 8 of the MTW to quit the IWW. For eight years the IWW had shown that it could exercise job control in a vital industry. More important, in its drive to organize underprivileged workers everywhere, it had continued the campaign begun in the Southern lumber industry to enroll Negro members.

So, on the eve of the First World War, the IWW was at last starting to carve itself a place in industries spurned by the AF of L, which remained unorganized until the CIO was formed in the 1930s. As it became more secure the IWW began to enter into those bargains and agreements with the employers that it had scorned ten years before. It also formed alliances with other political groups, not only the socialists, but

[49] *Ibid.,* 336.

the AF of L, the foreign-language federations, the women's emancipation movement, even, on occasions, propagandists for birth control. The Everett defense league was a typical example of this type of cooperation, and its letterheads listed fifty such organizations.

But for the First World War and its disastrous consequences for radical and socialist groups, it is possible the Wobblies might have made themselves the permanent spokesmen for semi-skilled and unskilled workers. But the IWW was persistently hounded and persecuted during the war, by the judiciary at both state and Federal level, and by self-appointed vigilante groups formed during the wave of xenophobia and war hysteria which swept the country after America entered the European conflict in 1917.

The IWW, with its radical doctrines and its natural opposition to war, which it regarded as a capitalist device for carving up the international markets, was especially vulnerable to this kind of attack. Moreover, its substantial membership of recent immigrants provided a ready-made target for super-patriots. This wave of persecution culminated in the jailing of over a hundred IWW leaders on charges of conspiracy in 1918. The trial and conviction of Joe Hill, the IWW's folk poet, and the lynching of two other Wobblies, Wesley Everest and Frank Little, served to dramatize what the IWW suffered during these stormy years.

7

THREE MARTYRS

WESLEY EVEREST

Torn and defiant as a wind-lashed reed,
Wounded he faced you as he stood at bay;
You dared not lynch him in the light of day,
But on your dungeon stones you let him bleed;
Night came . . . and you black vigilants of Greed . . .
Like human wolves, seized hard upon your prey,
Tortured and killed . . . and silently slunk away
Without one qualm of horror at the deed.

Once . . . long ago . . . do you remember how
You hailed Him king for soldiers to deride—
You placed a scroll above His bleeding brow
And spat upon Him, scourged Him, crucified . . .
A rebel unto Caesar—then as now
Alone, thorn-crowned, a spear wound in His side!

RALPH CHAPLIN

As the blood of the early Christian martyrs nourished the Church, so the sacrifices of its members gave strength and courage to the Industrial Workers of the World. Thousands of men (and some women too) were beaten and jailed for their beliefs; many died as they struggled to build "the grand industrial band." Yet only three achieved the supreme consolation of martyrdom: Frank Little, Wesley Everest, and Joe Hill. For a generation or more after their deaths, in IWW halls from coast to coast, photographs of Little, Everest, and Hill, faded, yellowing, and tattered, hung together as inspiration to Wobblies everywhere. In appearance and effect these pictures were like the triptychs found in medieval churches. These men died, the pictures seemed to say, so that the IWW might live.

Joe Hill's picture was almost invariably at the center of the group, and there was no doubt that he was the IWW's central martyr. On the face of it this is surprising. While both Frank Little and Wesley Everest were victims of brutal lynch mobs, Hill was executed after trial and conviction under due process of law for a sordid murder. Moreover, Little, a gifted, militant organizer who had led many famous strikes, was a member of the IWW's General Executive Board; while Everest, though less eminent, had a fine war record in France in 1918 and represented all the best qualities of the lumberjack. By contrast Hill was neither a leader nor a typical rank and file member. Though uneducated and unassuming, he was an intellectual.

Joe Hill was a folk poet. Born in Jevla, Sweden, in 1882, his real name appears to have been Joel Emmanuel Haaglund.[1] Though he may have been the illegitimate son of a prominent man, his early life is shrouded in mystery. Apparently he came to the United States in 1901. Wandering around the country looking for work, he assumed the name by which he became universally famous and started writing songs and parodies on the backs of laundry tickets and envelopes. Set to well-known melodies of the day, these songs mirrored the struggle of a whole generation of wage workers: they were songs for the inarticulate. Their author knew that a man fights better when he can sing and laugh.

So, as they struggled to found labor unions, thousands of ordinary men and women found themselves singing the coarse, homespun, wryly humorous, angry and sardonic words Joe Hill set to traditional tunes in such famous songs as *Casey Jones the Union Scab* and *The Preacher and the Slave*. Reprinted in rank and file newspapers or on song cards distributed during strikes, they made Joe Hill's name familiar to a host of workers who had never met him. Sung at demonstrations and on picket duty, in employment lines and jails, they swept the land. The chorus of *A Little Talk with Golden* became the marching song of the textile strikers at Lawrence in 1912. The wry skepticism, uncompromising militancy and passion of Hill's songs reflected perfectly the aspirations of wage workers seeking a better deal.

Perhaps the best assessment of Hill's writing was made by Ralph Chaplin, another Wobbly poet and contemporary of Hill. Chaplin's own song, *Solidarity Forever,* set to the tune of *John Brown's Body,* has a powerful chorus, ending with the affirmation "For the union makes us strong," which became the marching tune of the Congress of Industrial Organizations

[1] Ture Nerman, *Joe Hill* (Stockholm, 1951), 3. See also 190–91 below for a discussion of the reliability of all biographical data about Hill.

in the 1930s. He described Hill's work as "coarse as homespun and fine as silk; full of lilting laughter and keen-edged satire; full of fine rage and finer tenderness; simple, forceful and sublime songs; songs of and for the worker, written in the only language he can understand and set to the music of Joe Hill's own heart."[2]

Yet despite the world-wide popularity of his songs, the Joe Hill legend started only when he was arrested for the murder of a Salt Lake City grocer. During the trial Hill's name became the center of a controversy, which still rages, over his guilt or innocence. Special campaigns were launched, petitions organized, rallies and demonstrations held. Before it ended the Joe Hill case involved the Swedish Embassy, the Mormon Church, the State Department, and President Woodrow Wilson; it aroused the whole American labor movement and countless other plain people all over the world whose sense of justice had been outraged by Hill's trial and conviction.

These appeals and petitions were of no avail; and on the morning of November 19, 1915, a five-man firing squad, one bearing a rifle loaded with blanks, executed Hill in the yard of Utah State Penitentiary at Salt Lake City. In accordance with Hill's last requests, the IWW carried his coffin out of Utah to Chicago. Thirty thousand people attended the funeral at Graceland Cemetery, where graveside eulogies were delivered in nine European tongues.[3] His ashes were scattered in every state of the Union and in many overseas countries on May Day 1916.

Since then, the legend has grown prodigiously. Hundreds of books, articles, monographs, plays, and poems have been written about it. After the Wall Street crash in 1929 Hill's

2 Chaplin, 'Joe Hill, a Biography,' *Industrial Pioneer* (November 1923).
3 'In Memoriam Joe Hill,' funeral program, in the Labadie Collection at the University of Michigan, Ann Arbor.

phrase "pie in the sky" became the international slogan of the unemployed. In the 1930s a new generation of militant industrial unionists sang his verses and kept his name alive as they fought the bloodiest battles in American labor history to found the CIO. During the 1950s Earl Robinson's ballad, a setting of a poem written by Alfred Hayes in 1925 called *I Dreamed I Saw Joe Hill Last Night,* sung by Paul Robeson in many lands, introduced the legend to a third generation.

Novelists, playwrights, poets, and scholars have accorded Hill a place among the great American folk heroes, comparing him with John Henry, Johnny Appleseed, and Paul Bunyan. In his book *Nineteen Nineteen,* John Dos Passos devoted a whole chapter to Hill. "Used to play the concertina outside the bunkhouse door after supper, evenings," Dos Passos explained.[4] "Had a knack of setting rebel words to tunes." Another writer has dubbed him "the twentieth century's first egghead, he-man folk hero."[5] Joe Hill has become something more than a labor movement martyr. He is a type of Arthurian figure of the proletariat, who will return from the grave to help working men everywhere beat the boss. In the haunting chorus of the song by Robinson and Hayes, Joe Hill says "I never died."

How can one explain this myth? First, Hill was just the sort of obscure figure to whom legend clings. Virtually nothing is known about him. Uncertainty exists even about his real name, for while modern scholars prefer Joel Haaglund, his contemporaries knew him as Joseph Hillstrom, the name he took after reaching the United States. Most of the biographical information about Hill included in the popular picture of him was based on a story told to Ralph Chaplin, when he was editor of *Solidarity,* by a drunken sailor called John Holland, who claimed to be

[4] John Dos Passos, *Nineteen Nineteen* (New York, 1931), 422.
[5] Zapeta Modesto (Barry Nichol) 'Joe Hill, Some Notes on an American Culture Hero,' *Wobbly* (Berkeley, 1963), 9.

Hill's cousin.[6] Hill was in jail when Chaplin heard this intoxicated tale, so it is unlikely that his cousin, if such Holland was, would have spoken ill of him at such a time.

Hill himself was evasive about his background, perhaps because he really was illegitimate, perhaps because he was the stick-up man his enemies believed. In jail he shrugged off all personal inquiries, revealing only that he was a "citizen of the world" born on "the planet, Earth."[7] Tall, slender, with strikingly blond hair and deep blue eyes set in a long, thin, haunted face, he was still in his teens when he came to the United States. He may have learned English at the YMCA in Sweden, or working as a seaman on cargo ships sailing between Stockholm and Hull. After reaching the United States he drifted from job to job, a typical rootless migratory worker who, rather less typically, neither smoke nor drank, and was never seen in a fight.

He did not join the IWW until 1910, when he became a member of the San Pedro local in California. This gave him less than four years active membership, part of which was spent fighting for the rebel army during the Mexican revolution in 1911. Though by no means a leading Wobbly, Hill was unquestionably active in the cause of industrial unionism. He took part in the San Diego free speech fight in 1912, where he was beaten up and permanently scarred. Indeed, his body was a mass of scars. The prison ledger at Salt Lake City shows that Hill had four gunshot wounds, three on his face and neck and one on his right forearm.[8] Were all of these earned in the cause of industrial unionism? Or did some of them result from private, possibly criminal, adventures?

6 Wallace Stegner, 'The Case Against Joe Hill,' *New Republic,* January 5, 1948, 21.
7 Joe Hill to Oscar Larson, September 30, 1915.
8 Wallace Stegner, *The Preacher and the Slave* (Boston, 1950), 235.

He was working in the port of San Pedro, California, when the stevedores struck in 1912, and apparently took part in the abortive bid of some enterprising Wobblies to found a workers' commune in Baja California. Soon Joe Hill found himself on most employers' black lists all down the West Coast. The fact that it was virtually impossible for him to get a job in the Pacific shore states probably explains his move to Salt Lake City in the summer of 1913. Although Local 69 needed an organizer, there is no direct evidence that the IWW sent Hill there to fill the vacancy. Similarly there is no direct evidence that he took part in the successful strike at the Bingham United Construction Company shortly after his arrival in Utah. Perhaps his reputation followed him from California and no boss would hire him; or perhaps, as Wallace Stegner argues[9] Hill was already making a living from holdups and had no need of a job.

At all events, Hill remained unemployed the whole time he was in Utah. But although lacking visible means of support, he was usually well dressed and had money in his pocket.[10] Moreover, he had been arrested after a holdup in California, but then released because the police had insufficient evidence against him. Hints that he was carrying on love affairs with women also began to appear.[11] None of this circumstantial evidence and rumor about his private life need have been a threat to his safety in Salt Lake City. But his little red IWW membership card did endanger him. City hall politics in recent years had made IWW members especially vulnerable to attack.

Politics in Salt Lake City were traditionally the preserve of members of the Mormon Church, who had first settled in the

[9] *Ibid., passim* and *New Republic, op. cit.*

[10] Stegner, *New Republic, op. cit.*, and conversation with Ashleigh, November 19, 1965.

[11] Stegner, *New Republic, op. cit.*, and below, 198.

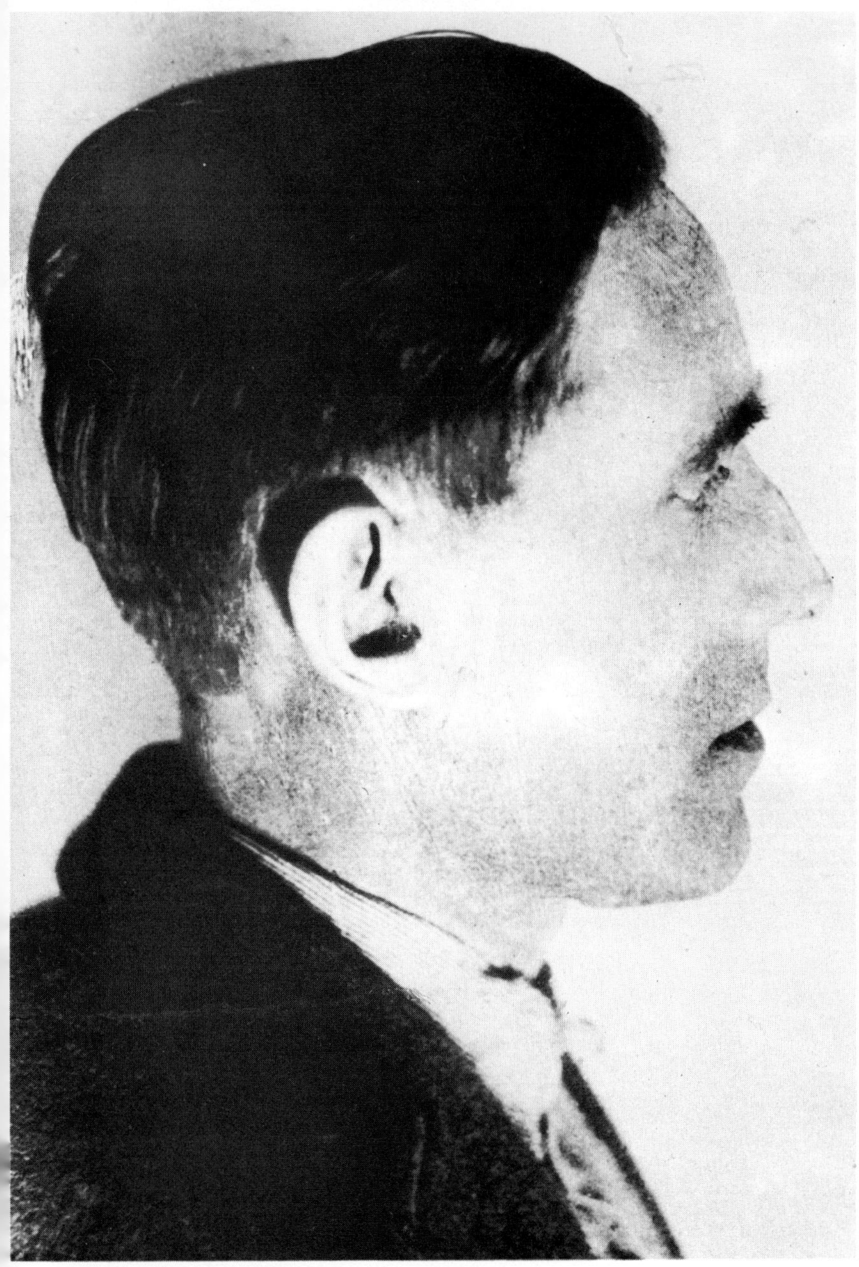

Joe Hill, "the man who never died." His last words were "Don't waste time mourning. Organize."

Joe Hill's funeral in Chicago.

A trainload of striking miners being deported from Bisbee, Arizona, into the desert of New Mexico in July 1917.

Frank Little, "half Indian, half white man, all IWW." Two days after this picture was taken, on August 1, 1917, Little was lynched.

Salt Lake area in the 1840s. But for some time before Hill's arrival the city had been run by an anti-Mormon group organized by the extreme right wing, business-oriented American Party. The American Party in Utah had been formed in reaction to the dominance of the Mormon community, symbolized when Reed Smoot, an elder of the Mormon Church, won a closely contested race for the United States Senate in 1908. After this, his opponents banded together to form a fusion ticket which swept the Mormons out of city hall for the first time in history.

Business may have been firmly in the saddle, but no millennium appeared. Indeed, American Party predominance was accompanied by a sharp increase in graft and corruption of all kinds, as well as much more labor unrest and violence. Disgust at the seeming consequences of the "Babylonian captivity" helped create another fusion ticket, this time between the Mormons and other political elements opposed to business leadership. By 1913 this coalition had ended the American Party's rule. In this atmosphere of compromise and intrigue Utah's Governor William Spry, a Mormon with a narrowly defined but demanding sense of duty, expressed his determination to "clean up the state" and "sweep out lawless elements, whether they be corrupt businessmen, I W W agitators, or whatever name they call themselves."[12]

Thus Joe Hill's arrival in Salt Lake City could scarcely have been more provocative had it been carefully calculated to provoke rather than purely fortuitous, as it seems to have been. The blow fell in January 1914. Hill, still unemployed, though working unpaid for Local 69, was arrested and charged with murdering John Morrison and his seventeen-year-old son Alving

[12] O. Ryan, 'Salt Lake City—A Municipal Democracy,' *Harper's Weekly*, October 4, 1913, *passim*.

in their grocery store on the night of January 10, 1914. Morrison, a former policeman, had been threatened and attacked several times before, and as no money was stolen in this fatal raid the presumption was that this had been a grudge killing. Two masked men were responsible, and Morrison's other son, fourteen-year-old Merlin, who survived the incident, testified that as they raced into the shop, one of them cried, "We've got you now," and opened fire.[13]

Merlin maintained that his brother fired one shot before he died, and that as the taller of the two men rushed from the store he clutched at his chest and screamed "Oh God! I'm shot!" Later that same night Dr. Frank McHugh treated Hill for a gunshot wound in his left lung. While dressing Hill's wounds, Dr. McHugh noticed a revolver in his shoulder holster, but when the police arrested Hill he was unarmed and they never found the murder weapon. Hill explained he had been in a quarrel over a married woman, and kept to this story throughout the trial, although adamantly refusing to name her. So another link was fashioned in the Joe Hill legend: that of a Galahad who went to his death rather than save himself by ruining a lady's reputation.

Throughout the trial, which became a *cause célèbre* in American legal history rivaled only by the Sacco and Vanzetti affair of the 1920s, Hill added virtually nothing to the story he told the doctor. He said he had disposed of the gun McHugh saw after leaving his surgery. But he refused to name the woman he claimed to have quarreled over, or the man he said shot him. Almost his only cooperative act after his arrest was to take the police to the gunsmith where he bought the revolver. This, he claimed confidently, would prove the gun was of a

[13] Barrie Stavis, *The Man Who Never Died* (New York, 1951), 29.

different caliber from the murder weapon; but the records at the store did not list the caliber of the revolver he had purchased—an omission that evidently rattled Hill.

The trial before Judge M. L. Ritchie seems to have been completely fair, though it is difficult to assess now because a full trial record no longer exists, and perhaps never existed.[14] The all-male jury was well-balanced, consisting of five businessmen, five laborers, and two farmers. The two defense attorneys, Frank B. Scott and E. E. McDougall, were competent and well-briefed, and their objections were upheld by the trial judge more often than they were denied. Yet halfway through the trial, in a dramatic courtroom outburst, Hill fired his lawyers, claiming they were not cross-examining the State's witness properly—though Hill's refusal to testify or to tell them anything privately did not help them.

The IWW then hired Judge O. N. Hilton, a sixty-seven-year-old labor attorney of formidable experience, to continue Hill's defense, which he did after a ten-day adjournment for him to master the unfamiliar brief. The prosecution's argument was riddled with inconsistencies and *non sequiturs*. As Hilton set to work on these Hill sat, calm and impassive after his outburst, watching the proceedings as if they in no way concerned him. None of the witnesses, not even Merlin Morrison, identified Hill as one of the killers. Although the bullet that wounded Hill passed through his body, the Morrison gun fired only plain

[14] James O. Morris, *The Joe Hill Case,* unpublished monograph in the Labadie Collection, University of Michigan, Ann Arbor, 123. For a partial transcript see *In the Third Judicial District Court of Utah in and for the Salt Lake City Court, State of Utah v. Joseph Hillstrom,* no. 3523, vol. ii, transcript of evidence 497–506, and *State v. Hillstrom,* 46 Utah 346 (1915). Morris provides an excellent summary of the trial, 21–66. An opposing view to Morris's can be found in Philip S. Foner, *The Case of Joe Hill* (New York, 1965). The incomplete transcript was important when the trial went to appeal—see Judge O. N. Hilton's remarks, below, 200.

lead bullets and no lead slug was found at the store, though six steel-jacketed bullets were found, two near Morrison's body and four near Alving's. The bulletholes in Hill's coat were four inches lower than those in his body, and his lawyers argued that Hill had had his hands up, thus stretching his jacket, when he was shot.

Yet Hill's own case was little more convincing. His refusal to name the woman he claimed to have fought over may have been chivalrous. Still, with his life at stake, it seems strange that no woman came forward to save her lover, or that no man was ever found who had been in a gunfight with Hill on the night in question. Even stranger was Hill's silence about his roommate, Otto Applequist, suspected of being the second gunman, who vanished at 3 A.M. on the morning after the murder and was never seen again. Applequist himself had had a hand dressed for gunshot wounds in September 1913, at the same time that John Morrison, the murdered grocer, had driven off an earlier bandit raid with gunfire.[15] Possibly Applequist was the man Hill fought. He may have killed him and then disposed of the body. No one can say now—although a wounded man like Hill would have had great difficulty in disposing of a corpse. In law Hill was under no obligation to say anything: the prosecution had to prove his guilt beyond reasonable doubt. In practice the jury thought his silence unconvincing and found Hill guilty. Judge Ritchie sentenced him to death.

Few who have studied the Hill case believe he was proved guilty beyond a reasonable doubt in court. Yet was he guilty in fact? That mystery remains unsolved. His lawyers were in no doubt. "The main thing the state had against Hill," they said after the trial, "was that he was an IWW and *therefore sure to be guilty*. Hill tried to keep the IWW out of it . . . but

[15] Stegner, *New Republic, op. cit.*

the papers fastened it upon him."[16] True, the local press was hot for conviction before the trial began, and hounded Hill until his death. But there is no evidence of any conspiracy to frame him.

Indeed, it seems Hill was unknown to the police. In the three days which elapsed between the killing and Hill's arrest, Salt Lake City detectives rounded up twelve other men and questioned them closely. When they finally burst into Hill's room at the home of the Eselius family, where local Wobblies used to meet, they shot Hill in the hand, though he was unarmed and lying on his bed under sedation from Dr. McHugh. But this piece of brutality seems to have been normal police practice in Salt Lake City, rather than an unsuccessful attempt to close the case by killing the prime suspect.[17]

What about motive? Many people who knew Hill found it inconceivable that he could have been mixed up in such a sordid and apparently senseless killing. But one student of the case, Wallace Stegner, having dismissed Ralph Chaplin's account of Joe Hill's character as hearsay, himself relies on hearsay evidence in asserting that Hill killed Morrison to avenge a friend Morrison had shot dead when he was in the police.[18] Stegner is even more sweeping in his condemnation of Hill as a cheap crook, but again relies on hearsay—and at two removes. "A Wobbly editor once told [Stewart] Holbrook [who wrote much about the IWW] that every Wob in the know was aware of Hill's character, but that he was blown up into a martyr for the sake of the cause," Stegner says, adding "and every old-timer I have found admits that he was a stick-up man."[19]

[16] *The Voice of the People,* May 21, 1914, quoted by Morris, *op. cit.*, 1 (italics in original).
[17] Stegner, *New Republic, op. cit.*
[18] *Ibid.*
[19] *Ibid.* The author has found no old-timers who think Hill guilty.

When it appeared in the magazine the *New Republic* in 1948, Stegner's outburst created a sensation and a Friends of Joe Hill Committee was formed to rescue Hill's reputation.[20] They met the question about the silence of Hill's alleged lover with the argument "some women, involved in clandestine affairs, will go to any length to avoid admitting such indiscretions and consider their 'honor' more important than anything else—even human life."[21] Much of the committee's defense of Hill's memory flows from this assertion, though they argue alternatively that the woman may have intended to come forward, but then have died or been killed.

Aside from partisan controversy two conflicting points are clear: there is some evidence that Hill was infatuated at the time Morrison was murdered and Hill wounded; and Hill lied to the Pardon Board and the Supreme Court when his case went there on appeal. The evidence that Hill may have been in love with an unknown woman at the time of the killing is contained in some love songs written by him while he was in Salt Lake City, which were found at the home of his friends, the Eselius family. In sharp contrast to the usual abrasive style of Hill's Wobbly songs, these are sentimental love lyrics called *Come and Take a Joy Ride in My Aeroplane* and *Oh, Please Let Me Dance This Waltz with You.*[22]

Hill's incriminating statements before the Pardon Board and the Supreme Court are more important and more revealing. Both courts insisted that to prove his innocence Hill had to testify. In the course of this testimony, the first statement he had made since his arrest nearly two years before, he said, "At

[20] *'The Case for Joe Hill,' New Republic,* November 15, 1948. This article was published in full in the *Industrial Worker,* November 13, 1948.
[21] *Ibid.*
[22] Salt Lake *Tribune,* June 21, 1914, quoted by Morris, *op. cit.,* 132 and n; see also Stegner, *The Preacher and the Slave, op. cit.,* 243.

the time I was shot I was unarmed. I threw my hands into the air just before the bullet struck me."[23] Yet the defense had never contested the fact that Hill had carried a gun into Dr. McHugh's surgery. Therefore, he must have been armed when he was shot—unless one accepts the unlikely hypothesis that he went home and collected his gun *before* calling on the doctor to treat a bullet wound that had penetrated right through his body.

There is a second discrepancy in Hill's story. During the trial his lawyers had argued that Hill had been forced to raise his hands by the woman's husband and was then shot—not, as Hill later swore, that he had thrown his hands into the air in an instinctive gesture the instant he was shot. The four inch gap between the wound and the holes in Hill's coat is a problem, but it can be explained. Merlin Morrison testified that the taller of the two masked raiders shot his brother Alving dead while his victim was crouching behind the shop counter, and that he received a bullet in return. To aim at him, the killer had to lean over the counter, so stretching his coat. This would almost certainly have caused a gap between the holes in his clothes and his body like the gap the police found on Hill when they picked him up. This possibility has another implication: the bullet, if it passed through the killer's body at close range, would have lodged in the ceiling—the only place the police did not search at the store.[24]

Hill did not try to explain why his roommate, Otto Applequist, had left town the morning after the murder and vanished without trace. This sudden disappearance lends some slight plausibility to the suggestion that the wounded assassin cried "Otto!" as he left the store rather than "Oh God!" which

[23] Deseret *Evening News,* October 4, 1915, quoted by Morris, *op. cit.,* 190.
[24] Morris, *op. cit.,* 129.

Merlin said he heard.[25] Yet despite the unsatisfactory nature of some of Hill's evidence on appeal, his attorney, O. N. Hilton, was genuinely shocked when the appeal was rejected. "The decision of the Supreme Court surprised me greatly," he said, "but the reason why the verdict was affirmed is, I think, on account of the rotten records made by the lower courts."[26]

Nearly two years elapsed between Hill's arrest and execution, and while the case went through all the many stages of appeal both the IWW and Hill himself were busy fighting the conviction. In the process the legend of Joe Hill was finally created. The fight for his life became international. In January 1915 the British IWW demanded his release. In July, the Australian IWW followed suit. At a mass meeting, 30,000 Australian workers adopted a resolution calling on Governor Spry to free Hill, and the Australian IWW's GEB followed this up with a letter in the same vein to the Salt Lake City *Evening Telegram*.[27] The Salt Lake City papers were getting fifty letters a day from all over the world expressing concern at the way Hill had been treated.

The reaction to this world-wide pressure varied. At first Governor Spry and the authorities in Utah were determined not to truckle to these demands. But later some responsible people began to argue that to make Hill a martyr by executing him would be playing into the IWW's hands. At the end of September 1915, Spry finally compromised and granted a stay of execution for thirty days. The Wobblies were jubilant.

Charles Ashleigh, who had been active in the AWO campaigns in the grain belt during the past two years, wrote in *Soli-*

[25] *Ibid.*
[26] Chaplin, *op. cit.*, 214. See also above 195 and n. 14 for the inaccurate and incomplete nature of the court records.
[27] Salt Lake City *Evening Telegram*, September 4, 1915, quoted by Stavis, *op. cit.*, 62.

darity, "The reprieve of Joe Hill is one of the strongest tributes ever paid to the indomitable energy of the IWW . . . The night of September 30, thousands of harvest hands tossed restlessly in their primitive couches . . . talking fitfully of the one thing uppermost in their minds: 'Would Hill die or not?' Here in Minneapolis, around the slave market, the name of Joe Hill is on everyone's lips. And everywhere among the workers the triumphant sentiment, 'We have done it.' "[28]

A leading figure in all the activity to free Hill was Gurley Flynn, and in gratitude Hill dedicated his song *The Rebel Girl* to her. Their correspondence while Hill was awaiting execution indicates nothing more than a platonic relationship, and they were together for only one hour in their lives, just before Hill's death, when she visited him in jail with guards present. She took up the question of Hill's sentence with President Wilson, who gave her a sympathetic hearing and wired the governor asking him to reconsider the case.[29] Spry curtly rejected this request as "unwarranted interference" in the affairs of the state of Utah.

The platonic note in the Hill-Flynn letters wavers a little near the end. "You have been more to me than a fellow worker," he told her.[30] "You have been an inspiration, and when I composed the Rebel Girl you were right there and helped me all the time." Another letter to Gurley Flynn raises the question of whether Hill was seeking martyrdom. He had once reminded her that he had reached the age at which Christ was crucified; now he added, "I have said that I'd have a trial or die trying."[31] While the campaign to free him mounted out-

28 *Solidarity*, October 2, 1915.
29 Stavis, *op. cit.*, 72; Flynn, *op. cit.*, 254.
30 Stavis, *op. cit.*, 96. Hill's correspondence can be read in Philip S. Foner, *The Letters of Joe Hill* (New York, 1965).
31 *Ibid.*, 74.

side the jail, Joe Hill kept busy. Articles, poems and songs flowed from his pen. His coolness under strain was remarkable. His lawyer, Judge Hilton, commented, "Never before have I seen a condemned man bear up so well under the . . . knowledge of certain death."[32] The Salt Lake City *Herald-Republican*, which had opposed Hill, the IWW and the way Governor Spry had granted a stay of execution, sent a reporter to obtain a last interview with Hill the day before he died. The newsman was deeply impressed by his courage. He had come to mock, but he remained to praise.[33]

The same day, Hill scribbled his last will and testament in the form of a moving poem.

My will is easy to decide
For there is nothing to divide.
My kin don't need to fuss and moan
"Moss does not cling to rolling stone."

My body? Oh! If I could choose,
I would to ashes it reduce
And let the merry breezes blow
My dust to where some flowers grow.

Perhaps some fading flower then
Would come to life and bloom again.
This is my last and final will
Good luck to all of you

JOE HILL.

He gave this poem, together with his silk scarf, to Ed Rowan, another IWW organizer. He wrote his last letter to Gurley Flynn, and his philosophy is summed up in a note to Ben

[32] *Ibid.*, 93.
[33] *Ibid.*, 92.

Williams, editor of *Solidarity,* which emphasized the need for proletarian unity and industrial unionism.

In Utah, a condemned man has the choice between hanging and shooting—a remnant of the customs of the Old West. Joe Hill chose the firing squad. He asked permission to face his executioners on November 19, 1915, without a blindfold and not strapped to the death chair.[34] The legend says he gave the order to fire himself, but this appears to have been a final act of defiance after fighting off his captors in his cell with a broom handle.[35] He wired his last words to Bill Haywood. "Goodbye, Bill. I die a true blue rebel. Don't waste time in mourning. Organize." With that undaunted curtain line, Joe Hill transformed himself from man into myth. It became the watchword of all who struggled to build labor unions in the next generation.

Without question the Joe Hill legend owes much to the fact that Hill had a poet's knack of self-dramatization. But there was more to it than that. Joe Hill was not proved guilty beyond all reasonable doubt in court. Thus it became easier for the I W W to discredit the whole system of bourgeois justice by concentrating on this one case. Was Hill guilty in fact? It is hard to fault the judgment of James O. Morris in one of the most careful and dispassionate studies of the case, which concludes that while Hill was not proved guilty in court he nevertheless did murder the Morrisons.[36]

Morris argues that while Hill's alibi was near perfect, it was simply an ingenious invention which happened to fit the known facts almost perfectly. "The resigned, defiant obstinacy of Hill protected no one but himself," he adds.[37] "There was

[34] Salt Lake City *Evening Telegram,* September 20, 1915.
[35] Stegner, *New Republic, op. cit.,* 23.
[36] Morris, *op. cit.,* 129.
[37] *Ibid.,* 133.

nothing magnificent, no aspiration to martyrdom, no noble spirit whatsoever behind his desire for a new trial. He did not prove his innocence because he could not. Guilt dictated silence, not honor nor a fanatical belief in the principle of fair trial. He did not dare fake evidence to support his alibi . . . He faced disgrace and very likely death too, on the one hand, and death alone on the other. Reluctantly, and probably with a deeply tormented soul, he chose death."[38] From this agonized choice grew the legend of the martyred troubadour of labor.

The most recent scholarly re-examination of the Joe Hill affair is Philip S. Foner's exhaustive study.[39] Dr. Foner's conclusion, after a thorough examination of all the available sources, is that Hill was the innocent victim of a conspiracy. Dr. Foner shows that the identification and ballistic evidence was most unsatisfactory, and reveals many other discrepencies in the prosecution's case. He argues that the trial was unfair because Judge Ritchie's conduct was sufficient grounds for a mistrial, while his summing-up ran completely contrary to precedent in the state of Utah concerning the law of circumstantial evidence.

Dr. Foner also believes a fair trial was impossible because the authorities in Utah—the Mormon Church, the copper trust, the newspapers and the police—were bitterly opposed to the IWW and determined to convict Hill as soon as they discovered he was a member of the union. In short, Dr. Foner's book is a lucid statement of what may be called "the traditional view" of the Hill affair. Readers alone can judge whether he makes out with his case.

His evidence that a conspiracy existed does not seem strong, and tends to overlook the fundamental fact that Joe Hill had

[38] *Ibid.*, 133.
[39] *The Case of Joe Hill* (New York, 1965).

to be found guilty by a jury. In the Haywood trial at Boise in 1907, and in several other cases, the authorities were as determined as they were in the Hill case to convict IWW defendants—yet juries acquitted them. The fact that the authorities were prejudiced does not prove that they conspired to deprive Hill of his constitutional rights or send him to his death, and there is no evidence—as there is in other cases involving the IWW—that efforts were made to tamper with the jury.

Moreover, Dr. Foner fails to discuss fully the weaknesses in Hill's own case. He does not note the two vital discrepancies in Hill's statement before the Pardon Board, in which he said he was unarmed and had his hands raised at the time he was shot. Why did he throw his gun away after leaving Dr. McHugh's surgery? Why did Otto Applequist leave town on the night of the murders? And how did Applequist get his gunshot wounds when Morrison's store was last attacked on September 20, 1913? Dr. Foner believes Hill died for an abstract principle: that a man must be proved guilty beyond a reasonable doubt. A reasonable doubt about Hill's guilt should have existed in the minds of any fair jury. His conviction was doubtful; and his death sentence should almost certainly have been commuted. But fifty years after the case it is hard for an impartial observer not to admit that a reasonable doubt exists about Hill's innocence too.

Joe Hill was really a far less authentic hero than Frank Little. After Big Bill Haywood, Little was perhaps the IWW's most dynamic figure. Like Haywood, he had only one good eye, and like him too he had Indian blood.[40] Lacking Haywood's oratorical skill, Little was nevertheless the toughest,

[40] Chaplin, *op. cit.*, 113.

most courageous and impulsive leader the IWW ever had. He joined the IWW in 1906, was active in the free speech fights at Missoula, Fresno, and Spokane, and went on to organize the lumberjacks, metal miners, oil field workers and harvest bindle stiffs all over the West and Southwest.

By 1916 he was a member of the General Executive Board and a powerful advocate of militant action. He favored the strong-arm methods employed by the AWO in the harvest fields and advocated sabotage of farming equipment in areas where the AWO met tough resistance from the employers. He was also a vehement opponent of the First World War. When hostilities broke out in Europe in August 1914 it put the IWW in a quandary. The IWW opposed war in general. But half the leadership thought this view was not shared by the overwhelming majority of wage workers whom they hoped to organize, and that their policy toward the war must be tempered to suit the mood of these workers.

To Haywood the war was a puzzling irrelevance which was best ignored. "What is this war all about?" he once asked Frank Bohn, a firm supporter of the Allies.[41] Those who supported Little felt the war was a gigantic capitalist plot which must be opposed more vigorously than other aspects of capitalism. This conflict between the two wings became much sharper when America finally joined the Allies in April 1917. But it was never resolved. Antiwar pamphlets like *The Deadly Parallel* were withdrawn, and IWW members went off to fight in France. Yet the Wobblies hedged on their attitude to sabotage in time of war, and no policy decision was ever taken.[42]

[41] Author's interview with Bohn, January 29, 1966.

[42] Ironically, the Socialist Party of America, which (though hopelessly split) officially opposed the war, was not prosecuted for antiwar conspiracy, while the IWW was brought to trial in 1918. See chapter 8, below.

Little's outspoken opposition to the war won him many enemies both inside and outside the union. Yet he refused to compromise. In the summer of 1917, the GEB debated the movement's attitude toward hostilities. Little argued that "the IWW is opposed to all wars, and we must use all our power to prevent the workers from joining the army."[43] Chaplin warned Little that opposing the draft and organizing draft riots, like the ones in Oklahoma known as the Green Corn Rebellion, would mean the end of the IWW, but Little was unabashed. "Better to go out in a blaze of glory," was his defiant reply "than give in."[44] Little then wrote a passionate antiwar statement which appeared in *Solidarity* on July 28, 1917, only three days before he died.

Although Little's antiwar attitude was very unpopular it was not super-patriotism that motivated his murderers. They were almost certainly agents of the copper trust who wanted to rid themselves of a dangerous IWW agitator in a dangerous industry, where 190 men had died in a single industrial accident at the Speculator Mine in June 1917. Frank Little had been a tireless organizer in the metal mines of Arizona and Montana in 1916–17. He brought his own men out in protest against wartime wage cuts, which accompanied wartime increases in the price of copper. In July 1917 he was called into action again when 1200 Arizona metal miners, including 104 Wobblies, were rounded up by armed members of the Bisbee Loyalty League and shipped into the desert in cattle trucks before being imprisoned without charge.[45]

Back in Butte, Montana, at the end of July, Little helped organize another strike of metal miners against the Anaconda

[43] Evidence and cross-examination of Haywood in *US v. William D. Haywood* (Chicago, n.d.), 212.
[44] Chaplin, *op. cit.*, 209.
[45] Telegrams between Grover Perry and Frank Little, July 1917, in the Labadie Collection, University of Michigan, Ann Arbor.

Company. He had broken a leg in Oklahoma on his way back from Bisbee, but still managed to shout scorn and defiance at a threatening crowd of company guards. Later, in the early hours of August 1, 1917, the company guards were revenged. Six masked men, heavily armed, broke into Little's hotel room, beat him up, dragged him down in his pajamas to their car, tied him by a rope to the rear fender and dragged him along the dirt track to the Milwaukee Railroad trestle several miles out of town. There, in the harsh light of their car's headlamps, they hanged him, and pinned a notice to his lifeless body saying *"First and last warning."*[46] This act of savage barbarity shocked Butte and the entire labor movement. The police kept up a pretense of looking for the man they called their prime suspect, a mentally deranged drug addict from the Western underworld, but no serious attempt was made to bring Little's murderers to justice.

Frank Little's claims to be remembered by the Wobblies probably outstrip those of anyone else. He was a prominent member of the GEB, completely innocent of any crime save that of trying to organize his fellow workers, who was brutally killed by an armed mob. Yet for some reason Little is the least remembered of the IWW's martyrs. Perhaps that is because he was an extremist, an outspoken advocate of sabotage and opposition to the First World War, who died just as the IWW was trying to avoid persecution by playing down its revolutionary character and posing as nothing more than a militant industrial union. Perhaps it was simply that soon after Little's death the IWW found itself in court on trial for its very existence, so that the demands of this defense campaign took first place over any efforts to keep Frank Little's name alive.

[46] George R. Tomkins, quoted by John Steuben, *The Truth About Butte* (New York, 1940), 89–90; Butte *Miner,* August 2, 1917.

Whatever the reason, Little is not such a hallowed figure as the Wobblies' third martyr, Wesley Everest. Though he was just an ordinary lumberjack and rank and file IWW card holder, Everest had one outstanding characteristic: he had served as a soldier in France at a time when the IWW was accused in Federal courts of conspiracy to oppose the American war effort. Everest was murdered by a lynch mob in November 1919 at Centralia, Washington, a state which had experienced perpetual industrial upheaval for the past three or four years. The Everett massacre in 1916 had been just one episode in a long story of free speech fights, strikes, reprisals, and labor unrest, which culminated in the Seattle general strike of 1919.

Toward the end of 1919 the lumber trust in Centralia decided they had had enough of the IWW and planned to run it out of town. Accordingly, they held a meeting which gave the president of the Southwest Washington Lumbermen's Association power to create a secret committee for this purpose. The trust even warned the IWW of its intention in the Washington daily newspapers.[47] Their chosen instrument for breaking up the IWW was the American Legion. Earlier in 1919 Legion members had entered the IWW hall at Centralia and beaten up Wobblies with gas pipes and rubber hoses. The IWW, forewarned of the lumber trust's intentions, fortified their hall and prepared for a siege.

The clash came on Armistice Day, November 11, 1919. The Legion paraded through the town in strength, some of them armed with rubber hoses and gas pipes. As they passed the Wobbly hall firing broke out. It was never proved who fired first, nor whether the firing began before or after the Legion began rushing the IWW hall. Legion men stormed the build-

[47] Eugene Barnett, unpublished statement at Cornell University Industrial and Labor Relations School library, 7–8.

ing, and in the affray three of them were killed. Everest, in army uniform, was inside the IWW hall when the League burst in, and told a comrade, "I fought for democracy in France and I'm going to fight for it here. The first man that comes in this hall, why, he's going to get it."[48]

Everest was a crack shot. He emptied the magazine of his rifle into the marauding crowd, dropped it and ran for the woods with his pistol. The mob followed. Everest ran for the River Skookumchuck, started to wade across and then found the current too strong. Up to his waist in water he stopped, turned and said he would submit to arrest by the police. But the mob was on him in a flash. Everest shot from the hip four times before his gun jammed, tugged at the trigger again, took careful aim and shot the leading man dead. His victim was another ex-soldier, Dale Hubbard, the nephew of the lumber trust boss in Centralia who had planned the raid.

Then Everest threw the gun into the river and fought the mob with his fists. Overpowered, he snarled defiance. "You haven't the guts to hang a man in the daytime," he told them. He was right, but the mob did drag him back to town behind a car and suspend him from a telegraph pole before locking him in jail. That night the city lights were turned off, and the mob smashed down the jailhouse door. "Tell the boys I died for my class," Everest said to his cell mates as he was dragged outside. Everest was flung on the floor of a car, castrated, and then driven to the Chehalis River bridge, where he was hanged and then riddled with bullets. His body was buried in a nameless grave.[49]

After Everest's death a reign of terror swept the whole state

[48] *Ibid.*, 12.

[49] Dos Passos, *op. cit.*, 457–61 is the most dramatic account of Everest's death, based largely on Ralph Chaplin, *The Centralia Conspiracy* (Chicago, 1920). See also Jensen, *Lumber and Labor, op. cit.*, 138.

of Washington. A posse of vigilantes arrested hundreds of Wobblies, and eventually eleven were indicted for killing the man who commanded the American Legion Parade. No attempt was made to bring Everest's killers to justice, but the trial of the Wobblies was scarcely in the highest traditions of Anglo-Saxon justice. First the case was tried before Judge John M. Wilson, who had delivered a funeral speech for the Legion men who died in the affray which contained a furious attack on the IWW. Then it was tried in Montesano, Grays Harbor County, a predominantly business area just a few miles from Centralia.[50]

Hostility here to the IWW had grown so intense since Armistice Day that a fair trial was virtually impossible. Judge Wilson himself admitted as much before it opened, but then changed his mind. The trial atmosphere can be judged from the fact that the Legion raised $11,750 from employers to pay fifty Legionnaires $4 a day to occupy the front of the courtroom in uniform. Three witnesses who testified that the Legion attacked the IWW hall before the shooting started were arrested for perjury as they left the stand, and the defense counsel, George Vanderveer, practically came to blows with the sheriff.[51] Despite this, the jury acquitted one defendant, declared another insane, brought in manslaughter verdicts against two more and found the rest guilty only of second degree murder, instead of first degree murder as the prosecution asked. Judge Wilson declared this verdict unacceptable, and sent the jury out for another two hours. This time they found the men guilty of second degree murder. They were sentenced to from twenty-five to forty years in Walla Walla Penitentiary. Four years later, nine of the jurors said in public, six of them under

[50] *Industrial Worker,* September 23, 1922; Harvey O'Connor, *Revolution in Seattle* (New York, 1964), 187–88.
[51] O'Connor, *op. cit.,* 188.

oath, that they had reached their verdict because of pressure from the lumber trust.[52]

The Centralia affair may have helped smash the IWW in the Washington timber forests, but it left a nasty taste behind. In the 1930s, a dispassionate inquiry into the killings and the trial that followed came to the only fair conclusion. "The six IWWs in Walla Walla Penitentiary are paying the penalty for their part in a tragedy the guilt for which is by no means their's alone. They alone were indicted, they alone have been punished.[53] Later, these prisoners were paroled. The price they paid, some fifteen years in prison, was perhaps not so high as that paid by Wesley Everest, whose murderers were never punished. So Everest became the third of a group of martyrs whose individual sufferings were part of the burden of persecution the IWW as a whole had to bear after 1917.

52 Walker C. Smith, *The Centralia Case* (Chicago, 1923), 122.

53 Federal Council of Churches of Christ in America, *The Centralia Case: a joint report on the Armistic Day Tragedy at Centralia, Washington, November 1919* (New York, 1930), 45–46.

8

THE GREAT TRIAL

I LOVE MY FLAG

I love my flag, I do, I do,
Which floats upon the breeze
I also love my arms and legs,
And neck and nose and knees.
One little shell might spoil them all
Or give them such a twist
They would be of no use to me
I guess I won't enlist.

I love my country, yes, I do,
I hope her folks do well.
Without our arms and legs and things,
I think we'd look like hell.
Young men with faces half shot off
Are unfit to be kissed,
I've read in books it spoils their looks;
I guess I won't enlist.

ANONYMOUS, *Industrial Worker*
April 14, 1917

The First World War did not initially divide the IWW as much as it divided the American socialist movement. The great European conflict split the socialists from the start, and they never really recovered their unity. The strong German element in American socialism had provided its backbone since the 1850s; with a few exceptions they favored the Central Powers. The Russian element, led by Morris Hillquit, supported the Germans because they believed, rightly as it turned out, that German defeat of Czardom would result in revolution in Russia. Moderate, reformist American socialists, who viewed the militarism and nationalism of the German Reich with suspicion, tended to favor the Allied Powers.

For the Wobblies the war, in its early years at any rate, was an irrelevance compared with the class struggle. They continued their organizing drives in the grain belt and the Far West, and the years between 1914–17 saw the IWW's period of greatest growth. In 1916, the tenth annual convention denounced war in general and stated that it hoped to prevent war by proclaiming "anti-militarist propaganda in time of peace, thus promoting Class Solidarity among the workers of the entire world, and, in time of war, the General Strike in all industries"[1]—an attitude typical of left wing socialism in both America and Europe before the First World War.

But when, on April 6, 1917, the United States entered the war on the Allied side the IWW General Executive Board in Chicago found itself facing many perplexing problems. As

[1] *Proceedings of the Tenth Annual Convention of the IWW* (Chicago, 1916), 110.

patriotism swept the nation, the common enemy overseas replaced the class enemy at home in the minds of many American workers. The IWW believed that "of all the idiotic and perverted ideas accepted by the workers from that class who live upon their misery, patriotism is the worst." But when America joined hostilities the IWW failed to put its antimilitarism into practice. Haywood told one Wobbly who wrote to the GEB demanding a general strike against militarism and war, "Of course, it is impossible for this office . . . to take action on your individual initiative. However I have placed your communication on file for future reference."[2]

Frank Little alone of the GEB favored direct action against the war—and he was murdered four months after America became involved. For more than ten years the IWW had used the industrial strike as its major revolutionary weapon. The battles had often been long and bitter, and the lines between the classes clearly drawn. Now, in a nation at war, the strike had become a more indiscriminately dangerous weapon. Conflict between masters and men in the Arizona copper mines, or the Washington timber forests, could affect the lives of American soldiers fighting on the bloody battlefields of Flanders or France. As past-masters of propaganda, the GEB knew that wartime strikes would be wildly unpopular.

However, the IWW's attitude to the American declaration of war was divided. A minority faction favored all-out opposition to the war by every means, including the general strike and defiance of the draft. This group consisted mainly of Irish and Finnish elements in the Mesabi metal mines of Minnesota, who hated Britain and Russia because they were suppressing national liberation movements in their homelands. The major-

[2] Philip Taft, 'The Federal Trials of the IWW,' *Labor History*, vol. 3, no. i (Winter, 1962), 59 and n.

ity, led by Haywood and the rest of the GEB, felt that opposition to the war would lead to persecution and sidetrack the IWW from its real work into some futile, pacifist backwater.[3]

The dilemma of the antiwar group is revealed in a letter from Walter Nef, head of the AWO, to one of his organizers. "We are against the war," Nef wrote, "but not organized and can do nothing." *Solidarity* said editorially: "We are unalterably opposed to war and conscription," but added the significant qualifying phrase, "*had we the power* we would stop every ship, train, mine and mill, every food and supply plant—every wheel of industry."[4]

These doubts about the IWW's strength caused Haywood to counsel caution. Grover Perry, a prominent member of the rising generation of IWW organizers, told him, "I may be thrown into jail at any time for refusal to enlist," adding, "without conscription there would not be enough men to make pall bearers for Jack Johnson."[5] So when Little urged a stronger stand against enlistment, Haywood replied, "Keep a cool head; do not talk. A good many feel as you do but the world war is of small importance compared to the great class war." Haywood concluded, "I am at a loss as to definite steps to be taken against the war."[6]

After much heart-searching and debate, the GEB decided to carry on with a policy of industrial activity in specially selected areas, where prolonged withdrawal of labor would soon force the employers to negotiate about conditions of work. Many of these industrial battles were fought in Arizona, Mon-

[3] See letters, minutes and other IWW documents in *U S Circuit Court of Appeals, 7th District,* October 1919.
[4] *Solidarity,* May 12, 1917 (author's italics).
[5] Grover Perry to Haywood, May 11, 1917. Jack Johnson was a Negro boxer and from 1908–15 heavyweight champion of the world.
[6] Haywood to Little, May 6, 1917.

tana, and Washington, for copper and timber were two vital war materials and employers who had to meet delivery dates to fulfill government contracts could not stand prolonged strikes.

Yet there is no evidence that IWW strikes were designed to interfere with the war effort. They were simply a means of trying to improve pay and conditions. There were also indications, since the success of the AWO, that the IWW was starting to abandon its revolutionary extremism in favor of the more moderate policies of an ordinary industrial union. Still, many businessmen, and some politicians, were becoming thoroughly alarmed about the IWW.

Newspapers implied that its strikes were backed by German gold, and Senator Henry F. Ashurst, a Wilsonian Democrat from Arizona, claimed the letters IWW stood for "Imperial Wilhelm's Warriors."[7] This sort of attitude forgot, or ignored, the fact that on the Philadelphia waterfront, by the Great Lakes and in the mighty Du Pont armament industries, where the IWW also had active Locals, industrial relations were peaceful because pay and conditions were much better than those offered migratory workers in the West.

In some parts of the West the IWW laid itself open to the suspicion of treason. In a letter from Seattle in August 1917 Haywood outlined his tactics there. "We have the good will of the German people here," he wrote, "and we feel sure [they] are in sympathy with our cause. We do not call them Germans, however, but refer to them as Fellow Workers."[8] This sort of attitude was quite harmless. But it made respectable, middle class Americans share the views of Senator William H. King, the conservative Republican from Utah, who

[7] Taft, *op. cit.,* 60.
[8] Haywood to Ralph Chaplin, August 2, 1917.

said of the IWW "I say it is a treasonable organization . . . because it is giving aid and comfort to the enemies of the Republic."[9]

The IWW was most certainly not financed by the German secret service. Some German agents may have tried to infiltrate and use the organization, as they did other popular movements in Britain, Ireland and the United States. But the government accountant who examined the IWW's finances for the Department of Justice refuted the charge that IWW organizing drives were paid for by German gold.[10]

However, though the IWW did not organize any resistance to mobilization, there was some opposition to the draft from other advocates of One Big Union in Texas and Oklahoma, then one of the most radical regions of America. In what became known as the Green Corn Rebellion, some two hundred tenant farmers from a 35,000-strong organization called the Workingman's Union marched on Sasakwa, Oklahoma, in August 1917, armed with ancient rifles to defy the draft, but then surrendered without a shot being fired. Their leaders, including H. H. "Rube" Munson, a former IWW organizer who had been expelled for criminal activity, were jailed for ten and five years, while most of the rank and file were sentenced to a year and a day in a federal penitentiary.[11]

Although, unlike the Socialist Party of America, the IWW never took a clear stand in opposition to the war, there nevertheless was a widespread public belief that the IWW meant to hinder the war effort at all costs. This belief, based on

[9] John D. Batdorf, *Menace of the IWW* (New York, 1916), 1.
[10] *William D. Haywood v. United States, U S Supreme Court,* October 1920, 760, 1, 421.
[11] Charles C. Bush, *The Green Corn Rebellion* (unpublished master's thesis, University of Oklahoma, 1932), 9 and n., 12 and n., 66–67. See also the *McAlester News Capitol* for the late summer and autumn of 1917 (esp. October 20).

incidents like the Green Corn Rebellion and doubts about the morality of striking in wartime, was, on the whole, groundless. But fanned by the xenophobic fears of a nation at war, and by some employers anxious to stamp out labor unions, the idea that the IWW was a subversive organization spread in newspaper editorials and correspondence columns across the land. In answer to this public unease, President Wilson appointed Judge J. Harry Covington to investigate the organization. Bill Haywood, as secretary-treasurer of the IWW, responded cooperatively, and immediately invited him to inspect the union's files. Instead, on September 5, 1917, agents of the Department of Justice staged simultaneous raids on forty-eight IWW Local halls across the entire nation, seizing five tons of letters, newspapers, propaganda pamphlets and other documents.

After it had been sifted by government agents, part of this material was presented to a Grand Jury of the United States Federal Court in Illinois, when 165 IWW leaders were indicted on five counts on September 28, 1917. They were charged with combining with Frank Little and "diverse other persons" unknown "by force to prevent, hinder and delay the execution" of eleven different Acts of Congress and Presidential Proclamations covering the war program. The second count charged the Wobbly leaders with conspiracy under Section 19 of the Criminal Code to injure, oppress, threaten, and intimidate those who wished to enjoy the Constitutional right and privilege of executing certain contracts without interference.

Count three of the indictment was of conspiracy under Section 37 of the Criminal Code to procure people to refuse to register for military service and to encourage desertion from the armed forces. Count four charged the IWW leaders with conspiracy to cause military insubordination, and the final count was of conspiracy to defraud employers who hired certain workers.[12] The following day, in a nation-wide sweep, a large number of those indicted were arrested.

From the very first moment it was clear that the IWW as an organization was being brought to justice. This led to a debate within the union about what attitude it should adopt toward the trial. Some Wobblies, believing that in the current climate of public opinion the trial would be little better than a judicial lynching, wanted to evade arrest. The leadership disagreed with this attitude, and Haywood and the IWW's chief counsel, George F. Vanderveer, the Seattle attorney, quickly decided that if the capitalists had made up their minds to punish the IWW under due process of law there was nothing they could do about it.

Accordingly, Haywood and Vanderveer decided to use the impending trial as a means of spreading IWW propaganda. They ordered all indicted members to submit to arrest[13]; an order that rebounded on Haywood's head several years later when he himself refused to submit to imprisonment and skipped bail. Following these orders, the indicted Wobblies soon surrendered.

The idea that the IWW should resist arrest had been expounded most forcefully by Gurley Flynn and Joseph Ettor. But they had been expelled from the IWW by the GEB for lack of solidarity in 1916. Their expulsion arose from an incident during the great IWW strike at Mesabi in northeastern Minnesota, the biggest iron-ore mining region in the world. Flynn, Ettor and Tresca, together with other IWW organizers of the caliber of Frank Little and George Andreytchine, a formidable Bulgarian destined to play a major role in IWW affairs in the 1920s, led a big strike of the predominantly East and South

[12] Taft, *op. cit.*, 61.
[13] *Defense News Bulletin*, December 1, 1917.

European miners. Flynn and Ettor defied GEB instructions and, in order to secure the release of five IWW organizers from arrest, had persuaded three striking Montenegrin miners to plead guilty to charges of killing a policeman during a riot.[14]

Now they made themselves even more unpopular. They managed to get their cases separated from the main group and were eventually released, along with Gurley Flynn's lover, Carlo Tresca, because the indictment did not cover their period of IWW membership. Arturo Giovannitti was also excused,[15] and others should have been, in particular Vincent St. John, who had left the IWW in 1914, when he resigned as secretary-treasurer to go prospecting in New Mexico.[16] The original charge had to be amended, since Frank Little had been murdered almost two months before.

While the defendants awaited trial in the verminous Cook County jail in Chicago, the defense sought to have the indictments quashed on the grounds that the testimony presented before the Grand Jury by government agents had been merely hearsay evidence. Vanderveer also submitted, as well he might, that the raids on IWW headquarters had been in flagrant violation of the Fourth and Fifth Amendments to the United States Constitution, which guarantee freedom from unreasonable search and arrest.[17]

On a less legalistic level, Vanderveer wired all the defendants informing them that the government would probably dismiss the indictments if the IWW agreed to renounce its beliefs and not make any propaganda out of the raids and arrests. Herbert Mahler, a defendant active on the Everett defense

[14] Taft, *op. cit.*, 61–62; Flynn, *op. cit.*, 225. Foner, *History of the Labor Movement*, *op. cit.*, 486–517 gives the best account of the Mesabi strike.

[15] Haywood, *op. cit.*, 269; Taft, *op. cit.*, 62.

[16] See chapter 6 above, and Taft, *op. cit.*, 75.

[17] Petition of George F. Vanderveer in *US v. Haywood et al.*, March 18, 1918.

committee in 1916, who was now helping to plan the defense of the IWW itself, believed that this idea had been suggested to President Wilson by such IWW-sympathizers as Carelton Parker, author of a pioneer study of migratory workers, John Graham Brooks, an authority on syndicalism, and attorney Clarence Darrow. He thought their intervention and the agitation of socialists and other radicals had influenced this unusual offer.[18]

But the imprisoned Wobblies would not agree to these terms, and the offer came to nothing without anyone really discovering whether or not it was genuine. Meanwhile, those who were still out of prison quickly organized a defense fund. Gurley Flynn, who was freed on bail before she was finally released, raised $5000 in a few weeks from women alone, her most illustrious contributor being Fola La Follette, whose brother Robert M. was Wisconsin's leading politician. Though Mahler was nominally in charge of the defense committee, his activities were limited by the fact that he was also in jail, and most of the work was done by Gurley Flynn. Before he was released, the passionately pro-Ally Italian Giovannitti wrote to her, "Gurley, if you don't get me out of this, I'll come to court in uniform."[19]

Finally, on April 1, 1918, there appeared in the huge, white marble Federal courtroom in Chicago 101 members of the IWW charged with sabotage and conspiracy to obstruct the war. The trial, which lasted five months, was at that time the longest criminal trial in American legal history. Though 101 defendants were at the bar, it was an organization, indeed, a philosophy, that was being prosecuted. The leading prosecut-

[18] Taft, *op. cit.*, 62 and n.
[19] Flynn, *op. cit.*, 224; Haywood, *op. cit.*, 302–05. One defendant whose name seemed made for martyrdom, A. C. Christ, *did* appear in uniform. Significantly, he was excused.

ing attorney, a corporation lawyer from Utah named Frank K. Nebeker, admitted as much in his opening statement, when he said, "It is the IWW which is on trial here."

The type and number of the defendants also gave the great IWW trial a distinctive flavor. The men sat or lounged on rows of benches, which looked more like the bleachers at a baseball stadium, smoking, reading newspapers, dozing, and otherwise taking their ease. Spittoons were provided. The trial judge, Kenesaw Mountain Landis, often strolled around the court while the proceedings dragged on through the hot summer months. At one point, during the examination of some Mexican witnesses, it was found that the court interpreter was missing. One of the defendants, Charles Ashleigh, spoke fluent Spanish, and perhaps for the only time in the history of American jurisprudence, a defendant acted as court interpreter.

It took a journalist of genius like John Reed to capture the atmosphere, as he did in a series of articles for *The Masses*. Reed, the rumpled radical from Harvard, had recently returned from Russia where he had observed the Bolshevik Revolution at firsthand. Now he reported on the trial of a movement that many respectable Americans regarded as the equivalent of Bolshevism in the United States. His comment on Judge Landis was acid. "Small on the huge bench sits a wasted man with untidy white hair, an emaciated face in which two burning eyes are set like jewels, parchment-like skin split by a crack for a mouth; the face of Andrew Jackson three years dead."

Reed's picture of the Wobblies was a heroic one. "As for the prisoners," he wrote, "I doubt if ever in history there has been a sight just like them. One hundred and one lumberjacks, harvest hands, miners, editors . . . who believe the wealth of the world belongs to him who creates it . . . the outdoor men, hard-rock blasters, tree-fellers, wheat-binders, longshoremen, the boys who do the strong work of the world . . .

"To me, fresh from Russia, the scene was strangely familiar . . . The IWW trial . . . looked like a meeting of the Central Executive Committee of the All-Russian Soviet of Workers and Deputies in Petrograd!" Reed's view of the IWW as the American version of Bolshevism was shared by many Americans who feared and detested the Bolsheviks as passionately as Reed admired them. Thus the IWW, which had already become the victim of wartime hysteria, now found itself the target for a barrage of anti-Red feeling. The chances of getting a fair hearing from the jury, which had always been slender, disappeared entirely after the Bolshevik Revolution of November 1917.

In conducting the case for the prosecution Nebeker was assisted by a battery of attorneys, who were all on the staff of the Department of Justice on either a permanent basis or part-time. The IWW had hoped to hire its old champion Clarence Darrow for the defense, but though he offered the services of his staff he could not appear himself because of war work in Washington. So the IWW's counsel was George F. Vandervеer, who had made a great impression by his conduct of the Everett massacre case, assisted by Fred Moore, Otto Christensen, Caroline Lowe, and several others.

In his opening statement Nebeker spoke for three hours. He alluded to Haywood as "the evil genius" of the IWW's campaign to close American mines, factories and munitions plants. The union, he claimed, had conducted "unceasing, unremitting warfare on the employers,"[20] and he quoted from the IWW preamble to show the union believed the workers and employ-

[20] *US v. Haywood et al.*, I, 233.

ers had nothing in common. Nebeker further charged that direct action and sabotage were criminal activities, and that the IWW had corrupted honest workers with these pernicious doctrines. It had branded the war a capitalistic trick, adding that "all countries engaged in it are making war for capitalists. If the U.S. gets into the war, it will be a war for capitalists and against the interests of wage workers of the country."[21]

Witnesses were called to show that IWWs had discouraged them from joining the Army. A newspaperman who worked at Butte, Montana, named W. W. Wallister, testified that a few days before he was lynched Frank Little referred to American soldiers as "armed thugs" and "Pershing's yellowlegs."[22] Yet much of this kind of evidence was related to times and places not covered by the indictment.

Ralph Chaplin admitted part-authorship of the antiwar *Solidarity* pamphlet *The Deadly Parallel*, but said it was not circulated after United States entry into the fighting. Haywood's letters were read into the court record, but they showed only that the IWW's attitude to the war was confused. Haywood thought those members in Detroit who had voted to "keep cool and confine our agitation to job control" in case of war were wise. He added, "Now is the time for cool heads, sane judgment and earnest work. There is no need of going on record for or against any movement that arises from other sources."[23]

Nebeker quoted editorials from *Solidarity* and the Finnish-language IWW newspaper *Industrialisti* as evidence of IWW opposition to war and the draft, but generally members who wrote to head office asking for advice and guidance on war

[21] *Ibid.*, I, 272.
[22] *Ibid.*, I, 304.
[23] Haywood to James Rowan, April 5, 1917.

policy were told, "The General Organization has not taken any stand." IWWs who joined the Army lost their membership, but then so did members of all labor unions, including A F of L ones. Haywood himself told Tom Buckley, the head of Construction Workers Industrial Union 573, that "no official stand has been taken on the question of registration, believing that the individual member was the best judge of how to act upon this question, still nothing has been left undone to help out the boys evading registration."[24]

Nebeker's extensive quotation from the IWW documents seized by government agents only showed that Haywood had argued that the war was no concern of the IWW. "The fight of the IWW is one of the economic field," Haywood said, "and it is not for me, a man who could not be drafted for war, to tell others that they should go to war, or tell them they should not go to war."[25] The prosecution's most sensational evidence concerned the IWW's efforts to free Ford and Suhr, who had been tried and convicted of murder in California after the Wheatland hop riot of 1913. Nebeker had little difficulty in showing that the IWW had advocated wrecking and sabotage during the Ford and Suhr campaign, but once more this evidence was outside the period covered by the indictments.

After two months of argument, the government concluded its case on June 1. The trial raised issues that greatly excited liberal and progressive thought in the United States. The public was urged to insist on a fair trial by a group of liberal writers, headed by John Dewey, the philosopher, Carlton J. H. Hayes, the historian, Helen Keller, the blind deaf-mute who had learned to talk and became an IWW supporter, Thorstein

[24] Haywood to Buckley, June 7, 1917.
[25] *US v. Haywood et al.*, IV, 12, 611. Haywood could not be drafted because he was a diabetic, and also—at 48—too old.

Veblen, the economist, and Walter Weyl, the Progressive journalist. They did not have much success. Vanderveer, opening for the defense, began by trying to show that the IWW was the product of contemporary industrial conditions. He attempted to introduce as evidence the *Report of the Commission on Industrial Relations,* ordered in 1917 by President Wilson, which Vanderveer called "the Bible of the IWW."

This six-man commission, headed by Secretary of Labor William B. Wilson, had found that "the overwhelming mass of the laboring population is in no sense disloyal . . . With the exception of the sacrifices of the men in the armed services, the greatest sacrifices have come from those at the lower rung of the industrial ladder." Secretary Wilson also reported that while industrial unrest had greatly increased after America's entry into war, only three out of a total of 521 strikes since April 6, 1917 involved the IWW. These three were in the Arizona and Butte copper mines, and in the Washington shipyards. The other 519 strikes had all involved AF of L unions.

Such evidence was obviously very valuable to the IWW's case. But Judge Landis ruled it out of order. Vanderveer tried to continue his economic argument by discussing living and working conditions in the Loop, an area of Chicago where the Federal Court itself was situated. He emphasized that the IWW wished to change the social system only and had no interest in government. But Judge Landis again ruled that such evidence about wages, hours, and working conditions was inadmissable because the American industrial system was not on trial.

This ruling was a body blow to defense hopes of securing an acquittal, or at least of making propaganda from the trial. Nevertheless, Vanderveer made the best of a bad job. He called a succession of witnesses from farmers and lumber operators who thought highly of the IWW and testified that they repeatedly helped them put out fires, or clear landslips and blocked rivers and streams which were used to transport timber. He also called IWW members whose sons had gone to fight in France, who had bought Liberty Bonds, worked in arms factories or loaded munitions ships. He revealed that thousands of IWW members were now in the armed forces.

In court, Vanderveer called upon sixty-one of the defendants to testify. The first witness was James P. Thompson, a founder member of the IWW and a leading Wobbly propagandist. Nebeker's cross-examination of Thompson set the pattern for the line of questioning he adopted for all the other sixty witnesses. First Nebeker asked Thompson if he belonged to the IWW, and if he understood its doctrines, especially those relating to sabotage, and if he approved of them. He also asked him his views on free love.[26] This last question was simply an irrelevance designed to prejudice IWW in the eyes of respectable jurors.

The other questions were all intended to show that the IWW was not concerned with improving conditions, but was engaged in plotting sabotage and violent revolution. Nebeker was not entirely successful in this strategy. Many witnesses testified about conditions in the mines, farms, factories and logging camps where they had worked, thus reading into the record much of the testimony Judge Landis had ruled irrelevant. Moreover, this testimony showed that the IWW *was* concerned with improving working and living conditions.

One of the most stimulating witnesses in this long procession was J. T. (Red) Doran, the pugnacious, irrepressible Irishman, who was one of the IWW's most popular lecturers. Doran gave his usual long talk on political economy, with the aid of

[26] *US v. Haywood et al.*, II, 11, 169.

blackboard and chalk. It lasted for the best part of a day. When he finished, Doran wound up his remarks with a studied piece of clowning. "Usually we have questions and literature for sale and collections . . . but"—and here he gave a long look around the courtroom—"I think I can dispense with that today."[27] Even Judge Landis joined in the laughter.

Farmers, employers, and local newspaper editors spoke on behalf of the IWW, and members testified that they had never been advised to oppose the war. Only one defendant had refused to register; the rest had all conformed with the law.[28] The only evidence against most of the men in the dock was that they were members of the IWW. Midway through the trial many disinterested observers found themselves agreeing with the comment of one Progressive magazine that "The real crime of Haywood and most of the rest was conducting aggressive propaganda and a strike program on behalf of laborers who are interested solely in obtaining better conditions of life and labor.[29]

The highlight of the whole trial was the evidence and cross-examination of the most notorious defendant, William D. Haywood. This was probably Haywood's greatest ordeal; it was also admitted by friend and foe alike to be his finest hour. Haywood's testimony took three days to deliver. If the press and the public had been expecting to see a wild, loud-mouthed agitator, they must have been sadly disappointed. Big Bill gave his own testimony and answered Nebeker's searching cross-examination in a soft voice which was not always clearly audible in the cavernous courtroom.

"Gentle Bill Haywood" was how *The Nation* described him

[27] *Evidence of J. T. Red Doran in the case of US v. Haywood et al.* (Chicago n.d.), 90.
[28] *Haywood v. USA.* Briefs for Plaintiffs in Error, III, 410–11.
[29] *Public,* November 16, 1917.

after this performance, for Haywood spoke almost lyrically about his hopes and fears. "I have a dream," Haywood told Nebeker, "that there will be a new society sometime in which there will be no battle between capitalist and wage earner, but every man will have free access to land and its resources."[30] This emphasis on land is surely significant in view of Haywood's own bitter experience when his own ranch was taken by the government.

Under questioning, Haywood argued that sabotage did not necessarily mean the destruction of property, but only the withdrawal of labor. He said direct action meant action at the point of production and did not involve the use of violence or force He maintained this position despite Nebeker's efforts to break him down. To make his case Haywood explained that while the United States Constitution had been adopted by means of political action, the Revolution that brought it about had been an example of direct action.[31]

Asked whether or not the IWW's propaganda aimed "mainly at destroying the idea of patriotism in its generally accepted sense," Haywood replied, "No, the aim and purpose of the literature that was distributed was to disseminate the idea of industrial unionism, not to destroy but to build, to construct; the Industrial Workers of the World is not a destructive organization but a constructive one."[32] Nebeker himself quoted some of Haywood's aphorisms which summarized the IWW's attitude to the war, such as, "It's better to be a traitor to your country than a traitor to your class" or, "Why be a soldier? Be a man, join the IWW and fight on the job for yourself and your class."[33]

[30] Barnes, *op. cit.*, 52 and n.
[31] *US v Haywood et al.*, II, 260–61.
[32] *Ibid.*, II, 266.
[33] *Evidence and cross-examination of William D. Haywood*, 234.

In another exchange with Nebeker, Haywood was quite specific about the IWW's attitude toward patriotic impulses. "We realize that the workers have no country," he said, "and that the flags and symbols which once meant something to us have been seized by our employers. Today they mean nothing to us but oppression and tyranny." A Wobbly from the Northwest was even more pungent. "If you were a bum without a blanket," he said, "if you had left your wife and kids when you went West for a job and never located them since; if your job never kept you long enough in one place to vote; if you slept in a lousy bunkhouse and ate rotten food; if every person who represented law and order beat you up . . . how in hell do you expect a man to be patriotic."[34]

Nevertheless, Haywood found himself being driven on to the defensive by Nebeker's remorseless questioning. He told the prosecuting attorney that "Little did not represent the organization in his attitude on war and conscription. He confirmed Chaplin's testimony that his pamphlet, *The Deadly Parallel,* was never circulated from headquarters after war was declared."[35] Haywood later maintained that Gurley Flynn's controversial pamphlet *Sabotage* had also been withdrawn from circulation with the United States' entrance into the war. This pamphlet had defined sabotage as "the conscious withdrawal of the workers' efficiency" and added "If the workers consider sabotage necessary, that in itself makes sabotage moral."[36]

Haywood made some sensational charges against the capitalist class. One was that the lumber bosses had distributed cocaine and heroin in the Southern lumber camps, especially among Negro workers. "They knew that when they became

[34] *The Truth about the IWW,* 11–12.
[35] *Ibid.,* 28.
[36] Elizabeth Gurley Flynn, *Sabotage* (Cleveland, 1915), 5.

addicted to the drugs, that they were sure to return to their jobs," he said. "It was the strongest method of holding them —stronger even than the chains of chattel slavery or the whips of the turpentine bosses . . .[37]

By the end of his long testimony Haywood had established a real *rapport* with his adversary Nebeker. A typical exchange came when they discussed a pamphlet written by Vincent St. John, who had left the IWW in an unsuccessful search for gold in 1914. Nebeker: "This book has been revised since St. John became a capitalist, hasn't it?" Haywood: "He has not quite obtained that position in life yet . . ." Nebeker: "He is just struggling to that end?" Haywood: "That is all."[38]

The defense virtually rested its case on Haywood's testimony. All that followed seemed like an anticlimax. Vanderveer had begun drinking heavily out of court. Fred Moore suffered another of his nervous attacks and was missing for a week or so, and the IWW's case seemed to be falling apart at the seams. Vanderveer refused to sum up, and in the last week of August 1918, Judge Landis gave the jury their charge. After five months in court hearing evidence which ran to a million words the jury reached their verdict on 101 separate cases in less than an hour. They found all the defendants guilty.

If the verdict was something of an anticlimax, the sentences certainly were not. Haywood and fourteen other of the leading defendants were sentenced to twenty years in jail with fines of $30,000, thirty-three others were given ten years, another thirty-five five years and the rest shorter sentences. The total fines imposed amounted to over $2,500,000. Ben Fletcher, the Philadelphia waterfront workers' leader, and the only Negro in court, cracked a rather painful joke about the court's decision.

[37] *US v. Haywood et. al.*, II, 128–29.
[38] *Ibid.*, II, 276.

"Judge Landis has been using bad English today," he said. "His sentences are too long."

The defendants bore this heavy blow with courage and dignity. Ashleigh told Judge Landis: "The day that I leave jail I shall recommence those activities on behalf of humanity and the working class for which you are sentencing me today," and Chaplin simply said, "I am proud I climbed high enough for the lightning to strike me." Ashleigh probably spoke for all of them in describing the scene. "When the verdict came, we bore ourselves proudly as kings in the exalted dignity of a cause that knows no defeat–the cause of the working class. Just think of labor, powerful yet blind, stumbling, fumbling, hesitating–yet slowly awaking to its historic mission: that of fighting, in the world-wide arena of the class struggle, for the freedom of the whole world."[39] As the prisoners, shackled together, left Chicago under guard on a train for Leavenworth Penitentiary in Kansas, the millionaire socialist, William Bross Lloyd, stood at the end of the platform and bared his head in silent salute.

The war and then the Bolshevik Revolution in Russia led to a tidal wave of antiradical feeling in the United States. This antiradicalism led to a spate of prosecutions brought under due process of hastily enacted law.[40] But the IWW's enemies also indulged in some "direct action" of their own. The Wobblies and other dissidents faced the constant threat of beatings, deportation, shooting, and lynching.

When the IWW led strikes against wage cuts and soaring wartime profits in the Arizona metal mines, the copper trust and the local press denounced them as "pro-German." In July

[39] Ashleigh to his mother from Leavenworth, November 3, 1918.
[40] William Preston, Jr., *Aliens and Dissenters* (Cambridge, 1963), *passim*, discusses the whole period trenchantly.

1917, members of the Bisbee Loyalty League rounded up 1200 IWW organizers, strikers, and sympathizers at gun point, tried them at a "kangaroo court" and gave them the choice between returning to work or deportation from Arizona. Some Wobblies tried to telegraph for help, but the vigilantes intercepted the messages. The prisoners were herded onto a cattle train, sent under armed guard to New Mexico and kept without food and water in the desert for thirty-six hours. Then they were beaten up, sent to a Federal stockade and held there without charge for three months before being released.

President Wilson's investigation dismissed the charge that the strike had been seditious. The committee found that 426 of those deported were Wobblies, 351 AF of L members, and 360 non-unionists. Just over half were native-born or naturalized citizens, 62 had served with the armed forces, 472 were registered for military service, 205 had bought Liberty Bonds, and 520 subscribed to the Red Cross. A handful of the strikers were German; the rest of the foreign-born were mostly Slav and British.[41] The Bisbee deportation is a notorious example of what happens when a community takes the law into its own hands. But though a Federal jury later indicted twenty-one leaders of the Bisbee Loyalty League none was convicted.

Butte, Montana, was the scene of more anti-IWW activity. Between 1914–17 the Anaconda Company tried to break the power of organized labor in the great mining center by playing craft against industrial unions. Company spies infiltrated both the Butte Miners' Union and the IWW. Helped by such incidents as the Speculator mining disaster, in which 190 men died, they fomented unrest and made incendiary speeches which led to mob violence, rioting, dynamiting, and widespread public disorder. The city's socialist administration, elected in 1911,

[41] Kornbluh, *op. cit.*, 294.

was replaced in 1917 by martial law which was imposed frequently until 1921. Unions were smashed, IWW halls raided and Wobblies arrested and held without trial.

President Wilson appointed Burton K. Wheeler, a LaFollette Progressive, who became one of the nation's most prominent legislators, as United States District Attorney for Montana in an effort to bring law and order to Butte. An ardent defender of civil liberties, Wheeler refused to prosecute labor leaders, foreign-born workers, or Wobblies as spies. For these principles he was condemned by a "kangaroo court" and subjected to a vicious smear campaign as a "Bolshevik," an "advocate of free love," and a "nationalizer of women."[42] This unrest at Butte culminated in the "murder of Anaconda Hill" in April 1920 when armed company guards fired on pickets, killing one and wounding 14 others, possibly on the order of company officials.[43]

For Frank Little's brutal murder in 1917 had been a prelude to three years of mob rule and violence. Vigilante action quickly spread. In Red Lodge, Montana, and Tulsa, Oklahoma, later that year dozens of Wobblies were whipped, tarred and feathered, and then run out of town by mobs. Perhaps the climax to this anti-IWW hysteria came at Centralia on Armistice Day 1919 when the American Legion clashed with the IWW. Four men died in the affray, and that night Wesley Everest, an IWW war veteran, was lynched.

Judicial persecution hit other radicals too. Emma Goldman and Alexander Berkman, two notorious anarchists, had been jailed during the war, and though no move was made against the Socialist Party, which had passed a militant antiwar dec-

[42] Robert S. Allen, *Our Fair City* (New York, 1947), 314–15.

[43] The special edition of the Butte *Daily Bulletin* which said the company had ordered its guards to "Shoot the sons of bitches" was suppressed as soon as it appeared.

laration at a special 1917 convention in St. Louis, SPA headquarters in New York City were raided and the socialist leader Eugene Debs was sentenced to ten years in jail for encouraging opposition to the war effort.

Yet the IWW was the chief target for antiradicalism. The great trial had been a monumental disaster for the union. At one blow it had lost almost its entire leadership, for the only experienced IWW agitators to escape prosecution, Gurley Flynn and Joseph Ettor, had been expelled from the union during the Mesabi strike of 1916. Not only the leadership suffered at the hands of the law. On Lincoln's Birthday in 1919, fifty-four foreign-born IWW's were deported; and at two other show trials, in Kansas and California, seventy members were jailed for their beliefs.

At Wichita, Kansas, thirty-four Wobblies were arrested during an oilstrike in January 1917, and indicted in March of the following year for espionage and draft resistance. The trial did not begin until December 1918, and the men were kept for nearly two years in a filthy jail where the deputy jailer said he kept discipline by "knocking the guts out of those fellows." Eventually twenty-seven of the defendants were sentenced to one to nine years imprisonment and sent to Federal penitentiaries which must have seemed like heaven after the hell of the Wichita jailhouse.

The California IWW conspiracy trial was held in 1918 at Sacramento. Following the bombing of Governor William D. Stephens' home in December 1917, forty-six rank and file Wobblies were arrested and kept awaiting trial for five months in a disease-ridden jail where five of them died. When they finally appeared in court all but two of the defendants refused to take part in the proceedings and adopted what they called a "silent defense." Twenty-four of them were given ten years in prison, the remainder from one to five years. They left court singing Chaplin's "Solidarity Forever, for the Union Makes Us Strong" and wired the Chicago headquarters in imitation of Joe Hill's last telegram DON'T MOURN! ORGANIZE! ORGANIZE![44]

These trials were used as test cases. The District Attorney at Sacramento had made no secret of his intention of using the trial to prove that the IWW was an illegal organization so that the state could enact a criminal syndicalism law, which it did in 1919. Soon twenty-three other states, mostly Western ones, like Idaho and Washington, where the IWW was strongest, had followed California's lead. Thus the IWW found itself liable to prosecution all over the country. In California alone some five hundred arrests were made in the period from 1919–24, and 164 Wobblies sentenced to long terms of imprisonment. The trials were usually a farce, with the same three professional witnesses testifying in each case and often the same jurors appearing.[45]

The majority of Americans supported their leaders' efforts to stamp out radicalism. The most determined Red-chaser was undoubtedly President Wilson's Attorney General, A. Mitchell Palmer, who discovered a bomb planted at his own house. Sensing the public mood, and with one eye on the White House, Palmer used the powers granted him by the Deportation Act of 1918 to launch an unprecedented and totally unconstitutional series of nation-wide attacks on radical and socialist groups across the country.

The first of the notorious "Palmer Raids" came on November 7, 1919, the second anniversary of the Bolshevik Revolution, when radical organizations in eighteen cities were raided

[44] Charles A. Madison, *American Labor Leaders* (New York, 1950), 283–84.
[45] Unpublished memorandum by Vern Smith, an IWW member, in the Brissenden Collection, Industrial and Labor Relations Library, Cornell University, 3.

with much violence and forcible impounding of documents. Nearly 250 people were summarily deported, including Emma Goldman and Alexander Berkman. In January 1920 came an even bigger series of raids. About 10,000 people were arrested in raids in seventy cities. Members of the Amalgamated Clothing Workers, the International Ladies' Garment Workers, and the IWW came in for special attention.

The Palmer raids shocked the conscience of liberal America and led to a tremendous outcry. Assistant Secretary of Labor Louis F. Post canceled over 1500, or 71 percent of Palmer's deportation orders and tried to get Palmer impeached.[46] Eminent jurists, such as Felix Frankfurter and George W. Anderson, protested publicly, while a dozen leading lawyers drew up a report on the *Illegal Practices of the Department of Justice*. Even Palmer's assistant, J. Edgar Hoover, who later became head of the FBI, agreed the raids had been unconstitutional. "The activities of the Communists and ultra-radicals," Hoover wrote, "have not, up to the present time, constituted a violation of federal law, and consequently the Department of Justice, theoretically, has no right to investigate such activities."

Supreme Court Justice Louis D. Brandeis condemned criminal syndicalism laws, giving judgment in the famous case of Whitney v. California, "The fact that speech is likely to result in some violence or destruction of property is not enough to justify its suppression," Brandeis said. "There must be the probability of serious injury to the state. Among free men, the deterrents ordinarily to be applied to prevent crime are education and punishment for violations of the law, not abridgements of the rights of free speech and assembly."[47]

Yet public opinion made no such distinction. Reviewing the

[46] Stanley Coben, *A. Mitchell Palmer: Politician* (New York, 1963), 232–34.
[47] *Whitney v. California*, 274 US (7927).

history of criminal syndicalism legislation in the United States a later authority concluded, "Throughout the whole period . . . we find the press the great motivating power which created through its news and editorial columns a distorted and vicious picture of the IWW, their legal persecution by the United States Government and the enactment of criminal syndicalism laws against them."[48]

Despite this anti-Red frenzy, the IWW managed to keep alive. Though the AWO was down to only 4000 members, the lumber workers still had close to 20,000, while in Chicago and the Eastern cities the foreign-language branches and the recruiting unions were active. The IWW's eleventh annual convention, which met in May 1919, was the first since 1916. It heard that membership was just over 33,000, and that two English-language weekly newspapers and an English monthly magazine, a Finnish daily newspaper and seven weeklies, plus two monthlies in other languages were still appearing with IWW news and views. But with over $100,000 still to pay in lawyers' fees, $29,000 for the relief of prisoners families and nearly $9000 in witnesses' fees to find from assets of only $78,000, the IWW was in financial trouble.[49]

Worse was to follow. After the Chicago trial the IWW took its case to the United States Court of Appeal. Several of the leading prisoners were allowed bail on sureties of $100,000. In October 1920 the Court upheld the convictions on counts three and four only—conspiracy to resist the draft and cause military insubordination. The sentences stood. Instead of returning to Leavenworth, Haywood and nine other defendants on bail refused to surrender.

[48] Eldridge Foster Dowell, *A History of Criminal Syndicalism* (Baltimore, 1939), 37.

[49] Thompson, *op. cit.*, 130.

Haywood's flight to Soviet Russia was a terrible shock to the rank and file of the IWW. True, he was a sick man and faced a long sentence. For this reason, and because the Russian Communists said they wanted him in Moscow, an inner circle of IWW leaders in prison decided to let him go. But the union as a whole never forgave him for deserting them, especially as he was the one who had ordered them all to submit to arrest in 1917. Otto Christensen, the IWW attorney who had conducted the case in the Appeal Court, denounced Haywood's flight as "the act of a coward," adding, "It will harm the cause of amnesty for political prisoners for which we are working. He will certainly be disowned by the IWW and its sympathizers."[50] Certainly, the IWW and its sympathizers lost a lot of money because Haywood and the others skipped bail. The union raised some $80,000 to pay back the bondsmen. William Bross Lloyd, a wealthy member of the newly formed Communist Labor Party, was Haywood's principal backer, but many who lost money were poor people, like Mary Marcy, who was ruined and took her own life shortly afterward.

All the frustrations pent up during years of persecution seemed to burst on Haywood's head after his flight to Moscow. At the IWW convention in May 1921 Roy Martin accused him of sailing in order to escape prosecution for a $35,000 shortage of funds. This accusation—which was neither substantiated nor investigated—nearly caused a riot. Yet even according to Gurley Flynn, who sympathized with Big Bill, the Wobblies as a whole were "pretty sore" about his sudden departure. The irony is that it was unnecessary. Within a few years all the IWW political prisoners had been granted amnesty.

Haywood wrote from Russia: "I shall return to America when I have finished the work assigned to me by the Interna-

[50] New York *Call,* April 22, 1922.

tional Council of Trade and Industrial Unions and when the interests of the workers demand my return."[51] Although the Bolsheviks never found any task which could use the great ability of this natural-born revolutionary giant, he did not return. After an abortive attempt to found a workers' colony in the Kuznetsk Basin, he took to drinking again at the Lux Hotel in Moscow, where he died in 1928, a lost and lonely old man. But while the Communist International found nothing for Haywood to do, their interest in him complicated the last, mortal crisis within the ranks of the IWW. For it showed that they hoped to use the organization as the spearhead of the Bolshevik Revolution in the United States.

[51] *New York Times,* April 30, 1921.

9

THE END OF THE I W W

BILL BAILEY

Bill Bailey belonged to every radical party
That ever came to be
Till he finally decided to start his own party
So he wouldn't disagree
He got himself an office with a sign outside the door
With Marxist League in letters red
And to everyone who came around
These were the words he said:

(CHORUS)

Oh you may be a friend of Bill Foster
Earl Browder and you may agree
You may get along with Emma Goldman
And with the S L P
You may be an old-time Wobbly
And think Bill Haywood's fine
Yes you may be a comrade to all of those folks
But you ain't no comrade of mine.

ANONYMOUS from *Songs for Sectarians*

The great Chicago trial of 1918 had been a major reverse for the Industrial Workers of the World. And the climate of public opinion in the years immediately after the Armistice, combining antiradicalism with xenophobia, was bitterly hostile to any organization like the IWW. The wave of mass arrests and deportations during the period of the Palmer raids created fresh problems.

Yet the situation was not entirely without redeeming features. The antiradical mood of most Americans was a reaction against the militant radicalism of a minority. The First World War had ended in a wave of revolutions in Europe and elsewhere which the IWW warmly welcomed. Soldiers returning from the front brought back some of these revolutionary attitudes, which were often strengthened as they struggled to readjust to peacetime conditions in which jobs were not easily obtained and prices rose far more rapidly than wages.

Indeed to some anxious observers it seemed as if revolution, led by the IWW, might be sweeping North America too. Early in 1919 the IWW was prominent in the general strikes at Seattle, Vancouver and Winnipeg.[1] All three failed, but only after a formidable display of proletarian solidarity. A workers', soldiers', and sailors' council, in direct imitation of the Bolshevik Soviets, was established in Seattle, and the idea spread quickly to Butte, Montana, and Toledo, Ohio, where the IWW organized more strikes. This small-scale revolution

[1] Robert Friedheim, *The Seattle General Strike* (Washington, 1964), gives a dispassionate account of these events; O'Connor, *op. cit.*, is a vivid personal memoir.

was followed in 1919 by the notorious policemen's strike at Boston, which Governor Calvin Coolidge crushed without difficulty.

The Amalgamated Clothing Workers won a forty-four hour week; the textile workers and lumberjacks an eight hour day. In the timber forests of Washington bindle stiffs burned their blankets and clashed with employers in a series of incidents which culminated in the Centralia tragedy when Wesley Everest was killed. Then, in September 1919, the unions shut down the steel industry for three months in a strike led by a former Wobbly, William Z. Foster.

But the IWW, far from being on the brink of leading a revolution in the postwar years, was within sight of total disintegration as a revolutionary movement. When the IWW leadership was jailed in 1918 the union lost most of its leading centralizers, the victors in the internal battles of 1912–14. Those who replaced them after 1918 tended to be decentralizing anarcho-syndicalists. The centralizers, who admired good organization and discipline, favored friendship with the Third (Communist) International. The decentralizers, who hated all political entanglements, were uncompromisingly hostile. Thus the Kremlin's efforts to capture the IWW for the Communist cause reopened the old centralization issue. And they added a third group—the Communists—to the battle. This three-way conflict was aggravated by a new, emotional issue: the attitude of the factions to those political prisoners who accepted release from Leavenworth Penitentiary.

After 1917 the Wobblies were being outflanked on the extreme left of the political spectrum by the Communists, who emerged from a split in the Socialist Party of America. The success of the Bolshevik Revolution in 1917 had provided a new focus for the world revolutionary cause. Fired by the formation of the Third International in Moscow in March 1919 the left wing of the SPA tried to capture the party's machinery. The differences between the leadership and the left wing of the SPA were partly ideological, but they also sprang from personal conflicts and a significant ethnic division. The rank and file of the left wing was drawn largely from the foreign-language federations, especially the East European elements, who were particularly sensitive to the revolutionary events in their homelands. In the months after 1917 the Slavonic federations grew until they constituted 53 percent of the party's total membership of 108,000 in 1919. For the first time the English-speaking groups found themselves outnumbered.[2]

The right wing leadership reacted promptly to this left wing revolt by calling an emergency convention in Chicago in August 1919. Here they managed to retain the loyalty of some of the left-wingers, leaving the Russian, Ukrainian, Polish, Hungarian, Lithuanian, and Lettish groups to quit the SPA and found the Communist Party at the headquarters of the Russian Federation.[3] A minority of the foreign-language federations, led by native-born left-wingers like John Reed and Benjamin Gitlow, marched out to form their own extremist group, the Communist Labor Party, in an IWW hall on Throop Street.[4]

This schism in the Communist ranks lasted until 1923. Before the breach healed both parties were driven underground at the end of 1919 by the Palmer raids. Communist propaganda called on the American working class to "seize the streets"; but there was no response for two years and both Communist factions waned. In 1921 the Workers' Party of

[2] Shannon, *op. cit.*, 128.

[3] Theodore Draper, *The Roots of American Communism* (New York, 1957), 176.

[4] *Ibid.*, 179.

America was formed as the legal "above ground" counterpart of both parties. Finally, in 1923, the underground was dissolved and the parties formally united.

In these years the history of the IWW centered on its relations with Moscow and world Communism. This was clear from the very outset. John Reed, the leader of the CLP, who had organized the 1913 Paterson pageant for the IWW, urged his former comrades to join forces with him. After the SPA convention in 1919 which gave birth to the CLP he told Gurley Flynn excitedly "Gurley, we've got it! A real working class socialist party at last![5] Reed went to Moscow to work with the Third International and died there of typhus in 1921, becoming the first American to be buried in the Kremlin. Bill Haywood was to be the second, although half of his remains were buried in Chicago.

But though strongly influenced by the Russian Revolution Gurley Flynn, like many Wobblies, hesitated to join a political party, and did not finally throw in her lot with the Communist Party until 1937. Others greeted the new Communist movement enthusiastically. Haywood was a fervent supporter of the Soviets,[6] while Harrison George, another Chicago trial defendant, wrote a pamphlet called *Red Dawn* which was uncritically pro-Bolshevik. George Andreytchine, the Bulgarian-born IWW who fled to Russia with Haywood in 1921, was also a convinced Communist. Charles Ashleigh joined the party in prison, and other leaders who did the same, apart from Andreytchine and Haywood, included George Hardy, the seaman's organizer, Sam Scarlett, who joined in Canada, and Roy Brown of the lumber workers.[7]

The first shots in this final conflict over Communism were

[5] Flynn, *op. cit.*, 271.
[6] Haywood, *op. cit.*, 361.
[7] Interview with Ashleigh, November 19, 1965.

fired in 1919, when the GEB spelled out its sympathy for the Third International in a motion supporting left wing unity. But the following year the IWW elected a new GEB which rapidly reversed this policy.[8] The new leadership rejected the Third International's invitation to attend its Second Congress in the Kremlin in July 1920. This congress not only drew up twenty-one conditions for affiliation, which became known as the "Moscow theses." It also created the International Council of Trade and Industrial Unions to organize the international working class on Communist principles.

This new body—which was soon renamed the Red International of Labor Unions—also invited the IWW to attend its conference in 1921. This time the IWW accepted. When George Hardy returned from a preliminary conference of syndicalist and other revolutionary trade unions in Berlin urging the IWW to affiliate, the GEB decided to put the whole question of affiliation before the membership. This referendum proved a fiasco. Though a majority apparently supported the GEB's line of non-affiliation, there were so many protests that the GEB was forced to concede that the questions had been badly phrased and declare the referendum void.[9]

Relations between the IWW and the Communists were further strained by the "Philadelphia situation." The Philadelphia longshoremen's Local had been the most stable element in the Marine Transport Workers Section of the IWW since 1913. In 1920 they struck for 20 cents an hour increase. The strike dragged on all summer, while the MTW defeated Communist efforts to take over the union. In August the Communists claimed the union was loading munitions for the interventionist troops in Russia. The GEB suspended the

[8] Gambs, *op. cit.*, 77.

[9] *One Big Union Monthly*, vol. iii, no. i (January 1921), 51.

Philadelphia Local pending inquiries, and the issue became an American version of the *Jolly George* affair in Britain.

The new GEB elected in 1921 found the Communist charge that arms had been loaded was groundless and reinstated the Local. But the damage had been done. Ben Fletcher, the Negro Philadelphia waterfront leader jailed at Chicago in 1918, was hurt by the IWW's apparent willingness to suspend his Local at Communist behest. So he used a long-standing dispute about initiation fees and transferability of membership as an excuse for quitting the IWW and joining the AF of L. Fletcher's reaction was bitter. "The history of the Philadelphia longshoremen's connection with the IWW is one of unswerving loyalty . . ." he wrote.[10] "Some have died while hundreds have been jailed as its standard bearers."

The departure of Andreytchine, Haywood, and others for Moscow in 1921 did not improve the IWW's relations with the Communists. Nevertheless, the GEB stood by its decision to send a delegate to the RILU's Kremlin conference and agreed to follow his recommendations. It even seemed eager to start negotiations with the RILU on a friendly basis by sacking John Sandgren, the bitterly anti-Bolshevik editor of the *One Big Union Monthly*. Sandgren was an anarchist who had become Hardy's most outspoken opponent in the fight over affiliation. The GEB apologized for the anti-Soviet tone of recent numbers of the magazine and replaced Sandgren with Henry Van Dorn.[11]

The IWW sent George Williams, who was not closely associated with either faction of the IWW, as its delegate to the RILU conference. Williams had supported affiliation before he went to Moscow, but his experiences there changed his

[10] Ben H. Fletcher, "Philadelphia Waterfront Unionism," *Messenger*, June 1923, 140–41.
[11] *One Big Union Monthly*, vol. iii, no. i (January 1921), 5.

mind. In Moscow he met five other members of the American trade union delegation, including William Z. Foster and Earl Browder of the Communist Party. He also met the exiled Haywood, who told him, "This is not a political party . . . This is really an independent movement . . . I see in this Red International the culmination of the aims and aspirations of the IWW."[12] But Williams found little evidence of this independence.

Indeed, everything that happened in Moscow convinced him that the RILU, far from being independent, was simply a Communist organization. All the members of the RILU's executive bureau were Communists. Andreytchine, the only American on the executive, was regarded by the Bolsheviks as an influential member of the IWW. In fact, he had been selected by a secret caucus of American Communists in Moscow, including Haywood and John Reed.[13] Gordon Cascaden, the Canadian representative, was denied a vote and granted only consultative status by the credentials committee because he represented the anarchist wing of the One Big Union and regarded Lenin's idea of the dictatorship of the proletariat as merely a new form of state oppression.[14]

But Williams' biggest objection to the RILU conference was over policy. Initially, the Third International had favored dual unionism and backed organizations like the IWW against existing trade union organizations such as the AF of L. But after the publication of Lenin's pamphlet *Left Wing Communism: An Infantile Disorder* the Communists switched to the united front policy of trying to capture "bourgeois" political parties and trade unions, which Foster had advocated

[12] *Liberator*, vol. 4, no. 9 (September 1921), 11–12.
[13] G. H. Williams, *Report on the First Congress of the Red Trades Union International* (Chicago, 1921), 10.
[14] *Ibid.*, 23–24.

for years. Accordingly, the RILU was asking the IWW to disband and start boring from within the AF of L like Foster and his Communist-dominated Trade Union Educational League.

Williams refused to acquiesce in this policy of self-destruction. "There was no doubt in my mind," he reported,[15] "that this first Congress . . . was to be a sincere effort to form an International of the revolutionary labor bodies of the world and . . . that it would be independent . . . From the storm that arose in the IWW over the question of balloting for endorsement of the Third International . . . it was evident that the membership wanted nothing to do with a political faction."

Accordingly, when Williams returned to the United States he submitted a very hostile report on what he had seen and heard in Moscow. He called on the IWW to reject the overtures of the RILU. The GEB unanimously endorsed his proposals and rejected affiliation. "The history of American unionism testifies to the destructive influence of labor politics and labor politicians," the GEB wrote.[16] "Experience has proven that when politics moves into a union effectiveness moves out, and hope for the workers moves out with it."

In December 1921 the GEB issued its official rejection of affiliation with the RILU, which it described as "not only undesirable but absolutely impossible."[17] The statement listed many reasons for its decision. First, the Congress had expressly condemned the policy and tactics of the IWW. Second, the RILU was a political organization dominated by the Communists—"It is, in fact, the Communist Party thinly disguised." It was determined to liquidate the IWW and all

[15] *Ibid.*, 13.
[16] *The IWW Reply to the Red Trades Union International* (Chicago, 1922), 21.
[17] *Ibid.*, 23.

labor organizations which refused to submit to its autocratic discipline. Moreover, the RILU was not representative of the international revolutionary labor movement.[18]

In his report Williams had urged the IWW to unite all the revolutionary syndicalist elements inside the RILU, such as the French, Italian, German, Scandinavian, Spanish, and South American syndicalists, into a new international of its own. Gordon Cascaden, the Canadian delegate in Moscow who was denied a vote, criticized the Russians for trying to divide the workers in North America and reached similar conclusions about the need for a syndicalist international.[19]

Henry Van Dorn, who had replaced the anti-Bolshevik Sandgren as editor of the *One Big Union Monthly*, agreed with Williams and Cascaden. "Andreytchine says that our choice lies between the Red International in Moscow and the Yellow International in Amsterdam," he wrote.[20] "But not so, fellow worker. We have also the choice of creating a Red Industrial International . . . located, let us say, in Chicago."

However, these efforts to persuade the IWW to establish its own Red Industrial International only aggravated its problems. The IWW now found itself caught between three distinct groups struggling for power within its ranks: the industrial unionists, who wanted the IWW to carry on as it always had: the Communists, who wanted it to dissolve itself and join the RILU; and the anarchists, even more distrustful of GEB leadership since the fiasco of the affiliation referendum, who wanted to found their own Red Industrial International or join the anarcho-syndicalist International with headquarters in Berlin.

From 1922–24 morale at general headquarters slowly col-

18 *Ibid.*, 31–35.

19 Gordon Cascaden, *Shall Unionism Die?* (Ontario, 1922).

20 *One Big Union Monthly*, vol. ii, no. ii (November 1920), 50–51.

lapsed as dissension and faction fighting increased. There was also a permanent financial problem. Small wonder that Philip Taft should write: "The last few years have been the most trying in the organization's history. We have been confronted with issues and problems such as we have never been called upon to face before."[21] Taft concluded that the financial problem could only be solved by the application of business methods to the union's affairs. But he had no solution for the faction fighting that threatened to break up the IWW.

Communist influence continued steadily throughout 1922–24, especially in the columns of *Industrial Solidarity* now being edited by Vern Smith. He wrote a series of articles in the summer and autumn of 1922 which argued the Communist case and asserted that the IWW had been launched by Marxists.[22] In October 1923, Smith published an article attacking the Berlin anarcho-syndicalist International and urging the IWW to reverse its policy by affiliating with the RILU. He wrote to C. E. Payne, the decentralizing editor of the *Industrial Worker,* asking him to print a similar argument. "I'm sure some such stand should be made as soon as possible, to avoid serious injury to the organization."[23]

Payne's reply was blunt and to the point, in the manner of the Far West. "You go to hell!" he told Smith. "If you think you can bluff me into printing anything like the screed you enclosed with your letter you are off your base . . . There is nothing too strong to say against your gang of cut throats. No one politician is any better at any time than any other. All are trying to ride to power on the backs of the workers . . ."[24]

In September 1923 the *Industrial Worker* reported a new

[21] *Industrial Worker,* May 13, 1922.
[22] *Industrial Solidarity,* July 29, 1922.
[23] Vern Smith to C. E. Payne, October 10, 1923.
[24] C. E. Payne to Vern Smith, October 14, 1923.

phase in the efforts of the RILU to capture the IWW in the shape of a letter from the International Seaman's Section of the RILU which tried to reopen the whole question of affiliation with Moscow. The GEB's reply was curt and un-cooperative.

Yet as Walter Smith, an IWW organizer in New York and Philadelphia, reported at the IWW's 1923 convention, the disruptive work of the Communists in their efforts to gain control of the union continued unabated.[25] The Communists, however, met fierce resistance from IWW members who feared Communist domination. Two decentralizers, Mick Raddock and Frank Bowerman, organized "breaker gangs" for beating up Communists during the affiliation dispute. The most eloquent anti-Bolshevik spokesman at this period was Jean Sanjour, who had just returned from Moscow where he worked for the Soviet press. In a whole series of articles throughout 1923 Sanjour attacked the Soviet government for persistent attacks on its own workers, which he said made the exploitation of American workers by the capitalists pale by comparison.

"Why do we not raise our voices against the persecution of workers in Soviet Russia now?" he asked.[26] "We know that those who are persecuted in Russia are as much guilty as the persecuted IWW . . . We are talking about socialists, revolutionists, anarchists . . . persecuted for expressing their opinions." Sanjour said his sources for these attacks were the bureau of the International Workingmen's Association in Berlin and anarcho-syndicalist papers like *Rabochi Put* and *Anarchichesky Vestnica* published in Germany by Russian revolutionaries who had been forced to leave the country.

Sanjour's articles took a strictly anarchist line. All govern-

[25] *Industrial Solidarity,* November 25, 1923.
[26] *Industrial Worker,* September 19, 1923.

ment was inherently evil, he argued. That was why the Soviet experiment had gone so sadly wrong. "That is the reason we talk against the Russian government, not against the workers of Russia nor against the Russian Revolution, but against the government."[27] In another article Sanjour warned that, "The experience of the struggle of the Russian proletarians in the so-called social revolution is a good warning to the working class of all the world."[28]

Sanjour asked many pertinent questions. "We say we will never forget Joe Hill, Frank Little, and Wesley Everest and the scores of our fellow workers murdered in prison and outside the prison walls," he declared. "And at the same time we find among our fellow workers those who are satisfied with the murder of our fellow workers in Russia. Are they not our fellow workers? Or do you think that our fellow workers are the hangmen of the Communist Party of Russia?"[29] The article concluded with the slogan "Workers of the world unite to get rid of *all oppressors*."

Payne and the other Western decentralizers supported Sanjour, but his views were bitterly attacked by other Wobblies like S. R. Darnley. He argued that Sanjour's stories of atrocities in Russia were all based on hearsay evidence and were untrue. "The ravings of Sanjour and C. E. Payne, together with the editorial comment on articles of a moderate nature, are calculated to arouse the disgust of any fair-minded individual."[30] After this the *Industrial Worker* ran a series of pro-Soviet articles called "Their views" alongside the anti-Soviet pieces headlined "Our views."

The main factions in the I W W at this period became closely

[27] *Industrial Worker,* September 1, 1923.
[28] *Industrial Worker,* August 28, 1923.
[29] *Industrial Worker,* September 5, 1923.
[30] *Industrial Worker,* September 11, 1923.

identified with two industrial unions. The anti-Bolshevik decentralizers worked through Industrial Union 120, controlled from the West Coast by Payne, who edited the *Industrial Worker,* Pat Cantwell, Matt Johnson and most of the Everett membership. The centralizers controlled Industrial Union 110, which operated from Minneapolis and was led by Tom Doyle, Tom Wallis, and Sam Forbes, who was released from Leavenworth early in 1923. When Herbert Mahler was also freed from jail later in the year he rapidly took command of the centralizing forces in IU 110.[31]

The fighting between these two factions often became bitter. The IWW had formed a General Defense Committee to direct the campaign to free the political prisoners, but its meetings frequently broke up in a riot and individual fist-fighting.[32] Much of this acrimony took place over the clemency issue. President Warren G. Harding had proved much more susceptible to the demands for a general amnesty for political prisoners than the stern, unbending Woodrow Wilson, and, in July 1922, Harding said he would give sympathetic consideration to individual pleas for clemency.

While the amnesty campaign moved toward a successful conclusion, the clemency issue raged within the IWW. The centralizers, backed by *Industrial Solidarity,* on the whole supported Ralph Chaplin and the other prisoners willing to take individual pardons. Harry Clarke and Bill Tiffany, both members of the GEB, led the Chaplin faction. The anti-clemency forces were led by James Rowan, Jack Lorton, and Patrick Quinlan, extreme anarcho-syndicalists who refused to compromise and heaped most of their vituperative abuse on the head of Chaplin as the most prominent of the forty-five "clem-

31 Memorandum on the split by Vern Smith, Brissenden Collection, Industrial and Labor Relations Library, Cornell University, 2.
32 *Ibid.,* 3.

ency hounds"—the men who accepted the June 1923 commutation. Chaplin, who left Leavenworth bitterly disillusioned and regretting his radical past, later became much more conservative and was converted to Roman Catholicism. The IWW press printed many letters from partisans of both sides and the discussion raged in the General Office Bulletin until the convention in November 1923.

This convention tried to settle the Leavenworth commutation controversy and end faction fighting within the IWW. It failed. Though it ruled in favor of the commuted men and tried to place a ban on further discussion the issue remained a live one. When the last of the Leavenworth men were released in December 1923 the controversy increased. Indeed, the release of all the prisoners was a prelude to the final split in 1924.

Many of those involved in this split had been personal enemies for years. This was especially true of the Leavenworth prisoners. Decentralizers like James Rowan, Mortimer Downing, Patrick Quinlan, and Red Doran had been at odds in prison with Chaplin, James Gallagher, John McDonald, and other centralizers long before commutation became an issue.[33] Once they were free they were able to carry on this feud within the ranks of the union.

The faction fighting over the clemency issue was exacerbated because the IWW's campaign to free the political prisoners had won widespread support from middle class America. Recrimination between revolutionary factions is usually embittered if one side attracts "bourgeois" sympathy. As wartime hysteria and the anti-Red scare faded with the election of Harding and the return to "normalcy" the public conscience became aroused by the case of the IWW convicts. As early as 1919 Albert DeSilver told President Wilson: "Whatever may be the pro-

[33] Smith Memorandum, *op. cit.*, 1.

priety of imprisoning heretics or dissenters in wartime, the continuance of their imprisonment in time of peace can serve no useful purpose."[34]

The amnesty campaign attracted much moderate left wing and Progressive opinion, and delegations to the White House included such figures as Senator Robert M. La Follette, Herbert Croly, the editor of the *New Republic*, Norman Thomas and Morris Hillquit of the Socialist Party, Jackson Ralston, the AF of L's chief attorney, and DeSilver himself. The Civil Liberties Union urged in 1922 that all political prisoners should be released, because "the sentences in war cases were unequal and often the product of hysteria."[35]

Senator William E. Borah, who had prosecuted Haywood in the Boise trial of 1907 and had no sympathy for the Wobblies, joined in the amnesty campaign. He maintained that no evidence had been offered "to justify a conviction . . . In other words . . . they were convicted under the compelling influence of the passions and fears which accompany wars."[36] Alexander S. Lomer, a captain in the Military Intelligence Division of the General Staff, examined the 44,000 page transcript of the 1918 Chicago trial and concluded that the evidence for conviction was woefully inadequate, especially in the case of Vincent St. John.

Charles Nagel, who had been Secretary of Commerce and Labor during President Taft's administration, said, "I have dismissed the last doubt about the justice or wisdom of the appeal for the release of the . . . prisoners . . . It is clear that these men were convicted under the law as a war necessity . . . They would probably be acquitted if tried under present conditions.

[34] Albert DeSilver to President Wilson, March 4, 1919.
[35] *New York Times*, January 20, 1922.
[36] *American Problems: Speeches by William E. Borah* (New York, 1924), 281.

. . . The very severe sentences were based, in large part, upon the charges . . . that were dismissed by the Court of Appeals."[37]

Church leaders from all over the country sent a delegation to Washington in July 1922 to press for immediate release and pickets were on constant patrol outside the office of Attorney General Harry M. Daugherty.[38] The AF of L and the Hearst newspaper chain joined in the campaign, and in the summer of 1923 Senator George Wharton Pepper, a Republican from Pennsylvania, raised the question of an unconditional pardon in the United States Senate.[39]

By the end of 1923 President Calvin Coolidge had released the last of the IWW prisoners. But this victory had been won at a terrible price. The best comment on the faction fighting came from the IWW's most gifted cartoonist, Maurice Becker, in the *Industrial Pioneer*. Becker showed the bloated figure of capitalism facing a determined IWW with a devil labeled "dissension" between them. Capitalism says: "I've raided 'em, framed 'em, jailed 'em and hanged 'em, but the IWW still stands. Now see what you can do." Just what dissension could do to the IWW soon became clear. Anti-Communism still raged, and helped add fuel to the union's funeral pyre. The 1923 convention had taken an uncompromising stand against the Third International and the RILU, and many prominent members were forced out because of Communist sympathies. Raddock and Bowerman, who had led the "breaker gangs" for beating up Communists during the affiliation controversy of 1921–22, organized their own General Industrial Union in Chicago in 1923 with its own independent powers for acting against Communists.[40]

[37] Unpublished letter in Brissenden Collection, Industrial and Labor Relations Library, Cornell University.
[38] *Industrial Solidarity*, June 24, 1922.
[39] *St. Louis Post-Dispatch*, June 17, 1923.
[40] Smith Memorandum, *op. cit.*, 8.

Though the GEB refused to grant a charter to this extreme anarcho-syndicalist decentralizing group it continued to exert pressure on union policy and pressed for the expulsion of leading Communists, like Harrison George and George Hardy. Raddock and Bowerman reorganized their "breaker gangs," beat up their opponents and raided their homes. The strike in the Oregon lumber region in September 1923 showed how far this anarchy had gone. The decentralizers in Centralia, led by Payne, called the strike, but many of the other branches refused to obey the call. The strike was a miserable failure.[41]

So the scene was set for the final schism at the union's convention in September 1924. On the surface the issue was the old one of centralization. But the personal rancor developed at Leavenworth, and the bad feelings caused by the strike in Oregon the year before, gave a new cutting edge to the old conflict which was enough to split the union. The 1923 convention had tried to reorganize the union along more centralized lines, with a stronger GEB and a general secretary, general organizer, and chairman for each industrial union.[42]

The decentralizers responded the following year with their own plan, which they called the Emergency Program. This called for nothing less than the abolition of the GEB and the reconstruction of the union on extremely decentralized lines with all power concentrated in the industrial unions. The decentralizers, led by Rowan, Ryan, Raddock, and Bowerman, further denounced the 1923 convention as illegal and void because it had not been properly convened and was packed with obedient Doyle supporters. They called on all branches to denounce the 1923 convention and accept their own Emergency Program.[43]

41 *Industrial Worker*, September 1923.
42 *Proceedings of the Fifteenth Annual Convention of the IWW* (Chicago, 1923).
43 *Proceedings of the Sixteenth Annual Convention of the IWW* (Chicago, 1924), 25.

Rowan succeeded in obtaining a court injunction restraining IWW headquarters officials from continuing to hold IWW property and money—yet another example of extreme revolutionaries calling in "the legal lackeys of capitalism" to help their cause. The 1924 convention was little better than a riot. The EPs, as the decentralizers called themselves after their Emergency Program, quickly took control of the meeting and forced the expulsion of Doyle and other members of the GEB. They even succeeded in forcing the headquarters group to move their offices from 1001 West Madison Street to 3333 West Belmont Street, Chicago.

As the IWW was breaking up at Chicago a committee of the RILU added to the chaos by trying to win over the centralizers.[44] Though the floor was denied them, the Communists approached many of the IWW's industrial departments hoping to win them over, but without success. Nevertheless, IWW membership, which had been falling steadily from its postwar high point of around 45,000 in 1922, went into an even steeper decline after the split. Though accurate figures are impossible to tabulate, as many as a quarter of these lost members may have joined the Communists, many of them outstanding organizers.[45] Apart from Haywood and Andreytchine, Harrison George, George Hardy, Charles Ashleigh and Roy Brown of the lumber workers joined the Communist Party in the 1920s, while Gurley Flynn and many others joined in the 1930s.

In contrast to this movement toward the Communist Party, there was also a loss to the extreme right. Harold Lord Varney, a young, upper class intellectual who joined the IWW and wrote a novel about it in 1919, became a Fascist sympathizer and spoke at meetings in support of Mussolini held in communities of Italian immigrants. The case of an Italian im-

[44] *American Labor Yearbook,* vol. 6 (New York, 1925), 107.
[45] Gambs, *op. cit.,* 89.

migrant, Edmondo Rossoni, is even more interesting. This former organizer for the MTW section of the IWW returned to Italy in 1921 and became Mussolini's secretary of the Confederation of Fascist Syndicates.

In July 1921, in company with other leading Italian Fascists, he succeeded in smashing the socialist unions which had controlled the Genoa waterfront and run cooperative societies and a system of job control which created two tiers of waterfront workers: the privileged group, who were certain of regular work, and the underprivileged, who were permanently out of a job.[46] Rossoni took control of Genoa by leading an underprivileged group who shared many of the characteristics that distinguished IWW adherents in the United States and elsewhere. But he led them in the direction of Fascism.

The EPs, who now considered themselves the "real" IWW, captured the 1924 convention. They soon discovered they had not captured the organization. They held their own conference at Utah in 1925, rewriting the constitution to provide full autonomy for industrial unions, abolishing payment of a per capita tax on all members to national headquarters, and passing a resolution against the ownership of property. The EPs produced their own paper, the *Industrial Unionist,* in Portland for a couple of years, but by 1926 it had ceased publication. The hold they had on the West Coast did not last long; and when the *New Unionist* appeared in Los Angeles in 1931 as the voice of the EPs it was the last gesture of defiance from a dying faction.

The Chicago IWW continued as the spokesmen of the Midwestern and East Coast Locals, with a sadly depleted but still doggedly loyal membership. In 1927 this group led a major strike in the coalfields of Colorado, when 10,000 stopped work

[46] A. Rossi, *The Rise of Italian Fascism* (London, 1938), 223–34.

for four months in protest against low wages and the hold a company union, established by the owners, exerted over their working life. Despite the pleas of IWW organizers at the outset, this strike ran the old familiar gamut of intimidation, violence, and martial law. Eventually, after sixteen weeks of unrelenting struggle, the miners won a dollar a day increase. It looked like a big victory. Yet the IWW had failed to win recognition; and the miners who left the broken company union joined the more powerful WFM rather than the rapidly declining IWW.

After the split the decline of the IWW was rapid and irrecoverable. "Something new, something qualitatively different is seen in the collapse of the IWW after 1924," Vern Smith observed.[47] By 1928 it had never been so weak. Membership had dropped below the 10,000 mark, and the GEB stopped publishing reports showing how much had been paid in dues. When a new general secretary took over at headquarters in 1932 he found the union had exactly $29 cash to pay back wages, run the office and meet printing costs.

The IWW still continued to command the loyal, unswerving support of a small band of idealistic supporters. The union was involved in the two year coal strike at Harlan County, Kentucky, which in the 1930s the AF of L, CIO, and Communist organizers who competed with each other to try to win command of the men regarded as the toughest place in America to organize. Some 18,000 miners were involved in the dispute, which was fought without quarter on either side. In one clash between pickets and company guards, one collier and three guards were killed. Later forty-four miners were indicted and convicted for murder. A vigorous campaign launched by the IWW helped avert the death penalty. The forty-four men

[47] Smith memorandum, *op. cit.*, 27.

Topping a huge tree in the Washington timber belt.

Wesley Everest, who was lynched in his Army uniform by members of the American Legion at Centralia, Washington, on Armistice Day, 1919.

George F. Vanderveer, "counsel for the damned," who defended the IWW at the great Chicago trial of 1918.

Mounted police attack Rudolph Dressel, an IWW organizer, during the Homestead, Pennsylvania, steel strike of 1919.

were jailed and some of them were not released until 1941. "Bloody Harlan" was the last of the IWW's major battle honors.

With membership reduced to a bare minimum, the IWW was unable to meet the challenge of the Great Depression and the New Deal. It was overtaken by the CIO, whose leaders borrowed many strike techniques first used by the Wobblies as they set about the task the IWW had pioneered of organizing workers on an industrial rather than a craft basis. The CIO succeeded where the IWW had failed: in mass-production industries, like steel, rubber, chemicals, and autos. A report in *Time* magazine captured, cruelly perhaps, the mood of the movement at its 1946 convention. "Thirty-nine men and a grandmotherly looking woman met in an office building on the North Side of Chicago to pass resolutions denouncing Capitalism, Fascism, Nazism, the CIO, the AF of L and the war . . . With that off their chests, the Industrial Workers of the World went home."[48]

But though the lion may have lost its claws, it was still capable of roaring from time to time. One of the last occasions when the IWW intervened to good effect came when its own reputation was blackened. When Wallace Stegner's article suggesting Joe Hill was guilty appeared in the *New Republic* in January 1948 the IWW formed the Friends of Joe Hill Committee, which picketed the *New Republic* offices until the magazine agreed to publish a synopsis of a very detailed defense of Hill produced by the IWW. By 1955—when the union celebrated its fiftieth birthday and Fred Thompson's official history appeared—it did not exercise job control in a single factory or plant.

Was the movement doomed to failure? But for the First

[48] *Time,* April 1, 1946, quoted by Kornbluh, *op. cit.,* 355.

World War, and the spate of antiradical feeling it unleashed, the Wobblies might have consolidated their pioneering work among the apparently unorganizable—the Western migratory workers, the Negroes in the timber forests and oil fields of the South and Southwest, the unskilled and illiterate, the most beaten down sections of labor who still remain unorganized today. They may have failed to unionize these workers; but they achieved as large a measure of success as anyone since.

From 1917–21, largely because of the war, the IWW became what it had been before on brief occasions when individual Wobblies were arrested: a full-time legal defense organization. The trials of nearly two hundred IWW members on charges of conspiracy and subversion, together with the harassment, arrest, imprisonment, and deportation of thousands of other dissidents, radicals, and revolutionaries, make unpleasant reading today. With the moral superiority of hindsight it is easy to condemn those who feared revolution and sought to crush it.

Today we can see that the threat was an empty one. But for Mitchell Palmer, President Wilson's Attorney General, revolution seemed very near when a bomb was planted in his home. Others knew the revolutionary specter was a turnip ghost; and by 1924 most Americans felt ashamed of the way the IWW had been treated. But by this time the movement had dug its own grave. The conflict between the anarchist decentralizers, the syndicalist headquarters faction, and the Communists striving to recruit the IWW into the Red International of Labor Unions eventually ended in the schism of 1924 from which the union never recovered.

Was the IWW even a genuine revolutionary movement? Clearly it was never a revolutionary threat; and despite public fears to the contrary, it is doubtful if its leaders took its revolutionary language too seriously. After 1912 the union became increasingly conservative in its methods, acting more like a hard-bargaining industrial union. Though its motto remained "abolition of the wage system" its actual demands during strikes seem moderate by today's standards. Perhaps some individual IWW members were revolutionary in their belief that men should be granted the same respect, security and dignity in the eyes of their fellows and the law whatever their race, religion, color, creed, or job—a belief which, despite pious lip service, is very far from being accepted today. However, the goal of creating general disorder through strikes which would lead to bloody revolution was never seriously contemplated by IWW leaders.

The IWW was primarily a revolutionary agitational body in its early years. But once the centralizers had won the struggle with the decentralizers from 1912–14 and established the AWO 400 it became primarily a militant union. Yet the Wobblies disagreed with other syndicalists, such as the French or Tom Mann. They kept an obstinate belief in the efficacy of dual unionism, as opposed to boring from within. For more than any other pioneer labor organization, the IWW laid the groundwork for the great organizing drives undertaken by the CIO among the unskilled and foreign-born in the mass production industries during the 1930s and 1940s.

True, the IWW had little or no success in organizing in steel, automobile, chemical, and rubber plants, which provided the core of the CIO's achievements. But many of its members, apprenticed in IWW free speech fights and strikes, toughened by persecution and imprisonment, survived to help form the CIO's industrial unions. John Panzner, who joined the IWW in 1905 and organized among the lumberjacks of the Far West and the metal miners of the Mesabi range, was typical of many others. He was one of the Wobblies sent to Leavenworth

Penitentiary, and after his release from jail in 1923 plunged straight back into the struggle for industrial unionism. In 1933 he joined the United Auto Workers, and remained a UAW organizer throughout the violent struggles of the 1930s which established industrial unionism in the auto industry.

Men like Panzner brought with them into the CIO the experience they had learned in years of organizing with the IWW. Wobbly strike techniques—in particular the sit-down strike—were used with great effect by CIO unions a generation later. The CIO succeeded where the IWW had failed for a whole number of complicated reasons. First, unionization was protected by the law during the New Deal period. Second, the CIO did not waste its energies and antagonize potential allies by talking about revolution when it was really concerned with improving living and working conditions. Third, and perhaps most important, it was organizing among workers who could be more easily reached by its propaganda. The predominantly immigrant workers in the mass production industries of the 1910s had been replaced in the 1930s by their children, educated in America, whose first language was English and whose first loyalty was to the United States.

Was the IWW part of the European revolutionary tradition, or was it an American phenomenon? Though it drew some of its ideas and much of its revolutionary vocabulary from European socialist and syndicalist writers, it was rooted in American experience and shaped by American events. Indeed, the IWW Locals which appeared in most other countries, like Canada, Britain, and Australia, slavishly followed all the American trends, debates, and schisms. Certainly the IWW preamble owed much to the syndicalist writers whom DeLeon, Trautmann, and Hagerty read avidly in the years between 1903–5. Yet discontent about social injustice in the United

States itself was the real driving force behind the demand for a new, militant industrial unionism which produced the IWW in 1905.

The form which this new kind of unionism took in the next few years owed everything to American conditions. Frontier society in the mines and logging regions of the West was unsophisticated. There were employers on one side and workers on the other. Law enforcement was often poor, and the two sides met each other regularly in head-on class conflict of the crudest kind. The closeness of the frontier, with its opportunity for overnight speculative fortunes, meant that a man could move from one class to the other very quickly. Thus Edward Boyce was a militant WFM leader in the 1890s, until he struck gold, while Vincent St. John gave up the pursuit of the millennium with the IWW in 1914 partly because of ill health, but also because of gold fever.

These were violent times, and the history of the IWW is inseparably linked with violence. Employers used force to discourage their workers from joining together, and the IWW met more determined resistance than most unions. But though they were, in theory, a revolutionary body committed to the overthrow of capitalism, the Wobblies were in no sense committed to violence as a philosophy of life. Moreover, no members were ever found guilty of planting dynamite or endangering life or property by acts of sabotage.

The IWW also had some criminal members: the Joe Hill case dramatized this aspect of the movement, which is one reason why the legend of Joe Hill is so important in understanding the appeal of the IWW. Some of the criminals who joined the union did so because it was the best way to separate the bindle stiff from his bank roll. When the IWW briefly began to make money, from 1915–17, other criminals joined to try to get at the profits. Some idealists accepted crime and criminals as simply another manifestation of opposition to capitalism. The Australian Wobblies went furthest in this direction, with their open welcome to criminals and their scheme of printing forged £5 notes to overthrow capitalism through inflation.

With its scorn for parliamentary democracy, and its belief in direct action and the general strike, the IWW appealed most strongly to weak, diverse, and divided groups in American society which shared certain characteristics. Those who supported the IWW rebellion felt a sense of alienation from industrial capitalism; they were usually voteless; and they were rootless, either because the nature of their work forced them to travel from place to place, or because their race and language separated them from the mainstream of American life.

Equally important, perhaps, the IWW left a mark in the field of civil liberties. The free speech fights, trials, and persecution at the hands of vigilante groups and state and Federal judiciaries awakened the conscience of many liberal Americans to the need to protect the rights of dissident groups and improve penal conditions. At a time when social dissidents are again making a mark on American life, in social protests ranging from civil rights to the war in Vietnam, this aspect of the IWW struggle has a certain topicality.

The IWW was also an international movement, which tried to spread the gospel of the One Big Union to working men of many nationalities who shared a common belief that they were the most despised sections of labor. While some IWWs clearly sought the power later used by John L. Lewis and other CIO leaders, others, especially in South American countries, anticipated national leaders of socialist revolutions, like Fidel Castro. In all these ways the IWW has an importance which goes beyond its achievements and failures. It was left to an implacable enemy, Senator William E. Borah, to sum up the elusive quality of the IWW.

"You cannot destroy the organization," he told members of the United States Senate in 1917. "It is an intangible proposition. It is something you cannot get at. You cannot reach it. You do not know where it is. It is not in writing. It is not in anything else. It is simply an understanding between men, and they act upon it without any evidence of existence whatsoever." Borah's statement sums up the strengths and weaknesses of the IWW—and helps explain its enduring fame. The IWW was as much an attitude to life as an industrial labor union.

For we have a glowing dream
Of how fair the world will seem
When each man can live life
Secure and free

runs the verse of one of Ralph Chaplin's songs. This vision of a fairer, juster, more decent life for the average wage worker was something the Wobblies worked for as if for a religious cause. In James Jones' novel *From Here to Eternity* one of the characters discusses his experiences in the IWW. "It was their vision that made them great," he says. "And it was their belief which made them powerful. And sing! You never heard anybody sing the way those guys sang! Nobody sings like that unless it's for a religion." This faith in the possibility of a better society must remain their justification—and their epitaph.

POSTSCRIPT: WORKERS OF THE WORLD

THE RED FLAG

Look 'round, the Frenchmen loves its blaze,
The sturdy German chants its praise;
In Moscow's vaults its hymns are sung,
Chicago swells its surging song.

James Connell

The founders of the IWW had always intended their movement to be international, reaching across the frontiers of capitalist nation states and uniting the working class of all lands in revolt. For this reason they sang *The Internationale*—anthem of international socialism before the Communists took it over after the Bolshevik Revolution—at the founding convention in 1905 and, as a more practical step, made union membership fully transferable, not only within the United States but for immigrants who held union cards from their homeland. Yet to make the IWW an international organization in fact as well as name proved more difficult, and its sections in countries outside the United States rarely exerted much lasting influence on trade unions.

However, the syndicalist threat remained a constant factor in the affairs of industrial nations from the early 1900s until the 1920s—from, say, the Charter of Amiens in France in 1906 until the General Strike in Britain in 1926, which was the last time the syndicalist idea of the universal strike was paraded seriously. After its failure the syndicalist threat never loomed so large again. Though the IWW made no impact in France, the home of syndicalist thinking, before 1914 it quickly caught on in English-speaking countries like Britain, Australia, New Zealand, South Africa, and Canada. There were also flourishing IWWs both south of the border in Mexico and also in Norway, where conditions—as in parts of Australia—were very similar to those in the American West.

The British section of the IWW, one of the first to be launched outside the United States, reflected faithfully most of the internal disputes and wrangles that divided the American movement. Initially the British branch of the Industrial Workers of the World grew out of the British Socialist Labor Party, which itself had been founded in 1902 by a breakaway faction of the Social Democratic Federation. This faction, led by the Clydeside Irishman James Connolly, was strongly influenced by the IWW.

The British SLP leadership sent a telegram of congratulation to the first IWW convention at Chicago in 1905, and a fierce controversy resulted over the role direct action and industrial unionism should play in British trades unionism. After this debate the transatlantic links grew stronger, and late in 1905 the SLP formed the British Advocates of Industrial Unionism in Glasgow in direct imitation of the IWW.

In 1908 the BAIU followed the lead of the American IWW once more and split into anarchist and syndicalist wings. The anarchists left and formed the Industrial League, which represented "pure" industrial unionism, opposed equally to bosses, trade unions, and any kind of political organization,[1] while the majority of the BAIU worked closely with the SLP and advocated action on both industrial and political fronts. In 1909 they reorganized under a new name—the Industrial Workers of Great Britain.

The IWGB met with some success in Glasgow and Edinburgh. Tom Bell, a leading figure in the SLP who helped launch the IWGB, claimed 4000 members in one factory, the Singer Sewing Machine Works at Kilbowie, Clydebank. This was an American-owned firm managed by an American, whose new techniques designed to increase production led in 1911 to a strike against wage cuts similar to the McKees Rocks dispute in Pennsylvania two years before.

[1] E. J. B. Allen, *Revolutionary Unionism* (Glasgow, 1909), sets out the aims of the anarchists in pamphlet form.

Like McKees Rocks, Lawrence, Paterson, and other American centers where the IWW met with some success, Glasgow was a city of great ethnic diversity. In 1900 it had a population of 750,000, of which about 20,000 were of Highland descent. The main divisions were between Catholics and Protestants, Irish and Scots, and Lowland and Highland Scots, as well as between the different Protestant sects, such as Presbyterians in various forms and Episcopalians.[2] Other racial groups included Poles and Lithuanians, who had been brought into help break earlier miners' strikes, some Scandinavian shipbuilders and Italian shopkeepers.[3]

Most of the 12,000 workers at Singer's went out, though the strike failed and its leaders were fired. Yet these men generally remained on Clydeside as a hard core of industrial discontent. Several of them helped form the Clyde Workers' Committee which led strikes during the First World War and merged into the Shop Stewards' Movement in the 1920s. One of them, Arthur MacManus, became first chairman of the British Communist Party in 1921.[4] Other Marxists active on Clydeside included Tom Bell, John Maclean, William Paul, Harry McShane, and William Gallacher. The latter, like Connolly a few years earlier, visited the United States in 1914 and came back an advocate of direct action and anti-Parliamentary activity[5]—an ironic result in view of the fact that he later sat in Parliament as a Communist M.P. for West Fife from 1935–50.

The IWW's influence on the British left culminated in Haywood's visit to Europe in 1910–11. Industrial unrest swept Britain that year. Strikes by seamen and firemen in Southampton had crippled every port in the country by June 1911;

[2] Robert Keith Middlemas, *The Clydesiders* (London, 1965), 28.
[3] *Ibid.*, 29.
[4] Tom Bell, *Pioneering Days* (London, 1941), 72–75.
[5] Middlemas, *op. cit.*, 50–51.

and the following month further strikes brought out the dockers, coal fillers, and carters. While Haywood attended the Conference of the Second International that year in Copenhagen he met Lenin, although the meeting did not seem to make much impression on the American.[6] He also talked with Rosa Luxemburg, Ramsay MacDonald, Keir Hardie, and Jean Jaurès, the leading figures of European socialism at that time. In England he met Albert Inkpin, William Hyndman, and Tom Bell, and was specially invited to Glasgow, the center of the syndicalist movement in Britain.[7]

The trip opened Haywood's eyes to a wider world, and his impact in Britain was immediate. The high point of his tour was his visit to South Wales during the bitter Cambrian Coal Combine struggle of 1910–11. Haywood approved of the striking colliers' decision to force the engine winders, pump operators, and pony drivers, who belonged to other unions, to strike in their support—a victory for industrial solidarity which did not prevent it from being a disastrous failure.

In 1913 Haywood went to Ireland, where the Irish Transport Workers, a new industrial union, had embarked on a desperate, eight month strike for better pay and conditions, and recognition of the union. Connolly and Jim Larkin had founded the Transport Workers in Belfast and Dublin as the nucleus of an Irish IWW uniting all the workers.[8] Larkin's experience of politics was not unlike Haywood's, and had similar results, for he had turned wholeheartedly to direct action in 1912 when he was debarred from taking his seat on Dublin Corporation. Later he visited the United States and watched the IWW at work there. During the 1913 strike he welcomed Haywood's help and advice. The strike failed; but the struggle

[6] Haywood, *op. cit.*, 233.
[7] *Ibid.*, 234.
[8] Emmett Larkin, *James Larkin* (Cambridge, 1964), 88–89.

of 20,000 Dublin transport workers made Larkin an international figure, just as Lawrence and Paterson had given Haywood a world-wide reputation for militancy. The activity of direct actionists in Britain coincided with the growth of direct action in the United States.

Yet the most significant feature of Wobbly activity in Britain was that it took place among the same culturally alienated groups who found direct action most attractive on the other side of the Atlantic. The IWGB was not strong in England as such. Its advocates were either Scottish, Irish, or Welsh, the "immigrant" workers from the Celtic fringe. MacManus was the son of a Fēniaū, Gallacher of mixed Anglo-Irish parentage. The English cities, like Liverpool and Birmingham, where the IWW was active, had large Irish minorities. Liverpool was known as "the capital of Ireland" and Jim Larkin had been born there.[9]

Tom Mann, champion of the London stevedores in their fight for the "dockers' tanner" in 1889, was a link man in a further development in the IWW story. Mann had become the leader of the "new unionists," the semiskilled and unskilled workers who began organizing in Britain in the 1890s. He had returned to Britain at the turn of the century after a long tour of Australia and New Zealand.[10] The industrial movement in Britain at this time was greatly stimulated by the Johannesburg strikes and the deportation of Archie Crawford and other South African labor leaders, while the miners' strikes at Broken Hill and other parts of Western Australia also struck a responsive chord in Britain.

On his tour of Australia, Mann discovered that while dual unionism was not an important issue, direct action was. So

[9] *Ibid.*, 3–4. I owe this point about the continuity of cultural alienation in Britain to Philip Williams, Fellow of Nuffield College, Oxford.
[10] Tom Mann, *Memoirs* (London, 1923), 254.

the IWW made headway in Australia after 1905. When Tom Mann left Sydney a few years before the prospects for industrial unionism had looked promising. Conditions in the new continent with its expanding frontier were often remarkably similar to life in the Far West where the American IWW won its first victories. Though many contrasts can be drawn between the American and Australian labor movements the Australian miners had much in common with the American Wobblies. Years of industrial struggle had prepared them for the blunt assertion in the IWW preamble that "the working class and the employing class have nothing in common."[11] From their own experience "the centering of the management of industries into fewer and fewer hands" was an observable fact. Yet in Australia unionism was influenced by a vital factor lacking in the United States: the existence of a large Labor Party capable of forming a government. The political issue in Australia was thus whether or not to affiliate with the Labor Party, not as in the United States, with one of two relatively powerless socialist parties. Direct-actionists in Australia aimed at strengthening the industrial unions and were scathing in their criticism of craft unions and the Labor Party. The opponents of direct action wished to revitalize the labor movement by federating existing unions and, while using the strike weapon as a last resort, relying in the main on the political arm of the Labor Party.

The debate on the political issue in Australia had begun in the 1890s, when the labor movement made a decision to intervene in politics. The growth of the Australian Labor Party was rapid; yet by 1907 disillusion with the cautious policies of the labor leadership was already widespread among trade union-

[11] Robin Gollan, *The Coalminers of New South Wales* (Melbourne, 1963), 123.

ists. From April until August 1904, J. C. Watson was Prime Minister of the world's first Labor government. But in power the Labor Party did nothing to halt the rapid fall in real wages. The result was a revolt against political action in favor of industrial unionism and a return to the bitter struggles and direct action of the 1890s.

One manifestation of this revolt was the IWW, which arrived on the Australian scene in 1907. It found a ready audience among miners already critical of the Labor Party and soured by six years of abortive arbitration in their disputes with the mineowners. Hitherto, militant socialist ideas had been kept alive by the Australian Socialist League, which tried unsuccessfully to make the Labor Party adopt a policy of nationalization and accept the need for urgent social change. The League finally left the Labor Party in 1898 and founded the Socialist Labor Party. After this, the revolutionary doctrines of the IWW reached the Australian workers through minority organizations like the Australian SLP.[12]

Like their comrades in Britain, SLP leaders in Australia were inspired to emulate the example of the American IWW, and in 1907 IWW clubs began to spring up all over Australia. They were especially influential among the coalminers in Newcastle and Melbourne. The socialists were forced to take notice of the IWW at a socialist unity conference in June 1907, attended by delegates from all the major cities, which decided that "the time has arrived for the reorganization of the Australian working class on the lines of the IWW."[13]

The Australian IWW, like its American counterpart, was most active among the semiskilled and unskilled nomadic workers roaming the new nation.[14] In the next few years the

[12] Robin Gollan, *Radical and Working Class Politics* (Melbourne, 1960), 189.
[13] Gollan, *The Coalminers, op. cit.*, 123.
[14] V. G. Childe, *How Labour Governs* (London, 1923), 115.

Australian IWW made much progress. Its message spread quickly through the labor movement. Its ideas were discussed in the Sydney Labor Council and the Melbourne Trades Hall Council in 1907, and in April 1908 the Trades Union Congress at Sydney debated at length a resolution, moved by the Newcastle Trades and Labor Council, "that the preamble and constitution of the Industrial Workers of the World [be adopted] as the basis of organization."[15]

Although this resolution was rejected by 55 votes to 23 in favor of an amendment proposing "the Federation of the whole of the labor organizations of Australasia," the IWW philosophy had been given serious consideration by the Australian labor movement. And in the coalfields it won acceptance. The Miners' Federation voted to incorporate the IWW preamble into its own constitution.

By July 1907, the coalminers of New South Wales and Victoria were being led by the Wobblies, and in the following year the IWW directed the Sydney transport strike. In the northern miners' lodges IWW influence was still very strong. When the Broken Hill miners went on strike in 1909 they were locked out for a year and their leaders put on trial for sedition.[16] The IWW tried to persuade the TUC to call a general strike in sympathy with the prisoners, but failed, and the men were jailed for eighteen months. The new spirit of militancy can best be judged by the strike rate during these years. Between 1901 and 1904 only two strikes lasted more than three days. In 1908 there were 223, in 1909 there were 151, and in 1910 there were 126, including the major struggles at Broken Hill and Newcastle.[17]

15 *Official Report of the Trades Union Congress* (Sydney, 1908), quoted by Gollan, *The Coalminers op. cit.*, 123; Childe, *op. cit.*, 119, gives a summary of this debate.
16 Childe, *op. cit.*, 120, 123.
17 Gollan, *Politics, op. cit.*, 213.

By 1914 there were four IWW Locals at Adelaide, Sydney, Broken Hill, and Port Pirie. Early in 1915 more Locals were established at Melbourne and Brisbane, and the following year in the Western goldfields, at Fremantle and in North Queensland. By 1916 the IWW had a dozen Locals in all with some 2000 members, while its weekly newspaper, *Direct Action,* founded in 1914, soon had a circulation of 16,000.[18]

In its first leader, *Direct Action* spelled out the IWW's editorial policy. "For the first time in Australia," it said, "a paper appears which stands for straight-out direct action principles, unhampered by the plausible theories of parliamentarians, whether revolutionary or otherwise . . . Every contributor, every supporter is a member of the wage-earning class, who is conscious of his slave status in society. . . . Parliamentarians who, from motives of timidity or self-interest, are content to move within the circles which the legal and moral code of capitalism allows . . . have been the real stumbling blocks to revolutionary education."[19]

When war broke out in Europe in 1914 the IWW's struggles in Australia took a new turn. Most Australian workers supported the war and were prepared to do their bit in the early stages. But after the heavy casualties suffered by Australian and New Zealand troops during the Gallipoli campaign in 1915 disillusion set in. Europe was a long way away and most Australian workers were not prepared to abandon the struggle for better conditions because the French army was in danger of defeat at Verdun.

But to the Labor government, and its Prime Minister W. M. Hughes, winning the war was of such paramount importance that all else seemed negligible. Accordingly, in 1916

[18] *Ibid.,* 151.
[19] *Direct Action,* January 1914, quoted by Childe, *op. cit.,* 155.

they decided to introduce conscription and so began a battle over military service which became central to Australian labor politics.[20]

The IWW was in the van of the attack on conscription. They enjoyed wide support among Australian workers, especially those of Irish Catholic descent whose sympathies were with James Connolly and the other leaders of the Easter Rising of 1916 in Dublin. An IWW organizer, Tom Barker, was repeatedly arrested for prejudicing recruiting. A typical IWW poster at the time read "Do you want conscription? While you are TALKING about what you will do at the BALLOT-BOX Hughes is ACTING and you will be called up next month and put under MILITARY LAW."[21]

Hundreds of Wobblies were arrested during 1916 under the Unlawful Associations Act of that year, while the War Precautions Act was used to close left wing newspapers which attacked Hughes' conscription plan, such as the Melbourne *Socialist* and *Ross's*. On September 30 police broke into the *Direct Action* offices and arrested the editor, Thomas Glynn, together with four other Wobblies, including Jim Larkin's brother Peter. They were charged with high treason. Membership books, dues stamps and £400 worth of literature were confiscated. Two other IWWs were later arrested and sentenced to death, but their sentence was commuted.[22] Hughes used the IWW opposition to conscription to try to persuade more moderate elements to support him, and there was no doubt he had some success.

The lengths to which some Wobblies were prepared to go in their opposition to conscription and the war clearly alarmed many who had hitherto been sympathetic to the movement.

[20] L. C. Jauncey, *The Story of Conscription in Australia* (London, 1935), is the best account of this episode.

[21] Quoted by Childe, *op. cit.*, 166 (emphasis in original).

[22] *Proceedings of the Tenth Convention of the IWW*, 1916 (Chicago, 1917), 21–22.

Attempts were made to set fire to factories and warehouses, and though Tom Barker was released from prison in an attempt to stop this sabotage, the fireraising still continued. True to the principles of Bakunin, but unlike Wobblies in most other countries, the Australian movement was not afraid to admit criminals to membership, regarding them as just another group who set at defiance the law and morality of capitalism.

The same sort of thinking was behind another extraordinary IWW venture at this time: the forging of currency. Wobblies like J. B. King, Louis and David Goldstein and others printed and circulated forged £5 notes, not to make money themselves but in the belief that this would hasten the collapse of capitalism, which they thought the war had brought to the brink of death. Inevitably, however, the criminals they willingly accepted as IWW members were lacking in this altruistic attitude and used the scheme to line their own pockets. The IWW was further discredited when two members murdered a young policeman at Tottenham in particularly brutal circumstances.[23]

Broken up and driven underground by a wave of arrests and persecution the IWW survived long enough to see conscription narrowly defeated in a referendum by 1,160,033 votes to 1,087,557.[24] Its influence remained a factor in the labor movement during the war and after it. Its antiwar propaganda prepared the way for the Australian Labor Party's peace proposals of 1917, the Labor Council's resolutions against recruiting and the Perth Conference decisions of 1918, when all members of the party voted to withdraw their support for the war effort until the Allies had offered peace to Germany on the basis of no annexations or indemnities.

The whole leftward movement of the Labor Party after the

[23] Childe, *op. cit.*, 159, 167.
[24] Gollan, *The Coalminers, op. cit.*, 142.

defeat of conscription, culminating in the formation of an industrial section in New South Wales, was partly inspired by the IWW. The union was also involved in the great coal strike of 1916 and the general strike of 1917. Finally, when the war was over, the Australian labor movement expressed its disgust with the Labor Party and political action as a whole by adopting the IWW idea of a militant, industrial form of labor organization unaffiliated to any party and scorning political action—the One Big Union.[25] Summing up the IWW story from a sympathetic point of view, Gordon Childe concluded, "Nobody has exercised a more profound influence on the whole outlook of labor in Australia."[26]

Compared with this turbulent tale of the IWW in Australia, the movement's progress in Canada was relatively peaceful. Canadian unions were usually no more than extensions of American ones, and this was the case to some extent with the IWW. The movement made its first appearance in Canada in 1906, organizing mainly among textile workers, metal miners, and lumberjacks.

Yet in Canada, unions as a whole, including the IWW, failed to make much headway for many reasons. At first the IWW branches in the West were successful. Their organizing campaigns among the metal miners, loggers, and unskilled workers enlisted 10,000 members by 1911, mostly in British Columbia and Alberta.[27] Links with Locals across the 49th parallel in the United States were much closer in the Western Provinces; and during 1912 the IWW conducted a major strike among building and construction workers employed on the Grand Trunk Pacific Railway. But in 1913 the Canadian wing suffered the

[25] Ian Bedford, "The One Big Union, 1918–23" *Initiative and Organization* (Sydney Studies in Politics 3, Melbourne, 1963), describes this venture.
[26] Childe, *op. cit.*, 147.
[27] H. A. Logan, *Trade Unions in Canada* (Toronto, 1948), 299.

same general decline which afflicted the movement as a whole, and failed to spring back again in 1914. At the end of the year a government report credited the IWW with only 465 members, and in 1915 its three remaining branches dissolved because of arrests and persecution during the war. Sporadic activity continued among isolated individual groups of radicals and industrial unionists, but the Canadian membership was hit by a wave of arrests similar to that which swept most of the American leadership into jail in 1917–18. An order-in-council of September 24, 1918, declared both the IWW and the Workers' International Industrial Union, as DeLeon's Detroit faction of the IWW was now known, unlawful organizations. The penalty for membership of the IWW was fixed at five years in jail, and though only one WIIU branch was prosecuted in this way several individual members suffered deportation.

In 1919 the ban on IWW membership was lifted. Two new branches were formed in Toronto and Kitchener, Ontario, and the IWW set about the task of re-establishing itself. It soon achieved some success, and the years from 1919–23 saw a wave of militant revolutionism sweeping across Canada.

But the Canadian IWW followed the American example and rejected the overtures of Moscow's Red International of Labor Unions. It disavowed all parliamentary action and pinned its faith on economic action through industrial unions. Its tactics were still the classic ones outlined in the Charter of Amiens of 1906: sabotage and strikes leading to a general strike and revolution. Its aim was the overthrow of the wage system, which it hoped to achieve by seizing the leadership of the Canadian labor movement.

This ambition seemed nearer fulfillment when the Lumber Workers' Industrial Union collapsed as an independent labor organization in 1921. But though it collapsed in Canada, the LWIU remained the loggers' biggest union in the United States. It differed from the Wobblies by engaging in political as well as industrial activity. In 1920 it claimed 23,000 members, and had led an unrelenting series of strikes for eighteen months.[28]

After affiliating to the One Big Union, which sprang into prominence in 1919 to challenge the IWW for the leadership of revolutionary unionism, the LWIU had taken part in the unsuccessful general strike of 1919 in Winnipeg and Vancouver. With Everett and Centralia just across the border from British Columbia, links with the militant movement among loggers in the United States were very strong. The battle for better wages, working conditions, bunkhouses, bedding and food reached a new peak of intensity and finally won big concessions. The greatest of these came when the eight hour day, which had been agreed as long ago as 1898, was finally conceded by all lumber firms in 1920.

Yet though the OBU made its membership cards interchangeable with IWW cards in the lumber industry, the sea ports and the Great Lakes area after the war, it was soon reduced to a few branches in the transport and lumber industries. After the demise of the LWIU, the IWW, the OBU and the Communists made takeover bids for LWIU members. Some sections of the OBU joined the Communist Red International; others made an abortive effort to refound the LWIU; while the remainder joined the American IWW.[29]

In Canada, as in the United States, the movement withered once peace and prosperity had returned. The Department of Labor reported that in 1926 the union consisted of six units

[28] Al Parkin, a member of the LWIU, quoted by Logan, *op. cit.*, 28.
[29] Logan, *op. cit.*, 301.

in all—a lumber workers' branch, a unit of Vancouver marine transport workers, a unit of agricultural workers in Calgary and units of lumber workers at Sudbury and Port Arthur—comprising a total of 5400 members.[30]

In 1931 the Canadian membership decided that the obvious decline of the American parent body after the split of 1923–24 was having an adverse effect on their own fortunes. They therefore persuaded the IWW convention at Chicago to establish an independent Canadian administration. This was formed in 1932, but all the new leadership could do was officiate at the last rites of the IWW in Canada.

IWW influence in the American continent extended into other South American states, like Mexico. In the early years of the twentieth century corrupt and barbarous dictatorships took a heavy toll in Mexico. In 1913, Emiliano Zapata confiscated the great estates of the south after a popular revolt. Standard Oil was deeply involved in Mexican politics, and the leaders of the Mexican Liberal Party, Ricardo Flores Magón and his brother Enrique, advocated the expulsion of Standard and other foreign-owned companies, as well as further expropriation. Magón had already spent twelve years in the United States, half of them in jail, where he was strongly influenced by IWW ideas.

From the outset of the Mexican rebellion he was a leading advocate of cooperation with other American revolutionary groups, like the Wobblies. In the early 1920s, Magón died in suspicious circumstances in Leavenworth Penitentiary. But in 1913 he was at the center of a tense struggle which developed as Mexican and American revolutionaries tried to evade border guards and join forces. This tension finally burst into open

[30] *Ibid.*, 300.

fighting in the "border bandits" incident. An American IWW lumber worker, Charles Cline, and fourteen Mexican rebels tried to cross the border from Texas at night. They fought off an attack by local Texas deputies and captured two of them, planning to use them as hostages to ensure safe conduct to the border, where they would have been released.

But one of their prisoners attacked a rebel and was killed. His killer fled and was never found. The other rebels were captured by vigilantes. One wounded man was kicked to death; the others were chained together by the neck and brought before a grand jury which included one of the captured deputies. The "border bandits" were given twenty-five years to life in jail, and served thirteen before they were given a full pardon by the liberal Democratic Governor of Texas, Mrs. James E. (Ma) Ferguson, in 1926.

The IWW left a militant legend in Mexico, where Mexican workers who had joined the IWW in the United States, like Magón, returned to help anarchists influenced by Spanish anarchism.[31] The story was the same in other South American countries where the state was either powerless, or unwilling, to intervene on the side of the workers in industrial affairs. So in Argentina, Uruguay, Bolivia, Chile, and Peru IWW ideas, often planted by American or Australian IWW seamen, like Tom Barker, survived and flourished for a time.

For example, in 1923 the IWW led a strike on the Peruvian Central Lines when a railwayman with twenty years good service was sacked. Within twenty-four hours the entire labor force on the railway system—engineers, firemen, brakemen, conductors, machinists, carpenters, laborers, and clerks—had

[31] Marjorie Ruth Clark, *Organized Labor in Mexico* (Chapel Hill, 1934), *passim;* Fanny F. Simon "Anarchism and Anarcho-syndicalism in South America," *The Hispanic-American Historical Review,* xxvi (1946), 38–59.

struck in accordance with the IWW motto "an injury to one is an injury to all." After two weeks the workman was reinstated, having first rejected a $50,000 bribe from the company to accept dismissal and send the strikers back to work.[32]

In Chile the IWW was very influential in the early 1920s among maritime, bakery, masonry, and leather workers, many of whom were of foreign origin. The union had seven affiliates and embraced 9000 workers in Santiago and seven maritime cities. The fact that its main strength was in seaports shows the importance of IWW propaganda and organizers coming from the United States and Australia on merchant ships.[33] In 1922 the IWW in South Africa led a strike of 11,000 miners in the Rand Goldfield. They were all arrested, and 850 were jailed for high treason.

The appeal of IWW ideas and methods was not restricted to English-speaking nations, nor to the American continent, though it was strongest there. They did make inroads in the Scandinavian countries, especially in Norway. In the early years of the century Norway was being transformed from an agricultural into an industrial economy. Its uprooted workers were remarkably similar to the migrating workers of the American IWW. They have been described as "men divorced from the stabilizing influence of permanent employment, property ownership, home life, social status, and the conventional forms of approbation, men who saw no reason why they should feel indebted to the established order of things and were ready to fight capitalism with the first weapons to hand."[34]

These weapons were provided by syndicalist agitators, like

[32] *Solidarity*, August 6, 1923.
[33] Moises Pablete Troncoso and Ben G. Burnett, *The Rise of the Latin American Labor Movement* (New York, 1960), 61–62; Robert J. Alexander, *Labor Relations in Argentina, Brazil and Chile* (New York, 1962), 254–56.
[34] Walter Galenson, *Labor in Norway* (Harvard, 1949), 61 n.

Martin Tranmael, who worked through the political arm of the labor movement. After 1905 the Norwegian Labor Party started to make rapid strides. In 1903 it had mustered only 23,000 votes; but in 1906 it won 43,000 votes, which rose to 91,000 in 1909 and 128,000 in 1912. There were ten labor members in the Norwegian Storting (or Parliament) in 1906, but twenty-three in 1912.

Tranmael was a young house-painter, who possessed remarkable political gifts. A brilliant speaker, an able journalist, and a passionate teetotaler and moralist, he was perhaps the best-loved figure in the history of Norwegian labor.[35] Like Willie Gallacher and James Connolly, he had acquired his theory of industrial action during a stay in the United States from 1903 to 1905.[36]

On returning he put the principles he had learned from the IWW into practice. "It was not fortuitous that the Norwegian syndicalists were so strongly attracted by the structure and methods of the IWW," says the Labor Party's official history, "nor that the philosophy of the two movements should have so much in common. The greater success of the Norwegian left wing opposition may perhaps be attributed to the fact that in Norway the new industrial workers constituted a much larger proportion of the nation's total labor force."[37]

In 1912 Tranmael brought the whole question of what part violence should play in direct action to public attention. In a speech, he argued that striking miners ought to stop work even if some dynamite might remain in the bore holes. He also indicated that such steps might give pause to possible strike breakers and blacklegs. In the "dynamite in the bore holes"

[35] F. Borkenau, *The Communist International* (London, 1938), 68

[36] *Det Norske Arbeiderpartis Historie*, ii, 77, quoted by Galenson, *op. cit.*, 59–60 n.

[37] *Ibid.*, quoted by Galenson, *op. cit.*, 61.

controversy which followed, Carl Jeppensen, conservative leader of the Labor Party, attacked Tranmael as an advocate of assassination.

Despite this resistance from the leadership, revolutionary socialism and syndicalism swept to power in the Norwegian Labor Party during the First World War. The chaotic conditions of the war and the resulting inflation had depressed the value of real wages rapidly and undermined the faith of the workers in the power of the traditional leaders of the trade unions and the Labor Party.

For a brief spell revolutionary socialism was dominant in Norway and the Norwegian Labor Party was the only large Western European social democratic party to accept the twenty-one conditions—the Moscow theses—and join the Third International. But the Norwegian Labor Party was unhappy with the "democratic centralism" of the Third International. The right wing soon broke away, and when Tranmael's efforts to assert the independence of the Norwegian party led to much worse relations with the Comintern the end was not far away. The Norwegian Party finally left the Third International in 1924, and IWW influence vanished.

So by 1924 the heart had gone out of the IWW in every country where its ideas had found some acceptance. It spluttered to life occasionally during the odd waterfront strike at South American seaports, but it was a moribund organization by the late 1920s, remaining alive only in legend and in the idea of the One Big Union. The rebels had failed. "We have been naught and we shall be all," sang the founders in 1905. Their successors did not fulfill this dream. Yet they had shown that ordinary working men could stand up for themselves in the face of misery and oppression—a lesson which was not lost on future generations.

A Note on Further Reading

No attempt has been made to include a full bibliography, since all references in the text are fully documented in footnotes. Moreover, other published works already include comprehensive bibliographies. The best are in Paul F. Brissenden's pioneer studies *The Launching of the I W W* (Berkeley, 1913) and *The I W W: A Study of American Syndicalism* (New York, 1920). John S. Gambs, *The Decline of the I W W* (New York, 1932), covers the later period. Joyce L. Kornbluh, ed., *Rebel Voices* (Ann Arbor, 1964), is a rich anthology of readings from I W W material which has a comprehensive list of sources and a book list for each chapter. It also has a wealth of illustrations.

Philip S. Foner, *A History of the Labor Movement in the United States,* volume IV, *The Industrial Workers of the World 1905–1917* (New York, 1965), deals in great detail with the I W W from the Marxist standpoint, but unfortunately stops short before the great Chicago trial. Fred Thompson, *The I W W: Its First Fifty Years* (Chicago, 1955), published as a fiftieth-anniversary tribute to the union, is the only book that attempts to tell the complete history of the I W W.

Other works which may be consulted are listed below.

LABOR

John R. Commons and Associates, *A History of Labor in the United States, 1896–1932* (New York, 1935), four volumes; Philip Taft, *The A F of L in the Time of Gompers* (New York, 1957); Joseph G. Rayback, *A History of American Labor* (New York, 1959); Henry Pelling, *American Labor* (Chicago, 1960); Maurice F. Neufield, *A Representative Bibliography of American Labor History* (Cornell, 1964).

SOCIALISM

Howard H. Quint, *The Forging of American Socialism* (Columbia, South Carolina, 1953); David A. Shannon, *The Socialist Party of Amer-*

ica (New York, 1955); Ira Kipnis, *The American Socialist Movement* (New York, 1952); Donald Drew Egbert and Stow Persons, eds., *Socialism and American Life* (New York, 1952), two volumes.

SYNDICALISM, ANARCHISM, AND COMMUNISM

Georges Sorel, *Reflections on Violence* (Paris, 1906); Louis L. Levine, *Syndicalism in France* (New York, 1912); Arthur D. Lewis, *Syndicalism and the General Strike* (London, 1912); John G. Brooks, *American Syndicalism* (New York, 1913); Elizabeth Gurley Flynn, *Sabotage* (Cleveland, 1915); Bertrand Russell, *Roads to Freedom: Socialism, Anarchism and Syndicalism* (London, 1918); George Woodcock, *Anarchism* (London, 1963); James Joll, *The Anarchists* (London, 1964); Theodore Draper, *The Roots of American Communism* (New York, 1957).

IMMIGRATION

John Higham, *Strangers in the Land* (New York, 1955); Oscar Handlin, *The Uprooted* (New York, 1955); ed., *Immigration as a Factor in American History* (New York, 1959); Maldwyn A. Jones, *American Immigration* (Chicago, 1960).

GENERAL

Carelton H. Parker, *The Casual Laborer and Other Essays* (New York, 1920); Nels Anderson, *The Hobo* (Chicago, 1923); Vernon H. Jensen, *Lumber and Labor* (New York, 1945); *Heritage of Conflict* (Cornell, 1950); Robert S. Allen, *Our Fair City* (New York, 1947); Ralph Bushnell Potts, *Seattle Heritage* (Seattle, 1955); Donald B. Cole, *Immigrant City: Lawrence, Massachusetts 1845–1921* (North Carolina, 1963); William Preston, *Aliens and Dissenters* (Cambridge, 1963); Harvey O'Connor, *Revolution in Seattle* (New York, 1964); Robert Friedheim, *The Seattle General Strike* (Washington, 1964); David H. Grover, *Debaters and Dynamiters* (Oregon State University, 1964); Philip S. Foner, *The Case of Joe Hill* (New York, 1965); *The Letters of Joe Hill* (New York, 1965).

AUTOBIOGRAPHY

William D. Haywood, *Bill Haywood's Book* (New York, 1929); Emma Goldman, *Living My Life* (London, 1931), two volumes; Mabel Dodge Luhan, *Movers and Shakers* (New York, 1936); Ralph Chaplin, *Wobbly* (Chicago, 1948); Elizabeth Gurley Flynn, *I Speak My Own Piece* (New York, 1955); George Hardy, *Those Stormy Years* (London, 1956).

IWW FICTION

Jack London, *The Iron Heel* (Chicago, 1901); Winston Churchill, *The Dwelling Place of Light* (New York, 1913); Harold Lord Varney, *Revolt* (New York, 1919); Zane Grey, *Desert of Wheat* (New York, 1919); Upton Sinclair, *Oil* (New York, 1927); Max Eastman, *Venture,* (New York, 1927); Charles Ashleigh, *Rambling Kid* (London, 1930); Robert Cantwell, *The Hills Around Centralia* (New York, 1935); John Dos Passos, *Nineteen Nineteen* (New York, 1931); Wallace Stegner, *The Preacher and the Slave* (Boston, 1950); Barrie Stavis, *The Man Who Never Died* (New York, 1951).

POETRY AND SONGS

Arturo Giovannitti, *Arrows in the Gale* (1914); Ralph Chaplin, *Bars and Shadows* (1922). Joe Glazer and Bill Friedland, *Songs of the Wobblies* (Labor Arts Label) have recorded many of the best-known I W W songs, and Joe Glazer has recorded the *Songs of Joe Hill* (Folkway Records). *The I W W Songbook* exists in many editions.

INDEX

INDEX